Pressure

Jeff Harrington

Published by Jeff Harrington, 2022.

PRESSURE

First edition. September 19, 2022.

Copyright © 2022 Jeff Harrington.

ISBN: 979-8215069547

Written by Jeff Harrington.

Acknowledgments

I am grateful to my parents for making sure everything medically that could be done for my eyes was pursued, including being transported to weekly Stanford appointments that were necessary for many years. I am thankful to Dr. Rosenthal, Dr. Egbert, Dr. Minckler, Dr. Baerveldt, and all the other ophthalmologists who were involved in treating my glaucoma condition. I know all the traditional surgical interventions and later the more experimental treatments that I endured were meant to save my eyesight. Unfortunately, the results of all these treatments did not ultimately save me from blindness; however, it did prolong my eyesight, providing me the time to complete my college course work.

When my vision was slowly disappearing throughout my teen years into my twenties, going from someone who was visually impaired to someone who was legally blind, to someone who was completely blind, throughout this decade of transitions, my family and friends were so supportive. There was never any discussion about taking me out of my mainstream high school and sending me to a special school for the blind. My friends made sure I had rides to and from high school, as well as to parties and other activities. Video games, sports competition, and reading were tasks I consciously avoided, but overall, I did not feel excluded.

I am grateful to Jill for her willingness to teach me the Orientation and Mobility skills that allowed me to regain my travel independence and qualify for a guide dog.

Len was my mentor who introduced me to computers with assistive technology that opened my eyes to so many possibilities.

I sincerely appreciate the Center for Neuro Educational Therapies (CNETs) for their open-mindedness and willingness to hire an OT who happens to be blind, providing me with my first professional job opportunity.

I was fortunate my parents had the financial means to purchase an electronic video magnifier, when I started college, and later, when I performed my OT internships, an accessible computer system, and paying Len to provide technical support/training, when I started my first job as an OT.

Amy and I met when I was 18, and she was my rock. when I began slipping into darkness, both emotionally and visually, during my early twenties. She was at my side during many of my surgeries and as my sight was fading away. Amy experienced my anger and despair firsthand, as I was trying to come to terms with this thing called blindness, which was quickly becoming my new reality.

The fact that Amy stayed with me during this time of loss is a testament to her patience, her positive attitude, and her love. I know this was not a fun time for either of us, and the fact we lived it together, I believe, made us a stronger couple. All I can say is...Thank You, Amy!

When I began writing this book, I was not sure whether the story that I was going to tell would be of interest to anyone. I had never written a book before, nor did I know how to go about it.

This story began for me at age 13 when my vision started to fail. After chronologically reliving the experiences through writing, I shared some of it with my mom. Probably not a true objective review coming from your own mom, but her encouragement did inspire me to keep going. Originally, I thought the story would end when I graduated from San Jose State University, but that was really just the beginning of my life living with blindness.

I want to thank my brother Michael Harrington, who has self-published several books, for providing guidance concerning how to get this manuscript of mine actually published. He pointed me to editing and publishing resources.

I also want to acknowledge the editors of this project, Laurel Ornitz and close family and friends, who helped with the corrections needed to get this book published. I appreciate you working with this rookie writers misspellings and grammatical errors.

ANNOTATION

This is a true story of my personal experience with progressive sight loss. It takes you through initial symptoms as a young teenager, to the glaucoma diagnosis, to the 10 years of medical intervention, including experimental treatment into early adulthood, to eventual blindness at age 23, to adapting to a life without sight, and to recognizing all the incredible support I have received along the way, from family, friends, government agencies, classmates, and coworkers. I also touch on how the COVID pandemic has been particularly challenging to those with sight loss.

Writing this story has given me an excuse to slow down, look back, and appreciate the significance of what I have been through.

No doubt that blindness is certainly a severe disability and living with the condition is challenging, but the public's perception of one's abilities is often filled with low expectations. All people deserve to be considered based on skills, experience, education, etc. And to simply dismiss someone based on assumptions is so sad. I hope that my story can serve as an example of what is possible if given an opportunity.

PREFACE

It was 2020, and life as I had ever known it had changed. The Coronavirus, physical distancing, remote working, political unrest, and fires were the new normal.

During this anxious time of disorder and uncertainty, I took the opportunity to reflect on where I am and how I got here—my journey battling to save my eye sight, living with blindness, and expressing my memories into words to tell my story.

The pandemic of 2020 had spread throughout the entire world. Adding to the unsettled times, race riots/protests were in the forefront throughout the country with the Black Lives Matter movement. The unemployment rate had risen from 7 percent to 13 percent, changing from 6 million to 13 million U.S. citizens out of work.

The presidential election of 2020 was dividing the country between Democrats and Republicans, between mask wearers and non-mask wearers, between those who support immediate re-opening of businesses/schools and those who feel isolation/distancing is the safer approach, and between those who believe in herd immunity and those who believe in developing vaccines.

Then there was the Republican-majority-run Senate's controversial decision to immediately move to approve President Trump's nominee for the Supreme Court vacancy—Ruth Bader Ginsburg had passed away on September 18, 2020, less than two months before the presidential election. In comparison, on February 13, 2016, Justice Antonin Scalia passed nearly nine months before the election, but in this case, the Republican-majority-run Senate refused to move forward on President Obama's nominee, stating, "The American people should have a voice in the selection of their next Supreme Court Justice. Therefore, this vacancy should not be filled until we have a new president," Senator McConnell said.

In addition, Sonoma County (Santa Rosa), where I have lived since 1992, was experiencing its fourth devastating wildfire event in the past four years. In 2020, the fire season started much earlier in August with the Walbridge Fire, which burned more than 55,000 acres, coming from a new direction out of the west, destroying 175 homes. In September, we had the second fire event of 2020, which originated in Napa County. Embers from that fire ignited a new break-out branch in Sonoma County, which was initially called the Shady Fire. This entire fire incident was re-categorized into one complex fire called the Glass Fire. It burned in excess of 67,000 acres, destroying 334 homes in Sonoma County.

In October of 2017, the Tubbs Fire burned nearly 38,000 acres, destroyed 5,600 structures (my sister's home being one of them), with 22 fatalities. In 2019, the Kincade Fire burned nearly 78,000 acres and nearly 190,000 Sonoma County residences were evacuated.

The pandemic has caused most of the country and world to shut down since mid-March, 2020. I have been working remotely in my position as the Lead Assistive Technology Specialist for the Earle Baum Center (EBC) of the Blind. The final one-third of my daughter's junior year, and now her senior year, of high school, has been limited to remote learning. Note that in the final six weeks of my daughter's senior year, she was able to participate in hybrid learning, which meant she could attend in-person instruction two times per week.

I cannot recall the number of weeks actually missed by her and her classmates, but since middle school, the reasons for cancelling school include flooding/unsafe roads, fires/evacuations, unhealthy air/pollution, rolling blackouts/power shut-offs, and now the Coronavirus/pandemic. Even though she has been participating only in remote learning, classes were once again cancelled due to the latest fire evacuations. So, not only is school restricted to remote learning, but now, due to the fire, the remote instruction was also cancelled for several days.

My wife continues to work as an occupational therapist at Memorial Hospital, assisting patients to rehabilitate from neuro, orthopedic, and other conditions. Amy undergoes thorough screening every time she reports to work, completing daily health questionnaires and temperature checks, and has been required to wear full Personal Protective Equipment (PPE), including a mask, a facial shield, and a gown during her workday.

The initial U.S. response to this life-threatening global pandemic could be described as poor at best. Medical recommendations of mask wearing and social distancing were not supported or taken seriously by government officials. Efforts put in place by state and local municipalities to impede the spreading of the virus, initially kept the infection rate down, but as physical-distancing rules were lifted and increased testing implemented, the infection rate has risen exponentially.

As a person who is blind, and in my role as an occupational therapist, the Coronavirus pandemic has proved to be particularly challenging for those with sight loss. It was kind of ironic that things really started to shut down on Friday, March 13, 2020. That day I was scheduled to provide remote training to a veteran who lived several hours away from the center. Little did I know at that time that remote working/training would become the norm for the entire country. The following week was my daughter Megan's spring break, which I had scheduled as my vacation time. I remember California was very proactive in implementing social-distancing measures. Megan and her friend, Beth, along with Beth's parents, had left at the very beginning of the March shut-down and had managed to visit UC Santa Barbara, along with Cal Poly San Luis Obispo, which was where we were going to meet Megan and continue with the college touring. We were planning to visit the campuses of Long Beach State and San Diego State Universities. By then, it was March 16 and even more of California was being shut down, including pretty much all colleges.

We cancelled our trip to Southern California, and as it turned out, my PTO time was spent on researching and developing an accessible remote system for continuing to deliver EBC services to visually impaired consumers in our community.

The average age of the clients that EBC serves is 78 years old. Many of these seniors with sight loss in our community were not smart phone users and did not use computers, but they still needed access to the services that EBC was going to continue to offer remotely.

The country was moving to a platform of remote learning and working. The Earle Baum Center needed a solution that would work for the demographic that needed our services, but at the same time the solution needed to work for our instructors. When implementing a solution for different levels of experience and skill sets, in my mind, the solution needed to work for the least-experienced person, and also needed to work for people with sight loss. Instructors at the EBC would be the ones facilitating the remote meetings, and as the host, there were additional responsibilities for managing a remote meeting. The host needs the ability to allow access to participants joining the meeting, the ability to mute/un-mute participants, lock the meeting, as well as record the meeting. Some of the EBC instructors have vision loss themselves and use assistive technology to access smart phones, computers, and tablets.

Third-party applications are not always designed with assistive software in mind. This means mainstream programs may not interact well with assistive software. I looked at different conferencing platforms and Zoom was the industry standard at the time. It offered a standard telephone, a smart phone, and computer access, meaning participants and staff could use any of these methods when joining or hosting a meeting.

Initially, Basic Free Zoom Accounts were created for EBC, which meant up to 100 people could join a meeting and the

40-minute meeting-length restriction was waived for schools and nonprofits. This meant that Basic Accounts could have meetings longer than 40 minutes without needing a paid account.

At the start of the pandemic, these Basic Accounts were in place, and the Tech Team of Jacques, Cathy, and Eli, along with me, worked very hard to get the hundreds of clients and staff comfortable with this new service delivery model. In order to join this new virtual meeting platform, a typical EBC participant would be required to dial an 11-digit number, 1, plus the area code, then the seven-digit number. Participants would then be prompted to enter the Meeting ID, which was an additional 10-digit number that the user had to enter into the telephone's keypad. The Meeting ID had to be entered in rapidly without delay. Participants who do not see well had trouble reading the number and getting it entered in quickly enough. If the numbers were not entered in quickly enough or a wrong number was pressed, then the process would need to be re-started. Participants who only had cell phones with touch screens found entering the phone number and Meeting ID to be even more difficult. To try and simplify the process, the Meeting IDs were kept the same for all classes.

The EBC Conference Rooms were also configured to not require a Pass Code, which would have been yet another number needing to be entered by the participant. This Pass-Code requirement that was optional at the beginning became a Zoom requirement within a month of using the conferencing platform.

Unfortunately, the Basic Accounts were problematic from the onset, and the 40-minute meeting-length restriction was enforced. Even though EBC was a 501c nonprofit organization, the meetings that we often conducted were ended automatically after 40 minutes. Contacting Zoom Technical Support to verify EBC's nonprofit status proved to be useless, as the company was inundated with requests due to the country's overwhelming demand for conferencing services. Further complicating the Basic Account access was the statement posted by Zoom that Basic Accounts may be prevented from using the telephone dial-up method as there were limited phone numbers available. This meant that Basic Account holders could be forced to use web-based access for meetings, which would not work for EBC clients and instructors.

EBC converted to a paid Account to ensure the telephone access feature would be available. Zoom began requiring Pass Codes or account holders needed to enable the Waiting Room feature. The Waiting Room meant no participant could join a meeting until the host had approved them. The Waiting Room feature could only be administered if the host was using the online method, i.e., smart phone, computer, or tablet. Hosting by telephone did not allow for the Waiting Room options.

By necessity, EBC was forced to create Pass Codes for all of its Zoom meetings. This additional requirement made it even more complicated for participants to join meetings. Some participants would not even try to join an EBC Zoom meeting due to all the numbers, while others would give up after being unsuccessful with entering the numbers.

For those participants who had a computer but did not have the skills to join the conference, they could be provided with remote-access support, and the EBC Tech staff could work with them directly just prior to the actual meeting, getting them placed into the Zoom meeting.

Helpful participants would also do three-way calling, where folks who had trouble joining meetings would be connected to another participant's call, who would enter the group of callers into the Conference Room together.

For smart phone users, EBC staff would create customized contacts that would be sent and saved on the participant's iPhones. These customized contacts could be activated with a voice command, and then the Zoom number, the Meeting ID, and the Pass Code would automatically be entered.

With the persistence of my coworker, Patricia, reminding me that many of the clients she was trying to work with were not successful joining the current Zoom rooms with the solutions that EBC had offered, I kept researching simpler solutions and found the Uber Conferencing service. This service could be configured without a Meeting ID or Pass-Code requirement. In addition, the number used for the meetings was in the EBC area code, meaning almost all of the participants would only need to dial a seven-digit number and they would be connected to the meeting room.

I knew being able to simplify the process and making it a familiar task, where you only needed to dial a standard number, would make the process familiar to most participants. In addition, the Uber Conferencing service could be configured to automatically call specific phone numbers at the time of the meeting, resulting in participants simply needing to answer their phone and press the #1 to be placed in the meeting. Adding the Uber Conferencing platform as a meeting option proved to be very successful.

There were safety measures put in place by public health officials requiring the community to practice social-distancing behaviors. What this meant was all citizens are expected to maintain a six-foot distance from those around you and wear a mask. This well-meaning social mandate is an impossible concept for someone with sight loss to follow. The long white cane is the primary tool used, which allows someone with vision loss to travel safely in their environment. By design, the white cane is an obstacle indicator; therefore, its job is to detect things in your path of travel, providing you with information about your surroundings.

Guide dogs are another mobility option used by some visually impaired people. These highly trained animals are taught to avoid obstacles in your path of travel, but the concept of keeping you six feet away has never been part of their training. In most cases, there would not even be six feet of open space available as you are led around most obstacles. If the obstruction is blocking the entire pathway, then the dogs have been trained to show you the obstacle by guiding you right up to it. Then by exploring with your feet or hands, you, as the handler, can make an informed decision and command your dog how to proceed.

Visual markings on the floor of many stores showing customers where to stand when they are waiting to check out are undetectable if you are unable to see. People with sight loss explore the world through touch and sound, and a frequent strategy utilized is a human guide. This is where someone with sight loss would request assistance from a sighted person by grasping their arm just above the elbow, particularly if you are in an unfamiliar area, such as a store.

Prior to COVID 19, I would regularly travel to the grocery store, where I knew, once I arrived, I could ask an employee for shopping assistance. I have chosen not to travel to the store independently since the outbreak. I have felt uncomfortable asking for help, thinking I would be putting myself or the store employee at risk.

Fortunately, I live with my sighted wife and daughter, who are able to shop for the family. I am also able to order online and have items delivered to my home. Other folks with vision loss do not have this same type of support or the skills to order online.

During this pandemic, I have heard from many of the clients who we serve concerning the unkind treatment they have received from some people in the community telling folks with vision loss to watch out or back off. Some folks have even gone as far as to threaten bodily harm if the visually impaired person does not get out of their way. It is safe to say that those with sight loss have been placed in an impossible position to comply with physical-distancing rules.

The events of 2020 have created enormous challenges for our communities, country, and world, and every one of us can play a role in getting us through. We all share the planet, live together in various communities, and have varying beliefs, and moving past these challenges is going to take cooperation by each of us. Focusing our energies on getting the pandemic under control, people back to work, and reopening schools to in-person instruction are goals that I think we all can embrace.

CHAPTER 1:
THINGS ARE UNCLEAR

It was January of 1979, and I was in the middle of my seventh-grade year, suffering from what most students called the mid-school blues. You know the feeling of being assigned too much homework, not enough break time to hang with friends, and wanting a girl friend, but not being confident enough for that.

I was just getting back into the swing of things after the Christmas holiday. In Mr. Crosson's typing class, we had learned the entire alphabet. We were beginning to type words and create complete sentences. As I viewed the lesson in the typing book that was to be transcribed, the words seemed fuzzy to me. My typing speed seemed slower than the other students, but I did not think much about it at the time.

In Mrs. Mark's Math class, I was working on the daily algebra assignment. I realized I was straining to see the problems on the overhead projector. I remember getting up from my seat to move closer to the screen, when suddenly, I heard Mrs. Mark's voice.

"Jeff, sit down! We are in the middle of a quiz."

A few days later, I was in P.E. class, playing softball. When I was up to bat, I swung at three under-hand pitches, striking out, managing only to hit air. I had played Little League baseball for the past four years, and had even made the all-star team, but you would not have believed that from the way I was performing now.

That night, I told my parents that my eyes were bothering me. An appointment was made for me to see the eye doctor, Dr. Wand, the following week. I had been seeing an ophthalmologist on an annual basis for farsightedness. The doctor had been prescribing glasses to me since early on in my life. When I got my first pair of glasses, my nose was not ready to support them , so a piece of tape was placed on the bridge of the glasses and the other end stuck on my forehead in between my eyes.

A couple of days before my appointment, I began worrying that I was making a big deal out of nothing. My eyes even seemed better, and I told my mom this, thinking she would cancel the appointment, but she didn't. The day of the appointment, I was nervous because there was nothing wrong, as far as I knew. I figured people would be angry with me thinking I had made things up just to miss school or something. Surprisingly, Dr. Wand explained that I had inflammation in both of my eyes and prescribed some medication, saying it should clear up in about a month.

A couple of months later, I began practicing for the upcoming Pony League tryouts, thinking everything was okay. I played catch with my dad and I became frustrated, while my dad became angry, because I was missing most of his throws.

"Stand still" my dad yelled, but I couldn't because the balls were bouncing off the garage door behind me, making quite a racket, instead of landing in my glove. I would not see the ball, as my dad released it, but would usually see a blurry object hurling toward me at the last second. My survival instinct would kick in at that point, and I would find myself jumping out of the way, throwing my glove where I had last seen the blur of the baseball coming at me—dodge ball with a baseball. I found it could have painful consequences.

"What's wrong?" my dad exclaimed.

"I can't see the ball clearly," I cried.

"Your eyes are fine now," he yelled, and began firing the ball harder at me. After being hit several times by the ball, my dad became quite concerned and realized my vision must still be clearing up.

It was thought that perhaps sitting out this baseball season would be a good idea since I was obviously still dealing with vision issues.

PRESSURE

The school year was ending, and everyone was ready for summer break, including me, especially since our family was going on a trip across the country to New York. My parents grew up in a town called Cortland, and many of our relatives were from that area.

When I received my final grades from seventh grade, however, I was surprised because my marks had dropped. I had gone from being a consistent B student to a C student in one semester. More important to me at the time was how my parents would react to the news, and I wondered how much fun my summer vacation would be now. Would attending summer school be suggested as a way for me to improve my grades?

My parents were more concerned than angry when they saw my report card, and another appointment was made for me to visit the ophthalmologist.

Dr. Wand explained that the inflammation was still present and prescribed new medication. He had reassured us that everything was okay, telling us to go on our vacation to the East Coast and not to worry. I was not too excited about putting more drops in my eyes because the medicine always seemed to be irritating and created a burning sensation.

In the back of my mind were memories that I had about taking eye medication and they were not fond ones.

As a child, my parents would have to put drops in my eyes to dilate them the night before I was to see the ophthalmologist. I would become anxious about the thought of medication being administered into my eyes by the doctor. I was older now and knew it was important to take the medicine, so I did it without complaining.

CHAPTER 2:
IT WAS A BLURRY VACATION

While we were vacationing at my grandma's house in New York, I continued to experience issues with my vision. I contributed the ongoing blurriness to the additional medication that had been prescribed.

The third day of our vacation was particularly memorable and scary. When I woke up, the entire room seemed to be filled with a heavy fog. Knowing that was impossible, I blinked and rubbed my eyes several times, trying to clear my vision. In a panic, I called out to my parents, and they arrived at my bedside in a moment.

"What's wrong?" my mom asked.

"It's my eyes; I can't see out of them," I exclaimed.

"Calm down," my dad said, "tell us what's happening."

I explained what I had experienced, and then my mom told me to shut my eyes and rest for a while. A few minutes passed, and my vision became clearer. To a person with normal sight, I am sure it would have still been quite blurry, but it seemed better to me. We were not familiar with any ophthalmologists in Cortland, things seemed to have improved from when I first had woken up, so nothing further was pursued. I continued to take my medicine and did not experience any noticeable issues during the remainder of the vacation.

My family returned home the following week, and once again, I found myself heading to Dr. Wand's office for an examination.

My visual acuity was measured, and Dr. Wand was very concerned with the results. During my previous annual check-up, my vision had been correctable to 20/30, but now my acuity had been reduced to 20/50. Dr. Wand said that the inflammation was still present, but it should not be interfering with my vision to that extreme.

The doctor began running different tests on my eyes, one of which was to measure the inner ocular pressure. To do this, Dr. Wand had to first put a topical anesthetic in each of my eyes to numb them. When the drops hit my eyes, there was a burning sensation, followed by tingling, and then it was as if the eye was gone. I mean that I could see out of it, but I could not feel it.

An instrument called a tonometer was attached to the slit lamp, which is where I always had placed my chin and forehead during previous examinations. This tonometer reminded me of a lighter that you would find in an automobile's dashboard. Instead of seeing an object with a round-shaped bright-orange color, you saw a similar-sized, round-shaped object with a light-blue color with a darker-colored center.

Dr. Wand used one of his hands to keep my lid open, and the other hand was operating the instrument, as he brought it closer and closer to my eye. All that I could think about was here comes this lighter thing that is going to torch my eye. It takes a lot of self-control to hold still while a probing light is being moved toward your eye. The dark-blue center came in contact with the front of my eye, and surprisingly I did not feel any discomfort. For the many seconds that the instrument remained in contact with my eye, I do not remember taking a breath.

Dr. Wand repeated the process on the other eye and said that he was not comfortable with the readings, so he wanted his colleague, Dr. Spier, to also measure the pressure in each of my eyes.

The dark center of the instrument needs to be lined up with the cornea of the eye, and my corneas were quite small, making it difficult to line up.

Dr. Spier measured the pressure in each eye, and then both doctors left my mom and me in the exam room to consult about their findings.

My heart was pounding when Dr. Wand re-entered the room a few minutes later. The doctor immediately gestured to my mom to follow him out of the exam room. Now there I was sitting alone wondering what was wrong with me. It must be really bad I thought, and no one wants to tell me.

The next thing I remember was standing at the reception desk at Dr. Wand's office, while the secretary gave my mom directions to Stanford Hospital. In my sixth-grade class, I remember there was a student who had been gone for quite a while, and we asked our teacher, Mr. Pope, about it. The teacher said he knew there must be a serious medical condition because the boy was at Stanford Hospital. Now I was also being sent to Stanford, so I knew there must be something seriously wrong with me as well.

CHAPTER 3:
REFERRED TO STANFORD FOR ANSWERS

During the drive to Stanford Hospital the next day, various paranoid thoughts began racing through my mind. Only seriously ill people go to Stanford. What is wrong with me? Do I have some incurable disease? Not understanding why my eyes are not functioning like they should, and experiencing vision issues, is a very unsettling feeling.

As we walked through the hospital toward the Eye Clinic, there was no conversation between my mother and me; I heard nothing, and saw nothing. I was like a zombie staring straight ahead, not moving a muscle, except for my feet, putting one in front of the other.

I was scheduled to see Dr. Rosenthal, who was a well-known ophthalmologist in his field, specializing in glaucoma treatment. Before I could see the doctor, paperwork needed to be completed, establishing me as a patient at the hospital.

Hospitals, I soon learned, are like any other business. They want to be paid, and they want to know who is going to be paying them, When we arrived at the second-floor Eye Clinic, we were immediately sent to the Admitting Department, which we were told was on the first floor.

It seemed a bit impersonal. You were here to receive intervention with some medical condition, and the hospital seemed more interested in what type of insurance coverage you had.

My mom and I set off to find the Admitting Office. The directions that we received from the lady in the Eye Clinic seemed straightforward enough. But when we encountered the maze of hallways going in different directions, we were lost.

Stanford's main facility (where the Eye Clinic is located) is quite large, consisting of three stories, spread out over several blocks, plus a basement, which I found by mistake one day, as a result of my progressive sight loss.

Stanford also has a prestigious children's hospital (Lucile Packard)[1], as well as the original Hoover Pavilion/Hospital.

By asking an official looking person for help, we were pointed to our destination of the Admitting Office.

A clipboard, full of forms, was handed to my mom. Each form needed to be filled out. Many of the questions were repetitive and the same answer would need to be entered on several of the forms. After the forms were completed and turned in, each one was reviewed for completeness.

We were rewarded with a red plastic Stanford Hospital card, which we were told should always be with us when we are visiting the hospital.

Apparently, every department in the hospital will ask you to present this red card as part of the check-in process. Having this red card in your possession appears to be more important for the hospital than you, the actual patient.

Somehow we weaved our way back through the hospital and ended up at the Eye Clinic. Sure enough, they asked to see the red card, and I presented it proudly, feeling like it was a VIP card made especially for me. I was not aware that every other patient had this same type of card. We were handed another clipboard full of forms that needed to be filled out. Believe it or not, two of the forms were identical to the ones we had just filled out at the Admitting Office. My mom pointed this out to the lady at the front desk. She

---

1.   https://www.google.com/
search?q=Is+Lucile+Packard+still+alive%3F&sa=X&ved=2ahUKEwjez63UjLvxAhWVlW
oFHXRyCdkQzmd6BAgIEAc

replied in an angry tone, I guess irritated that we had questioned her instructions.

"We keep separate files here ma'am," the receptionist said matter-of-factly to my mom, acting as though we should have known that.

A nurse called my name and I was led into an examining room. She introduced herself as Clair and said she wanted to check my prescription, verify medications I was taking, and make sure my new chart was in order before seeing Dr. Rosenthal. The lights in the room were being dimmed, and I was asked to read letters on a chart, covering one eye, then the other. I was asked to remove my glasses and read the eye chart again.

Once the nurse completed her preliminary tasks, she led me deeper into the clinic. I could no longer hear the chatter from the waiting room, and even the hospital's intercom paging system, which was continuously broadcasting some doctor's name, seemed to be fainter sounding in the background.

I was placed in another examining room surrounded by what would become the all too familiar ophthalmic equipment. My anxiety level was peaking now. I was still not interested in carrying on any type of conversation with my mom, and preferred to wait in silence for whatever would happen next. I was at a new hospital about to be seen by a new doctor, who was going to determine what was wrong with me. Was the doctor going to tell me that I had some terminal diagnosis? I was told Dr. Rosenthal would be arriving soon to perform an examination of my eyes.

Suddenly, the door to the examination room opened. A tall man with a black scraggly beard wearing a white lab coat appeared, with his tie hanging loosely around his neck. He was standing a bit hunched over. This man looked more like a mad scientist than a renowned ophthalmologist. Later I would learn that he had back issues, which caused him discomfort and made it difficult for him to stand up straight. He introduced himself as Dr. Rosenthal. I would not describe him as being real personable and wanting to carry on small talk. He had no real bedside manner. Creating an atmosphere where the patient was put at ease and provided with details concerning diagnostic testing that would be ordered was not what Dr. Rosenthal chose to focus on.

I learned quickly that Dr. Rosenthal was not a very patient man. His objective was to obtain information and test results promptly, to confirm a diagnosis and treatment plan for his patient.

Dr. Rosenthal got right down to the business of determining what was going on with my eyes. After answering several of his questions concerning my vision and the changes that I had been experiencing, I began to calm down and became more comfortable with this doctor who I understood wanted to help me.

The question and answer period ended almost as soon as it had started.

CHAPTER 4:
TESTS, TESTS & MORE TESTS

It was now time for the evaluation process to begin. I was subjected to a battery of diagnostic tests. The doctor began by measuring my inner ocular pressure, which I had just experienced with Dr. Wand the day before. This involved administering a topical anesthetic into both of my eyes, some sort of yellow dye was added to each eye, and then the tonometer was brought in contact with the front of my eye. My natural reaction to having this probe touching my eye was to blink. This blinking of my eyes interfered with Dr. Rosenthal's ability to accurately measure my pressure.

"Jeffrey, Jeffrey," I heard Dr. Rosenthal say, "you need to hold still". I was trying so hard not to blink, but honestly, I believe it was an involuntary response from my body having a foreign instrument forced into it.

Dr. Rosenthal, I quickly learned, would not give up until he had obtained the reliable pressure readings that were required. It took the doctor a few attempts with each eye, along with my conscious efforts not to move, and my very high eye pressure was confirmed.

The difficulty in measuring my eye pressures would be a constant theme for the ophthalmologists who were treating me. My eyes were naturally small, including my corneas. The tonometer was designed for more standard-size eyes, so getting the instrument to line up correctly was always a challenge. The resident doctors, and there were a lot of them at Stanford, since it was a teaching hospital, had the most difficulty measuring my pressure. My regular ophthalmologists learned to work with my eyes and became very successful obtaining accurate pressure readings.

Next, my eyes were dilated with additional topical medication, which caused a burning sensation upon contact. This medication prevented my pupils from naturally restricting and allowed high-intensity lights to pass through my eyes. This procedure was called ophthalmoscopy and allowed the doctor to view structures in the back of the eye.

Many different lights with extreme intensity were shined into my eyes. There is a variation of this type of examination, called indirect ophthalmoscopy, which was particularly memorable because it was not very pleasant. Dr. Rosenthal uses a condensing lens and a bright light mounted on his forehead. This type of exam allows the doctor to see the retina and other structures in great detail and in three dimensions. The worst part is when Dr. Rosenthal inserted the oversized lens directly into my eye. Before this stage of the exam, the lens that he was using was held externally in his hand, with no direct contact with my eyes. This lens that had just been inserted into my eye was coated with some kind of slimy solution, which allowed it to easily be manipulated while in my eye for optimal viewing of the innards of my eye. It was an uncomfortable and irritating experience.

By now, I had developed quite a headache, but there were still more tests to be performed.

After that, I went with a medical technician to have a Goldmann Visual Field Assessment. The purpose of this test was to measure my peripheral and central vision. To do this, I had to rest my chin and forehead in the standard eye examination position. One of my eyes was covered, while I was instructed to stare into a circular-shaped, half-dome-concaved movie screen. I was asked not to move my eye around and was required to stare straight ahead at a tiny bright light. A small metal washer-like object was placed in my hand. The technician instructed me to tap with the washer on the tabletop when I saw another light coming from the periphery or appearing in my central visual field. This test went on for 60 minutes (about 30 minutes per eye), and the only thing that changes is the size of the lights. Initially, the lights that must be spotted are very small and they get larger and larger as the test goes on. This was the longest, most tiresome, and boring test of the day, but probably the most revealing. It could tell if there was any visual field loss and to what degree.

The ultrasound examination came next and it was not fun either. Picture your eyelids being prevented from blinking by something called a speculum. This metal paper-clip-like device is positioned under your upper and lower lids. A funnel-reservoir-type container is placed over the eye. A glue-like substance is painted around the eye socket to create a water seal. The funnel reservoir is filled with water and your lids are held in a forced-open state, then the ultrasound machine is used to take images of the structures in my eye.

The final test of that day that I remember involved taking photographs of my eyes. This was the easiest test of the day because it did not involve medication or inserting objects into my eyes. I was asked to look at a lighted bull's-eye target, which assisted the technician in getting my eyes to look in the correct direction, giving the optimal angles for the photos to be taken.

Stanford is a teaching hospital, so during many of the tests, several resident doctors would be given the opportunity to measure my pressure, shine varying-intensity lights into my eyes, inserting and removing the oversized contact lens, when each doctor took his/her turn. Enduring each of these tests was quite an ordeal, but having them repeated, so that each doctor could take a look, was borderline torture for the patient.

CHAPTER 5:
DIAGNOSIS &
HOSPITALIZATION

A nurse led us back to Dr. Rosenthal's office, where he was waiting to discuss the test results. Dr. Rosenthal jumped right to the point and explained that I had a disease called glaucoma. I looked at him blankly, not having a clue what that meant, so he began to explain the condition. Basically, it is abnormally high inner ocular pressure. Cells in your eyes produce fluid and this fluid flows through your eyes, providing nutrition to the various structures, and eventually flows out of your eyes through blood vessels. In glaucoma, the fluid does not drain out of your eye quickly enough; therefore, the eyeball expands, putting pressure on the optic nerve. This increased pressure damages the nerve, and if it is not controlled, it will result in progressive permanent sight loss.

Glaucoma occurs because the eye is overproducing fluid, or there is a blockage inhibiting the fluid from leaving the eye, or there is a combination of the two. That day, Dr. Rosenthal had measured my inner ocular pressure and the reading was 50 millimeters of mercury (mm). A normal pressure is about 12 mm. Dr. Rosenthal said something needed to be done right away to decrease the pressure. According to the tests that had just been completed on me, irreversible damage had already occurred. He said medications were quite effective in treating glaucoma, that glaucoma can be controlled, but not cured.

I was admitted into the hospital that afternoon. My dad was contacted at work, and he left immediately for the hospital, meeting us at the Admitting Office. He arrived just as the clerk was putting identification bands around my wrist.

My dad, who is always joking, tried to keep things light, by asking the nurse: "Why do you put bands around both wrists?" And before the nurse even had time to respond, he answered his own question. "Is it in case the doctor cuts off one of his arms by mistake?" My dad said this, chuckling. That even brought a quick smile to my face, something I had not done for a while.

Soon I was being pushed in a wheelchair up to the pediatric ward, which was on the third floor of the hospital.

I remember thinking these people must think I am really sick; they will not even let me walk. I did not feel sick, except for the headache, which I had acquired because of all the tests I had endured that day.

I did not understand at the time, but my vision was already permanently impaired because of the uncontrolled eye pressure that I had already been experiencing for an undetermined period of time.

The diagnosis explained my blurry-vision issues that I had been experiencing for more than six months by now. The hospital setting did nothing to improve my mood. I had just been told that I have an incurable eye disease. The hallways seemed dark, the walls were white, the hospital personnel all wore white, and they wanted me to wear their white pajamas. I would not consider what they offered me to be pajamas, but rather, a gown that covered very little of my body. As a matter of fact, it did not even cover my back side. I figured this is how they get their patients to stay in bed who want to trounce around the hospital with their butt hanging out. I had no choice in the matter, because I had nothing else to wear, so I reluctantly put on the gown. My dad said I looked good in the dress, and I just glared at him. I think he got my message because he stopped making jokes after that.

I was placed in a ward with five other beds. There were machines in the room continuously buzzing and beeping, there were lights flashing on and off, and the entire room smelled liked cleaning detergent. Four of the beds in the room were occupied. In one of the beds, there was a boy who was lying in his bed motionless with tubes running in and out of his nose and arms. Another boy, who had no hair on his head, was sitting up watching television. A third boy had his right leg in a full cast being elevated in the air by cords that hung from the ceiling. The fourth person had the curtains pulled around his bed, so I could not see, but I could hear snoring coming from that direction.

It was early evening by now, and my brother and sister were at home probably wondering where everyone was. I was not scheduled to see any doctors until morning, so there was no need for both of my parents to be there. My dad said his goodbyes, and we told him if there was any news, he would hear from us.

CHAPTER 6:
PHARMACEUTICAL INTERVENTION BEGINS

The nurse administered the first round of medications that Dr. Rosenthal had prescribed, three different eye drops and a pill. I was looking forward to the medication because I wanted my pressure to lower so I could go home.

My mom stayed at the hospital that night, sleeping on a cot in the playroom with family members of other patients. Although I was extremely tired, I was not able to get much sleep. I was in a strange place with noises that were unfamiliar to me. There were carts going up and down the halls, they were continuously paging some doctor, and, of course, the nurses had to check each patient's vital signs every four hours or so. When people are admitted to the hospital, I thought they are supposed to get rest, but with all the noises and interruptions, how can anyone get a peaceful night of sleep?

The next morning, just as breakfast arrived, the transport person came to take me to the Eye Clinic, so even though I had quite an appetite, I would have to wait. The nurse had warned me that the Eye Clinic has a reputation for taking patients away right at mealtime. Luckily, my mom had gone out early that morning to buy me some real pajamas, so I could go to the Eye Clinic without exposing myself. My mom followed as I was being escorted in a wheelchair down to the clinic.

Dr. Rosenthal numbed my eyes and measured the pressure. He grumbled when he received the readings and announced that it had not decreased like he wanted it to. He wrote an order to increase the milligrams of the Diamox pill, which I was taking, and said, "See you tomorrow." Dr. Rosenthal is a renowned ophthalmologist, but his bed-side manner is abrupt. His approach is direct, appearing brutal at times. This would become more and more apparent to me as my contact with him increased.

When I returned to my room, the breakfast tray was still there, but the food was cold, and I did not eat much. I asked my mom: "If I am only going to be seen once a day, why can't I go home and come back each day?"

My mom agreed with me and said that we would ask that question tomorrow. I was tired of wearing my pajamas, I did not feel sick, so I put my regular clothes back on. My decision to wear my street clothes did not please the nursing staff, but I was more comfortable. The rest of the day I was pushed around in a wheelchair by my mom, which was hospital policy, exploring the pediatric floor. There was a pool table and various other games, but I was not interested in playing anything.

That afternoon, my dad arrived with additional clothes for me and a milkshake. I drank the shake so fast and it tasted great. My parents were happy to see that I was feeling better and had not lost my appetite. The dinner arrived, and I was able to eat it, while it was still warm, this time, but it did not seem to taste any better than my cold breakfast. I ate most of it anyway, so it must not have been too bad. After all, Stanford is a prestigious medical facility, not a restaurant.

My mom and dad left shortly after dinner, saying one of them would return tomorrow in time for my appointment with Dr. Rosenthal.

That night, my brother and sister called. As usual, they wanted to know every detail of what the doctors had done to me so far. I explained the various tests that had been performed, and my brother and sister's most frequent response to what I was saying was "No way" and "That's intense."

In the morning, I was once again wheeled to the Eye Clinic just as breakfast arrived. My pressure was measured, and the doctor reported that it had decreased further, but it was not back to normal. My mom questioned him about taking me home, saying that I could be brought back whenever necessary.

Dr. Rosenthal said matter-of-factly, "Do you realize he is on several different medications that need to be administered in both eyes at regularly scheduled times?"

After several minutes of debating, we convinced the doctor that we were confident enough to manage the medications without difficulty. He said if everything continued to progress positively, I could be discharged tomorrow.

My mom left shortly after our meeting with Dr. Rosenthal. She needed to get back to work because she had missed several days. She also knew I was more comfortable with the hospital setting now and figured I would be coming home tomorrow.

CHAPTER 7:
UNEXPECTED VISITORS & EXAMINATIONS

I was excited about the prospect of going home, but the day seemed to drag on. Around 1:00 p.m., a lab technician appeared at the foot of my bed, holding a tray full of tiny bottles.

He said, in a Dracula-like voice, "Are you Jeffrey?"

"Yes," I said.

"I need to take some of your blood," he continued, in that strange voice, I guess trying to be funny.

I thought what is so damn funny about sticking a needle in my arm? I questioned the technician, saying I was not aware of this test, but he assured me that it was to be done. Apparently, Dr. Rosenthal had ordered the test to measure the amount of medication that was in my bloodstream but had neglected to inform me about this lab work.

Another unexpected visitor arrived at my bedside. I do not recall the doctor's name, but I remember that he was bald with bushy eyebrows. He spoke with an accent that I interpreted to be Russian. This was back during the Cold War, when the United States considered the Soviet Union to be a dangerous enemy. This doctor wanted to isolate me and take me to some examining room, and I was not too thrilled with the idea. The nurse, sensing my reluctance, assured me that Dr. Rosenthal had written an additional order for this doctor to examine me. I was preparing for fight-or-flight mode.

I was led across the hall from my hospital room to a small examining room, where I was sure an interrogation would take place. When I entered the room, there was the doctor's female assistant, sitting reading what must have been my chart. I was asked to remove my street clothes, put on one of those fashionable gowns, and lie on the table. I was not too comfortable with the idea, especially since there was a female present, but I did as I was instructed. Just the other day, I had complained about those damn hospital gowns, but I was thankful now. At least part of my body would be covered. The doctor examined every inch of my body, while his assistant wrote notes in my chart. He measured the length and width of my fingers and toes, he looked at my teeth, asked about my dental history, pulled hair out of my head, and placed different textures on my skin to see the response. During the examination, the doctor would verbalize his findings, and his assistant would write it down. I was basically ignored; I felt more like a specimen than a human being.

Occasionally, I would be asked questions like, "Does anyone else in your family have a nose like yours?"

This doctor wrote a follow-up order for me to be taken to the Radiology Lab for X-rays. This is it, I thought. I am going to be nuked by this Russian doctor. As it turned out, he actually wanted pictures of my skeletal structure to view my bone development. Well, I survived my trip to Radiology.

CHAPTER 8:
BEING DISCHARGED
& SALVAGING THE SUMMER

Morning arrived and I was very energetic, anticipating my departure from the hospital. The transport person seemed to take a long time, but then again everything seemed like it was going slow on this day.

Finally, I was in the examining room waiting for Dr. Rosenthal to make his appearance. He apologized for making us wait and said he had just received the report from the doctor who had examined me yesterday. The doctor had concluded that I have a rare genetic syndrome called Ocular Digital Dental Dysplasia and that could be the cause of my congenitally based glaucoma. In English, that means that my eyes, fingers, and teeth did not develop fully prenatally. Dr. Rosenthal hypothesized that my eyes were producing fluid at a rate for a normal-sized eye, but because my eyes were smaller, they were unequipped to handle this normal output of eye fluid, resulting in elevated and damaging pressure.

This diagnosis made a lot of sense to me, as I look back. I was born with webbing between my 4th and 5th fingers. The pinky and ring fingers on my left hand were connected by skin, requiring me to have surgery when I was very young. The bone structure on my pinky finger was also misshapen. Further supporting this syndrome was my extensive dental history. As a young teenager, my molar teeth had significant decay issues. Crowns were required for all my top-and-bottom back teeth. Later, all these teeth that were crowned, eventually, also required root canals. I could tell a long story about the horrors of endodontic treatment, as I have a lot of memories of very painful teeth. I am also very thankful for the care that I received and the fact that my teeth were saved. Fortunately, my mom was an

Office Manager for a dental practice, so I had access to the dental care that I needed. My current dentist, Dr. Peterson, has never seen a patient like me with 20-plus root canals.

Dr. Rosenthal went on to measure the pressure and said that it was continuing to decrease. He said I could go home because things were on the right track, and I could not hold back the smile when I heard those words.

The nightmare was over for now, and I was returning home to salvage what was left of my summer vacation.

The days flew by between the time I left the hospital and the time I started my eighth-grade year. We spent the time shopping for clothes, gathering school supplies, and running from sporting event to sporting event, because every member of my family played on some athletic team, including my mom and dad.

CHAPTER 9:
RETURNING TO SCHOOL WITHOUT ACCOMMODATIONS

The school counselor and office staff were made aware of my serious eye condition and visual impairment, and the information was to be passed on to my classroom teachers. Unfortunately things did not go well and I did not receive the support that was needed.

For example, the ditto worksheets that the students work from are often of poor quality. I remember approaching my English teacher, Ms. Dorr, and asking, "Can I have another worksheet, this one is too faded, and I'm having trouble seeing it?"

"Try your best," my teacher said, and left it at that.

Not knowing any better and figuring it was my problem to deal with, I went back to my seat and would just stare at the blurry ditto sheet. I would ask my friends sitting around me for help, but my teacher would quickly reprimand me for talking.

"Jeff, be quiet! This is independent study time."

This was becoming my independent sleep time during English class. I could not see the work that had been assigned, I did not receive help, I was forbidden to ask for help, and so I would just sit in English class and zone out.

In my Math class, I was assigned to a seat in the back of the room. After straining to see the overhead projector during the first week of class, I asked my teacher if I could move closer to the front.

"Are you still having trouble with your eyes?" my teacher asked.

"Yes," I said, realizing she had no idea how serious this disease is and thinks it will suddenly just go away. Sight loss from glaucoma is irreversible. The hope is to control the pressure and maintain the remaining vision.

During the third week of school, my English teacher requested that each of us read out loud to the rest of the class. When it became my turn, I had never been so embarrassed in my life. I was straining so hard to see the words in the book, but they just would not come into focus. The words were stuttering out of my mouth, my heart was pounding, and my face was extremely hot, probably beet-red. The teacher finally intervened, saying I needed to work on my reading skills.

In P.E. class, my self-esteem was being shot to hell. When teams were chosen for different games, I was being picked last. I was not used to being selected last for a team and it really hurt. The various captains would say I do not want him on my team; he is just going to miss the ball. Or they might say, try and hit the ball for once this time—little did they know I was trying as hard as I could.

CHAPTER 10:
INCREASING DOSAGES &
ENROLLMENT IN SPECIAL EDUCATION

Meanwhile, I returned to Stanford for a check-up, and the news was depressing. My pressure had increased (30 mm), and although I had not noticed a vision change, the pressure was at a harmful level. The peripheral vision was probably being affected the most, and that is not usually consciously detectable. That is why they call glaucoma "the sneak thief of sight."

My credibility was being tested right away. Dr. Rosenthal wanted to know what medicines I was taking and how often. I could not pronounce the technical names of the medications but had developed a system based on the color of each bottle's lid. I do not think my system impressed the doctor. Dr. Rosenthal had no clue what I was talking about when I said I was taking the yellow-topped drop two times a day, the green-topped drop four times a day, the white-topped drop two times a day, and the pill twice a day, his confusion was clear to me, by his silence and shaking of his head. From that point on, I decided to learn the technical names of the medications that I was prescribed.

Dr. Rosenthal increased the dosage strengths of the Timoptic and Pilocarpine drops that I was already taking, as well as the Diamox pill, to the maximum dosage. He said I might experience side effects, such as burning eyes, blurry vision, headaches, diarrhea, loss of appetite, and numbness in the hands and feet, and that I was to return in two weeks for another check-up.

The first semester progress reports had been sent home and all my grades were poor; but worst of all, I had received an F in English class. Never had I come close to failing a class before, and I was in complete shock. This same English teacher also was my Art instructor. I received a D in Art, which was slightly better than a second F, but certainly not good.

Upon seeing my report card, my parents visited the school officials again.

Their solution was to enroll me in the Special Education Program. Everyone knew the classroom next to the library was for students with learning disabilities. When I was required to attend classes in that room, I felt very self-conscious thinking I was being given an additional label of being learning disabled.

Initially in this new classroom, I was asked to perform remedial work. The assignments were easy for me to complete . I was receiving a lot of one-on-one attention from the teacher's aides because material would be read out loud to me. I was not being challenged with the current curriculum. The attitude of the school, it seemed, was if you have a sensory impairment, then you must also have a cognitive impairment.

My new class schedule, meant less time hanging with my friends. They would discuss specific assignments, and various things that had happened during their classes. I was beginning to feel more and more left out. I withdrew from the things I enjoyed. I did not rush up to the Crunch Corral at break to meet my friends and chow down on a cinnamon roll and milk. The medicine was bothering my stomach, and I spent more of my break time using the toilet in the filthy bathrooms. I did not have much of an appetite and figured whatever I ate would go right through me anyway. I did not participate in lunch-time basketball games anymore because my performance was lacking, and I did not want to embarrass myself, or the team.

I returned to Stanford for a check-up. Dr. Rosenthal asked me how I was tolerating the Diamox. Knowing that the alternative to medication was surgery, I did not complain about the side effects.

My mom, however, admitted that my appetite was lacking and said I seemed to be spending more time in the bathroom. Dr. Rosenthal ordered a blood test to measure the levels of medicine in my bloodstream. The Chief Resident, Dr. Bachman, was also present in the examining room, and I remember him telling me to eat an orange a day. He said that would help to balance the chemical levels in my body.

My eye pressure had not increased, nor had it decreased from the last visit, like they had expected it to. Dr. Rosenthal said he did not understand why the medicine was not more effective in controlling my glaucoma. It was becoming common practice for Dr. Rosenthal to sit on his stool, shaking his head, while he stared at the ceiling, after he would examine me. He tentatively scheduled me for surgery on Friday of that week, saying if the pressure did not decrease, surgery would be performed.

Dr. Rosenthal would not actually perform the surgical procedure due to his back problems. He said I would meet the surgeon on Thursday when I returned.

He made it sound as if surgery was imminent, and that was the last thing I wanted to happen.

On Thursday, I would be seeing Dr. Bachman, the Chief Resident, who had been following my case from day one. He had accompanied Dr. Rosenthal during each of my previous appointments, often being the first to examine me. Dr. Bachman would immediately relay his findings to me, so when Dr. Rosenthal arrived, I would already know my status. Many of the other residents who examined me, only would tell me that Dr. Rosenthal will be in shortly. Dr. Rosenthal did not usually have clinic on Thursdays but said he would be checking up on me.

When I left Stanford that day, I was fearful, depressed, and had a negative attitude. I snapped at my mother in the car on the way home. I told her she had no right telling Dr. Rosenthal that the medicine was bothering me. My mom let me explode and vent my frustrations. She said simply the doctor needed to know. During the remaining 45 minutes of the drive back to our home in Scotts Valley, nothing was said.

The thought of surgery turned my insides out. I was willing to do anything to prevent surgery. I explained to my parents how frustrated I was about not having control over the situation. People who have heart trouble can change their diet and exercise. People with back trouble can perform stretching and strengthening exercises and learn body mechanics. I felt totally helpless because there was nothing I could do to combat my eye condition. My mom said that is not true. It is so important that you take your medicines regularly and on time. Most people who have glaucoma are elderly and they often forget to take their medications. I am one of those one-in-a-million cases and don't want to be, as it is extremely rare for someone my age to have glaucoma.

On the drives up to Stanford, I was always preoccupied with what the doctor's examination might bring. My mom and dad both were aware of this and they never pressed conversations. On the drive home, you could always tell what kind of appointment I had by my behavior. If I was talkative, weird, and asked for food, then the news was good. But if I was quiet, angry, and not even interested in an ice cream, then the news was usually bad.

CHAPTER 11:
AVOIDED SURGERY
& INTRODUCING LARGE PRINT

It was Thursday, and I found myself returning to the hospital for a second time this week. The short-cut that we were now using to get to the second-floor Eye Clinic took us a back way past Dr. Rosenthal's Office. Because this was not his clinic day, he was in his office, and he acknowledged us, as we passed. I had been sitting in the waiting room for about 10 minutes when Dr. Rosenthal appeared and asked if I had been seen yet. I said no. Dr. Rosenthal immediately turned around and headed down the hallway toward the examining rooms. I heard him yell, "DAVID!"

Dr. Bachman quickly appeared from one of the examining rooms.

"Jeffrey needs to be seen right away," Dr. Rosenthal barked.

Almost immediately a nurse led me into an examining room. Shortly after that, Dr. Bachman entered the room.

Usually the waiting room at the Eye Clinic is packed with patients. Patients have been known to wait literally hours before they are seen. During my previous appointments, the shortest wait that I had was one half hour. During my first appointment, I waited one and a half hours before I was seen. The important thing is that you receive quality care. Stanford is one of the finest hospitals in the nation, and the Ophthalmology Department is no exception to this rule.

Dr. Bachman could sense my anxiety, and instead of making small talk, he initiated the examination. My eyes were numbed once again, and he proceeded to measure my pressure. I knew this was the moment of truth. Depending on whatever number the tonometer displayed would determine whether an operation would be performed or not. A cheer came out of Dr. Bachman's mouth as he received the measurement from the machine. I pulled away from the chin rest and gave the doctor a high five. My pressure was down to 20 mm in both eyes; thus the need for surgery having been dodged.

It felt as if someone had just removed a ton of bricks off my shoulders and I was elated. As we were walking down the hall to exit the hospital, Dr. Rosenthal cut us off at his office. I relayed the news to him concerning the appointment. He seemed surprised, but also pleased with the news. He said I never cease to amaze him. My pressure goes up and down like a roller coaster without any apparent rhyme or reason. Dr. Rosenthal removed a small examining light from the pocket of his lab coat and began looking into my eyes right there in the hallway. He looked at both of my eyes, for a few seconds, and said, "Okay, see you next week."

On our return trip home from this visit, we stopped for Chinese lunch. This was becoming a habit for the Stanford goers. Whoever was the chosen one, usually my mom, would accompany me and pay for lunch. It was an excellent deal for me. I think that was my parents' way of making the Stanford trips a little bit more tolerable.

My parents felt helpless concerning my eye condition. They could not just kiss my eyes and make the glaucoma go away. My entire family would hurt emotionally as they saw what I was going through.

My appetite was excellent after this appointment, so you knew the doctor's report must have been good.

My parents were concerned about my academic performance because I had already missed many days of school this semester. Furthering their concerns was the minimal time they saw me spending on homework. I told them I was not usually given homework assignments, and if I were assigned something, I would complete it at school. My parents asked to see the work that I was currently doing at school. They were shocked to see the simplicity of the work.

My parents once again approached the school officials with their concerns. They did not understand why I was being assigned work below my grade level. They emphasized that I was visually impaired, and needed accommodations in order to complete my academic assignments. The school principal contacted the County Office of Education because they obviously did not know how to handle the situation.

The county had specific resources to assist visually impaired and blind students. There were credentialed teachers trained to work with the visually impaired. There were also books on tape, in large print, and in braille. They had various magnifying devices, large-print typewriters, and talking calculators.

I was provided with large-print textbooks and allowed to return to regular classes. I was excited about being back in class with my friends, instead of being isolated. It is so important at that age not to be different. It is detrimental to be taken from the mainstream and placed in a specialized setting.

At that age, children wear the same brand of clothes and tennis shoes, and they have the same hairstyle. You would not consider being different because it was not cool.

The large-print books that were given to me allowed me to see and read again. I remember working with a student teacher in my Civics class. We were trying to find the chapter that was assigned for the week, and because of the large-print, we needed to search through several volumes before finding the correct chapter. Storing the books proved to be challenging, especially since lockers had been removed at the junior high school over the summer.

CHAPTER 12:
THE FIRST OF MANY SURGERIES

Dr. Rosenthal scheduled me to return on a weekly basis. He said that my pressure had been too unpredictable and it would be dangerous to go more than a week without being checked.

By now I was figuring out the system at the Eye Clinic. Patients would check in at the front desk and sit down in the waiting area next to the main hallway. After an unpredictable amount of time, a nurse would escort you into a small examining room. The nurse would test your visual acuity, update your records, and ask if there had been any significant changes since your last visit. You were then led to a smaller waiting area adjacent to the doctors' examining rooms. You would wait here for an unknown period, until the doctor called your name.

I learned to bypass the main waiting room and immediately go and sit down in the smaller one. I would strategically place myself in a seat where I was easily visible to the doctors when they came out of the examining rooms. Dr. Rosenthal would usually spot me when he was seeing one of his other patients out. He would order his nurse to put me in the room that had just been vacated. Thus, I would bypass several pieces of the bureaucracy. Dr. Rosenthal would treat me like a VIP whenever I was at the Eye Clinic. He realized how far we traveled to see him; he could sense the fear we had regarding my complicated eye condition, so he made our visits to the Eye Clinic as pleasant as possible. Whenever the staff would have a lunch in, he would be sure to give us something we could take and eat on the way home.

"Your eye pressure is 30 mm today," Dr. Bachman reported.

My heart sunk into my stomach when I heard those words. A large lump was forming in my throat and all the fears that I had about surgery rushed back into my mind.

Another visual field assessment was performed on me that day. I found myself staring at a concaved half circle for an hour, tapping when I saw a light enter my visual field.

The test results were compared to my previous test and there were changes. Dr. Rosenthal said some of the variations between the results could be due to the test administrators. I had a different person administering the test to me this time and that could account for some of the variation, Dr. Rosenthal indicated, though that he believed the test showed a significant loss of vision. He said the bouncing up and down that my pressure had done over the past three months had been harmful.

I was scheduled for surgery on Friday of that week. Although I did not want it to happen, in the back of my mind, I knew it was inevitable, though. I was to return on Thursday morning for what they called pre-op. I was scheduled to see one of the Eye Clinic's resident doctors. From what I could tell, all the patients who were having eye surgery on Friday saw this one doctor. Apparently, that is one of the ways Stanford chooses to teach its clinicians. It also frees up the staff physicians from having to be bogged down performing the bureaucratic paperwork that is involved when a surgical procedure is indicated.

The week flew by and Thursday arrived much too soon. Once again, I was missing school to make a Stanford appointment. This time, however, I would be out several days recovering from the surgery. I gathered a week's worth of assignments from my teachers so I could keep up on my schoolwork. With a bundle of assignments under my arm, I went to the office to wait for my mom to pick me up.

My mom, who was habitually late to all her appointments, never was late getting me to Stanford. This time, I was hoping that my mom would be late or just plain forget to pick me up, but she was right on time. We arrived right on time for my appointment, but we had to wait and wait to be seen. This time, I did not bypass the main waiting room, as I knew I would not be seeing Dr. Rosenthal and I really did not want to expedite the surgery process. I sat in the waiting room silent just thinking about the surgery, hoping that a miracle would happen, and my pressure would decrease. Finally, after waiting about an hour, I was taken to begin the pre-op work-up. I realized why it had taken so long to see the doctor. The resident was very thorough. He would repeat several of the tests to assure accuracy. He tended to ask repetitive questions to my mom, acting as if I would not know the answers. I understood that my mom was the adult figure present, but I felt like I should have been given an opportunity to answer the questions. After all, the questions concerned me. I understand the purpose of letting the resident perform the work-up, but it is certainly not fun for the patient.

I underwent several of the same tests that Dr. Rosenthal had ordered on my first visit. This time, however, an inexperienced doctor was performing them, and it made for a long afternoon. The doctor attempted to measure my pressure multiple times, and so much time had elapsed during these tests that additional anesthetic drops had to be given. During one of the tests, the doctor requested that my mom hold my lid open, while he examined the eye. I remember being quite patient during the entire process, and I was even complimented about it by the doctor and later by my mom.

A tall, brown-haired, clean-shaven doctor entered the examining room. He shook my hand and introduced himself as Dr. Egbert. His handshake was gentle, but reassuring. Dr. Egbert, after greeting me, immediately went over and introduced himself to my parents. His voice was soothing, and it helped to reduce the tension that was in the air. He spoke with authority and experience, and an era of confidence quickly filled the room. Dr. Egbert explained that he and the Chief Resident, Dr. Bachman, would be performing the surgery on my eye.

Dr. Egbert was very cautious when he examined my eyes. The grip that he used to open my eyelids was gentle, but firm. Before he administered any medications into my eyes, Dr. Egbert made sure that I had a Kleenex so I would be able to blot my eyes. The other doctors who I had seen would always put the drops in my eyes first and then hand me a Kleenex. By that time, the excess medication would have already rolled halfway down my cheeks.

Dr. Egbert concluded his examination and said he concurred with Dr. Rosenthal's findings. Dr. Egbert took his time and explained in detail what the procedure would entail. He was careful to not overwhelm us with technical terms and spoke in a language that we could understand. So often doctors would huddle around me in the examining room, discussing my case, but talking way over my head; Dr. Egbert, however, encouraged us to ask questions and would pause periodically to make sure that we comprehended what was being said. Amazingly, he answered the question that I was most concerned with. Would there be any shots? He could not speak for any of the other doctors (the anesthesiologist or for Dr. Rosenthal) but assured me that he would not be giving me any shots.

He said they had elected to operate on the right eye because it was my dominate eye. Surgery is rarely performed on both eyes at the same time because of the risk of bilateral infection and the inconvenience to the patient. A procedure called a goniotomy would be performed. This was the least-intrusive surgical procedure that could be done. It involves the least amount of cutting and the eye recovers quickly. In the eye, there is a natural channel where the aqueous fluid flows, so it can leave the eye. During this operation, the surgeons will probe this channel and clear any blockages. The actual procedure only takes a minute or so. Most of the time that I am in the operating room will be spent lining everything up. The area that must be probed is microscopic and everything needs to be positioned perfectly before entering the eye.

Dr. Egbert was looking through my chart to make sure everything was in order before I was escorted to the Anesthesiology Department. He realized there was one document that was not in my chart. If this situation had occurred in Dr. Rosenthal's presence, shit would have hit the fan. Dr. Rosenthal would have become irate. He would have yelled at the resident doctor, then at his nurse, ordering her to retrieve the proper forms immediately. Dr. Egbert's reaction was calm, and he simply went to the appropriate staff member to get what he needed.

Dr. Rosenthal was the head of the Ophthalmology Department, and in that capacity, he had very high expectations for his staff. He was an extremely intelligent man and had set ways of how things were to be done. He did not tolerate what he perceived as incompetence by others, nor did he have patience when things did not go as planned.

Next, I found myself in the Anesthesiology Department, sitting and waiting to see yet another doctor. A nurse showed me to the bathroom and asked me to pee in the small cup that was just handed to me. I produced and had no trouble completed that task. My height was measured, and I was weighed and led to sit at a small table. Across the table from me was a lab technician smiling at me. I noticed immediately there was a tray full of tiny bottles that I recognized. The person who pretended to be Dracula when I was in the hospital before was carrying this same type of tray. This person across the table from me was going to withdraw blood from me, and she was apparently happy, smiling about it.

Well, my worst fears were coming true. I had already been poked with a needle by the lab technician; the anesthesiologist said he planned to start an intravenous line, from which he could administer the necessary medicine to put me to sleep, and he was uncertain whether pre-op medication would be prescribed. The anesthesiologist said he would be in contact with my doctor to see whether anything had been ordered. The way that I had it figured, I would only have to endure one more shot, the IV prior to surgery, because I had already spoken with Dr. Egbert.

It was early evening by now, and I was being pushed in a wheelchair up to the Pediatric Ward. I was placed in the same big room as before with five other beds. All the patients who had been there previously were gone. I wondered if they were discharged like I had been, or was it more tragic and had they passed away from their disease?

I remember very little about the hospital, probably because I had blocked out most of the memories. The nursing staff remembered me and welcomed me back, saying they were sorry we had to meet again, considering the circumstances.

A light dinner had been ordered for me, but I was not too hungry. They encouraged me to eat, saying I could not have anything to drink or eat after midnight due to my morning surgery. I forced down a few bites, so everyone would shut up and stop bothering me about it. I should have been exhausted from the day's ordeal, but I could not rest because my mind was racing. The entire surgery concept scared the hell out of me, and not knowing what to expect was a very uncomfortable feeling.

My mom elected to stay the night on a cot in the playroom so she would be there when I was being prepared for surgery. The nurse had told my mom that they would begin preparing me for surgery around 5:30 in the morning. I remember thinking, what does it mean when the nurses say they are going to prepare you for surgery? I felt like a piece of meat that was going to be part of a meal that the surgeons would be feasting on. Unfortunately, I was going to be the main course. I was going to be marinated by the nurses before being taken downstairs to the operating room, where I would be cooked and carved up.

I spent a long sleepless night. I was on edge the entire night and alerted to the slightest noises. Any time I heard footsteps coming down the hall, I was sure someone was coming for me. The room was dark so I could not see the clock. I kept track of time by the nurse's rounds. I knew they checked vital signs every four hours. There was the 8:00 p.m. check, the 12:00 a.m. check, and the 4:00 a.m. check. After the third evening check, I knew that the time was drawing near. Luckily, the surgery was scheduled for 7:00 a.m. and the anxiety would not have to be prolonged. It was hospital policy to operate on children first thing in the morning whenever possible. They understand the fear children have concerning surgery and they do not like to keep them from eating for an extended period.

The clatter of footsteps could be heard in the distance. The footsteps were getting louder and louder, so I knew someone was approaching the room. Out of the corner of my eye, I saw the dreaded white uniform pausing at the foot of my bed. I remember faking asleep, hoping that the nurse would just go away and leave me alone.

"Jeffrey, Jeffrey," I heard the nurse say. "it's time to get ready for surgery."

The nurse obviously was not going to disappear, so I had to stop faking and face reality. The nurse brought me a basin full of water. She presented me with a bottle of soap and told me to wash my face. The warm water felt good on my face and I paid special attention to the area around my right eye. I rubbed ever so gently with the washcloth around my eye and even gave my right eye a pat when I finished.

I was so afraid of swallowing any liquids that I would continuously blot the saliva from my tongue. I thought if I swallowed anything, even my own saliva, it would be harmful to me during the surgery.

The nurse brought one of those revealing gowns for me to wear. She said I needed to remove all my clothes, and she emphasized that my underwear would also have to be removed. This nurse had obviously been around the block a few times because she knew exactly what I was going to do. I was planning on leaving my underwear on, but she made it clear that they were to come off. There were little booties to put over your feet, but I had the damndest time trying to figure out how they went on.

My mom arrived around that time and could see how frustrated I was getting. She grabbed the bootie that I was not working with. She looked at it for a moment, and then handed me the bootie, having the place where the foot goes opened. I gave her the bootie that I was struggling with so she would figure that one out too.

My mom attempted to carry on a conversation with me, but I was not in the mood. I was giving her the classic one-word answers to her questions. I blotted some more saliva from my mouth, and my mom wanted to know why I was doing that. I explained my reasoning to her, and she could not hold back the laughter. She told me it was not necessary for me to do that. I got defensive because she had laughed at me. I told her she did not know for sure if it was necessary or not, and being stubborn, besides, I continued to blot my mouth.

The nurse entered the room and appeared to be hiding something behind her back. She said it was time for my shot and told me to roll over on my stomach. I thought the nurse was joking and I did not think it was funny. She pushed away the little bit of gown that was covering my bottom. I figured this was her way of checking to see that I had removed my underwear. I heard the nurse rip open some package, and then the odor of alcohol filled the room. She rubbed the alcohol pad on my bottom and suddenly the realization...

Oh my God, I thought. This lady is not kidding; she is going to give me a shot. A rush of adrenaline went through my body and the flight-or-fight response had kicked in. I wanted to run like hell, but being I was in no position to attempt that, I opted to stay and fight. I tensed my muscles, and right at that point, I felt the needle being driven into my backside. The medicine burned as it went in, and I did not take another breath, until the needle had been pulled out of my body.

"You're lucky," the nurse said. "It was almost necessary to give you two separate shots."

The large amount of medication that had been prescribed barely fit in one syringe.

That is funny, I thought, I do not feel very lucky right now. My butt was stinging, I still had the IV to endure, and I figured my eye would be hurting soon. I had Dr. Rosenthal to thank for that early-morning shot. Apparently, he had ordered this injection but did not let me know about it.

The bed rails were locked in the up position around me. Any hopes of escaping now were impossible. I felt like I was in prison, as I stared at the metal rails on either side of me.

Soon the powerful medications that Dr. Rosenthal had prescribed began taking their toll on me. First, my mouth became very dry, and then my entire body began to tingle. I was feeling the full effects of the muscle relaxers by now. My arms and legs were limp. I had no control over my limbs, and I could not voluntarily move them. I remember lying on the gurney outside the operating room, and I wanted to scratch my neck because it itched. I tried and tried, but I could not make either of my arms budge. It was so frustrating not being able to run my fingernails across my neck just a couple of times to sooth the irritation.

The tranquilizers were also doing their job. My eyelids were extremely heavy, but I would not allow them to shut, because I wanted to know what was going to happen to me next. I was quite drowsy, but I made myself stay awake, because I was afraid of what would happen to me if I fell asleep. I figured the doctors could not operate if I am awake.

The florescent lights began looking distorted to me. I felt as if the lights were right on top of me or I was floating up on the ceiling next to the lights. I heard voices in the distance, but they were muffled sounding and I could not comprehend what was being said. I do not know if the voices were directed toward me, but I was in no condition to carry on a conversation or even respond. I chose to just lie there in my half-conscious state and wait for the next step.

The next thing I remember was two men standing over me with blue pajamas, a shower cap on their head and a mask pulled down over their neck. I am totally spaced out, I thought. There are grown men huddling around my bed wearing pajamas. If they think this is a slumber party, then they are at the wrong place. One of the men asked me if my name was Jeffrey. I attempted to respond, but an unintelligible noise came from my mouth. Obviously, neither man understood me, because they grabbed my arm to check the identification band around my wrist to verify my identity.

I remember feeling my dad's hand patting my shoulder, wishing me good luck. I did not remember my dad arriving and wondered how long he had been there. My mom added her supportive pat, and I was off.

The two men wearing pajamas asked me to slide onto the gurney, which was next to my bed. One of the men grabbed me by my shoulders and the other man grabbed my feet, and they did most of the work getting me to the gurney. I do not remember the gurney starting to move, but as I lay on my back, staring at the ceiling, florescent lights would pass over me.

The elevator door opened, and the gurney was pushed inside. I wondered if I was too long for the elevator. Afraid that the door would shut on my feet; I attempted to bend my knees, but my muscles would not respond—when the door shut, I was relieved to know that my feet were still intact.

It was quiet and calming in the elevator, and I had the opportunity to take in what was happening. Why me? I thought. How could this be happening to me? Before I even had time to process that question, the door opened once again, and I knew I was on the surgery floor. I exited the elevator and was immediately pushed through an automatic door. A blast of cold air hit me, and it was quite sobering. I became more alert temporarily.

The odor of cleaning agents overwhelmed me. The sound of running water could be heard in the distance, where I presumed surgeons were busy scrubbing, talking to one another about their upcoming cases. Most of what they were saying was muffled, and those words that I could hear seemed like a different language.

I was becoming quite cold by now, and the thin blanket covering me was doing nothing to reduce the chill. The florescent lights had stopped moving above me, so I knew I had been parked somewhere.

As I lay there on the gurney outside the operating room, I was becoming drowsy again. My neck was becoming quite itchy, learning later, it was a reaction to the medication that I was given. I was working so hard to get my hand from my stomach to my neck so I could sooth the irritation. Out of shear necessity, I had managed to move my hand up to my chest, and knew relief was only a couple of inches away. This simple task was draining what little energy I had left.

I was startled rather suddenly by hands that were putting something on my head. I looked up and saw a person wearing a mask looking down at me. My mind began to race.

Am I already on the table? Is this guy about ready to carve into me? I better do something quick, I thought, so this guy will understand that I am still wide awake.

"Hello Jeffrey," a soothing female-sounding voice came from behind the blue mask.

She introduced herself as the head nurse, and I was surprised that it was a woman when I was expecting it to be my doctor; nevertheless, I was put at ease. Obviously, she was expecting me to be awake, so I knew they would not be starting the procedure right now.

A shower-cap-type hat had just been placed on my head, she explained. I wondered why she could not have explained that before she placed it on my head, so I would have expected it. With all the excitement, I had forgotten that I was trying to scratch my neck, and now, even though the irritation was flaring up again, I did not have the strength to do anything about it. My hands had managed to find their way back by my stomach, and there was no way they were moving from that spot this time.

The nurse began asking me a series of questions, and I realized I had answered these same questions the night before. Why the hell are they asking me these same questions? Is this a cognitive test to see how well half-conscious people perform? The nurse was rattling off questions like "Have you ever had any of the following: hepatitis, bronchitis, asthma, heart disease, tuberculosis, etc.?" In my present condition, I was not able to process the information as fast as the nurse was spitting it out at me. My answers were at least two or three diseases behind what she was asking. It did not seem to faze her, though. She was on a role, acting as if she had to get through this list in a certain period of time.

I was zoning out in my own little world for I do not know how long, resting quite comfortably, when I was aroused by movement. My gurney was being rolled into the operating room.

The doctor who was pushing me, I guess, noticed that my eyes had opened slightly and said, "We're ready for you, Jeffrey—you are now entering the fix-it room." He said this in an attempt to keep me calm.

PRESSURE

Why don't they just tell you the way it is? Instead, they make it sound like we are going into some shop where we are going to build dollhouses. It would have been all right if I had not been the dollhouse that was going to be put back together. Since I was the person who was going to be "fixed," I was not amused by the doctor's reference.

As I was being transferred from the gurney to the operating table, I was still drowsy, but very alert. It was if I was seeing things through a heavy fog. Everything that I could see was fuzzy, everything that I could hear was muffled, and everything that my mind was taking in was in slow motion, but I was able to process most of what was going on around me.

A nurse untied the gown from behind my back and removed my arms from the sleeve holes. She positioned my right arm by my side and pulled the blanket up around my waist, tucking my right arm against my side with the blanket being tucked snuggly under my body.

Two anesthesiologists began hooking me up to all the monitors. One of the doctors was busy placing electrodes all over my chest. At the same time, the other doctor was applying a blood-pressure cup to the upper part of my left arm and attaching a wire around my left index finger. Both doctors were talking to me. One of them was apologizing for something about cold electrodes, while the other one was saying the blood-pressure cup will inflate and deflate automatically.

The blood-pressure cup was inflated around my arm, so it would act as a tourniquet. I was then asked to open and close my fist several times, after which the doctor began slapping the dorsal surface of my hand. I had no idea why the doctor was doing that, but I did know that my arm was going numb from the lack of circulation and hoped the doctor would hurry up and complete whatever he was doing.

A package was ripped open and the alarming smell of alcohol filled the room. Even though I had not been told what was being done to me, the olfactory clue made it obvious.

Oh shit, I thought, I am being prepared for another shot. I have always been fearful of needles and continue to hate them to this day. When someone from the medical profession, I learned, takes the action of opening an alcohol package in your presence, it means an injection into your body is soon to follow.

"This might sting a little," the anesthesiologist said.

Why bother using the quantifier, "might"? The doctor knew damn well that it was going to hurt. Physicians and other healthcare professionals choose their words carefully, so they will not alarm the patient. I suspect that is what the anesthesiologist was doing when he said it "might" hurt. During my experiences, I have learned to ask a lot of questions. The more questions that I asked, the less surprises there were—doctors do not like to tell you about pain and discomfort, and leave out those types of details or use mild phrases like "It's a soft needle; you may feel a little pressure; this might burn slightly etc.," when they are describing specific procedures. If you do not ask detailed questions ahead of time, like I did not during the early days of my treatment, then you are going to be surprised.

The alcohol pad was used to scrub the posterior surface of my hand. The doctor straightened and spread out each of my fingers in search of a good vein. He spotted the one that he wanted and flicked it with his middle finger a couple of more times. I felt the prick of the needle, as it broke through the skin, followed by pressure and burning, as the IV needle was being manipulated into my vein. My hand began to tingle, and I was not sure if it was due to the tourniquet that was still in place or if it was a reaction from the IV that was now connected through the back of my hand. I was lying completely still, afraid to move, thinking if I did, the large needle would rip my hand apart. Finally, I did not feel anymore discomfort.

Tape was being wrapped around my hand to hold the IV line in place. The tourniquet was released, and I began regaining sensation down to my fingertips.

It must have been quite a sight, me lying there on the operating table. I had a shower cap on my head, an oxygen tube up my nose, with tubing extending across my face and around my ears, white circular electrodes covering my upper torso from my navel to my throat, with wires running to every individual electrode, a blood-pressure cup around my arm, which was actively inflating and deflating, an intravenous line running from a bag, which hung from the ceiling into a vein in my hand, and finally another wire extending from my index finger to an oximeter.

Preliminary medication was administered to me through the IV. Before the anesthesiologist even finished saying, "I just gave you something to help you relax," my eyes became extremely heavy, and I could no longer keep them open, as if I really needed anything else to help me relax. I was feeling quite relaxed because of the drugs I had already been given, and to give more was overkill.

Even though I could not open my eyes, I was still conscious enough to hear faint sounds around me. The anesthesiologist said he was going to put me to sleep now and asked me to take a deep breath. He then asked me to count backwards from 100. I do not remember making it to 99, before I was out.

CHAPTER 13:
RECOVERY ROOM
& DECEIVING SURGICAL RESULTS

I awoke to the sound of someone moaning. Confused and disoriented, I turned toward the noise, attempting to determine where it was coming from and where I was. There was a radio on in the background, and the DJ's voice was familiar to me. That is the station my parents always listen to, Frank Dill and Mike Cleary on KNBR. It was calming to hear a familiar voice, even if it was only on the radio. Finally, things were beginning to clear. I had been operated on, I remembered, and now the procedure must be over, because there was a patch covering my right eye.

The nurse seeing me become restless came to my bedside and said, "Jeffrey, you are in the Recovery Room—-your surgery is all done."

The nurse asked me if I knew where I was, what day it was, and who the president was. I remember thinking to myself that these questions are ridiculous. This lady must think I had some sort of brain surgery, and this is her way of testing me to see if my brain is still functioning. Well, as far as I knew, the surgeon had worked on my eye, and not my brain, so I answered the nurse's questions without difficulty.

My eye burned a little, but other than that, it felt pretty good. The natural reaction was to blink, but when I attempted to do so, I realized there was a patch covering my eye, reducing any movement.

There was a terrible taste in my mouth, and when I attempted to swallow, my throat was very sore. The oxygen tube that was in my nose felt like it was about two sizes too big for my nostrils. The blood-pressure cup was still acting like it had a mind of its own, as it inflated and deflated automatically. The IV line was still flowing into me, which inhibited me from moving, because I was afraid that I might knock it out.

The nurse offered me some apple juice, and I gladly accepted. The juice tasted great. It helped to rinse the horrible taste from my mouth, and the cold liquid soothed my throat as it went down.

The entire day's ordeal was beginning to catch up to me. My stomach was knotting up, and I was becoming nauseated. This is my body's way of saying you put me through hell today, and now I am going to get some pay-back. My hands were clammy, my face felt flushed, and my stomach continued to turn.

I broke into a cold sweat, the room began to spin, and up came the contents of my stomach. Revenge was served. Fortunately, my stomach was empty, except for the small amount of apple juice that I had just consumed. The nausea symptoms had passed for now, and I was resting comfortably.

The anesthesiologist came to my bedside to examine me. It was not a traditional examination. The anesthesiologist made a statement, saying "Obviously the surgery did not agree with you."

Because I chuckled at the doctor's remark; he concluded that I was stable and coherent enough to return to my room on the Pediatric Ward.

Two orderlies came to transport me from the Recovery Room to my hospital bed. On the trip back to my room, I began feeling nauseous again. My head was beginning to spin. These guys are driving this gurney like a maniac, I thought. There must not be any type of test to pass to become a gurney driver, because if there had been, there is no way these orderlies would have passed. It seemed like they were racing the gurney through the halls, doing occasional 360-degree turns. My body was responding to all of toxins that had been put into it, and it was attempting to get rid of them.

By the time I arrived in my room, my stomach was all knotted up again. My family was waiting there for me. I heard someone say, "He looks a little bit pale." Right about the time my sister asked me how I was feeling, I began to dry-heave. No words were necessary; my actions spoke for me. That episode summed up exactly how I was feeling.

The nurse said she was going to get me something to make me feel better.

More drugs, I thought. That is the last thing my body needs right now. The thing that made me sick in the first place was medicine, so how was giving me more medicine going to help?

The nurse returned with what she thought would make me feel better. She said, "I can give you this shot in your arm," acting as if I would be pleased by that, I guess, thinking the arm is better than my butt.

WRONG! I thought. There is no way the pain from a shot is going to make me feel better. I bargained with the nurse, pleaded with her not to give me the injection, saying if I became nauseous again, I would take the shot. The nurse went along with the deal. It is amazing how the threat of an injection can scare the nausea right out of you. I did not feel sick anymore and would not have admitted it if I had.

My parents informed me that Dr. Egbert said everything went well during the surgery. I dozed on and off during the rest of the day and through the night. My family, realizing that I was not very good company, left for home early that evening. I was awakened a few times during the day and night, so the nurses could measure my vital signs, and I could relieve my bladder. The nurses would not allow me to ambulate to the bathroom, so I had to relieve myself in bed. What I mean is the nurses provided me with a plastic container, but no instructions in its use. They pulled the curtain closed around my bed and told me to holler when I was finished. Now, to a normal person in their right mind, with good visual acuity, this thing probably would have been easy to figure out. But being that I was half conscious, barely able to open the non-patched eye that had limited vision, and had use of only one hand because the IV line was going into the other hand, made the task challenging, to say the least. Had the container that I was presented with been given to me opened on one end would have made this task much easier. Instead, I needed to become very familiar with a urinal, which I had no experience with and no visual memory to reference. I did discover that there was a removable lid on one end, and once I figured out how to open the lid, the task was completed successfully.

I had slept quite a bit during the past 24 hours, and as a result, I awoke early before sunrise. The IV was still flowing into me, I was wearing the fashionable surgical gown and I felt something rather sticky on my chest. When I examined the area more closely, I discovered an electrode still attached to me. There were no wires coming from it, so I assumed it had just been overlooked when I was being disconnected from all the machines. I ripped the electrode off, and no alarm sounded, so I figured I had not done any harm.

My eye was not hurting, but it was extremely irritated. It felt like someone had poured a bag of sand in my eye, and the natural reaction was to blink. That only seemed to stir everything up and make matters worse. The best thing I found to do was to keep the eye as still as possible. Of course, this was a lot easier said than done.

My dad and mom arrived early that morning and found me to be a lot more talkative today. The day before, I had said virtually nothing to my parents, and now I was rattling off one question after another, trying to make up for yesterday's silence. It was obvious that I was elated that the ordeal was over, and I had survived it.

I dressed my lower extremities but did not know what to do about my upper extremities. Because of the IV, I did not know how to remove the gown (which I so desperately wanted to get rid of).

I figured the gown would remain on me if the IV was attached to me. The nurse entered the room at that point, saying I looked much better today and complimented me on the progress I had made in dressing myself.

The nurse asked if I wanted to change the gown that I was wearing. It did not take me more than a split second to respond with a definite yes. She must have read my mind, I thought. This is double good luck, I figured. I am getting rid of the gown, and the only way to do that is to remove my IV. The nurse spoiled the good news by saying, "I won't be able to take out the IV yet because you haven't consumed enough fluids."

She disconnected the IV bag from the ceiling. I pulled my left arm out of the sleeve hole, and the nurse followed close behind with the IV line and bag. My mom handed me a real pajama top, and not the gown version of pajamas the hospital tries to pass off. The nurse did not seem to mind the casual switch my mom made, even though the nurse had laid out a fresh gown.

I was anxious for breakfast to come, because I was starving, and I wanted to get busy drinking, so I could get this damn IV out. Breakfast arrived, but so did a team of doctors. Dr. Egbert, Dr. Bachman, Dr. Sparks, and Dr. Bryant all squeezed in around my bed. Everyone exchanged greetings, and then it was down to serious business. It was interesting how Dr. Egbert stood back and let each of the other doctors admire his work. There was a definite pecking order that was followed. Dr. Bryant, being the newest resident, took his turn first. He got the distinct honor of removing the patch from my eye. The tape that held the patch in place was intertwined in my hair, and all eyes were on Dr. Bryant, as he pulled the tape away from my face and hair. He was working so carefully, trying to be gentle. The slower he worked though, the longer the discomfort lasted. I could feel each strand of hair being pulled, as the tape was being torn away. This was a case where ripping off the tape in one quick motion would have been preferred.

At last, the patch was removed from my face. It was quite stuffy under that patch, so it felt good to have the eye exposed to the open air. I immediately tried to open my eye to determine whether my eye was still functioning or not. The lid was swollen, so I only managed to open my lid a sliver. That was enough though because I could see light, and knew my eye was still working.

Dr. Bryant completed his examination. Then Dr. Sparks took his turn, shining different lights into my eyes. Dr. Bachman, who was the Chief Resident, took his look just before Dr. Egbert. He broke the uncomfortable silence in the room by saying everything looks good.

It was relieving to me to hear something, anything. The first two doctors had performed their examinations but had said nothing. I wondered whether things looked so bad to them that they did not want to say anything. Dr. Egbert took his turn, and he had an opportunity to evaluate his work. After his examination of my eye, he agreed with Dr. Bachman's assessment. It was reassuring to hear Dr. Egbert say everything looks good, because his opinion carried the most weight, in my mind.

Dr. Egbert proceeded to put some Polysporin ointment into my eye. This was to be put in my eye three times a day, he said, as he requested that one of the resident doctors put a fresh patch on my eye.

The experience of having the Polysporin put into my eye was not at all what I had expected. The gooey substance was surprisingly soothing. It acted as a lubricant, as it penetrated, making the sutures softer. Dr. Bachman placed the patch on my eye and began taping it to my face. This time, I took the responsibility of pulling my hair back out of the way as much as possible. Right about the time I thought he was done taping, Dr. Bachman placed a metal shield over the patch for protection and proceeded to tape that down. The doctors said they would be seeing me tomorrow in the Eye Clinic.

I wondered why Dr. Rosenthal was not a part of this team of doctors that had come to my bedside. It was Saturday, and I figured he probably does not work on weekends.

I started in on my breakfast again, which, of course, was cold by now. I managed to swallow a few bites before the nurse came in, announcing that Dr. Rosenthal wanted to see me right away in the Eye Clinic. That is weird, I thought. Why did Dr. Rosenthal not accompany the other doctors during the morning rounds at my bedside?

"This is not the first time he has made demands like this," the nurse grumbled. The nursing staff likes to have the orders written in the patient's chart, and they do not take kindly to doctors calling up and barking out orders, demanding immediate service. The nurse let me in on some inside information, which helped me to understand things a little better. Off the record, she said, "Dr. Rosenthal is not welcome on the Pediatric Ward anymore."

Apparently, Dr. Rosenthal had criticized the nursing staff one too many times, verbalizing his displeasure rather loudly, not seeming to care who might be around hearing his outburst. Dr. Rosenthal was told his conduct was not acceptable on the pediatric floor, and it would be appreciated if he would see his patients in the Eye Clinic, rather than on the floor.

A transport person was immediately dispatched to my room, and he arrived shortly after that. The orderly, upon seeing that I had an IV, extended a pole from behind the back rest of the wheelchair. He hung my IV from the pole, and then asked me to transfer from my bed into the wheelchair. We were on our way down the all-too-familiar route from the Pediatric Ward to the Eye Clinic.

The orderly parked me outside the only examining room that appeared to be open for business. All the other rooms were locked up, and this was the only one that had signs of life. I noticed a handful of people sitting in the waiting room when I rolled up. It reminded me of any other clinic day, but being that it was the weekend, it was pretty quiet. Fortunately, the orderly had notified Dr. Rosenthal upon our arrival. He dismissed the patient that he had been seeing out, and pushed me into the exam room.

Dr. Rosenthal did not know how to handle the IV contraption that was attached to me. I needed to sit in the examining chair, but there did not seem to be anything to hang my IV bag from. Dr. Rosenthal was quite anxious to examine my eyes, and he was becoming impatient with this IV situation. He slammed a few pieces of equipment around, I guess looking for something that might help him. He grew more and more irritated as the seconds passed and began scratching his head and rubbing his forehead profusely. What I interpreted as a minor inconvenience was becoming a major issue. The tension was building, and it was only a matter of time before the good doctor exploded.

"Haven't you eaten breakfast yet?!" Dr. Rosenthal said sternly.

"Yes, a little bit," I said rather timidly, hoping it was the right thing to say.

"Why haven't the nurses taken this thing out then?" he continued in that same tone, I think meaning to direct his frustration toward the nursing staff rather than me.

I shrugged my shoulders to answer the question, afraid to say anything at this point.

Dr. Rosenthal hesitated for a moment, and then proceeded to remove the IV from my hand. I cannot say that I argued with the man, because I wanted that thing out as bad as he wanted it out of the way. I was concerned about how it would feel when it was being removed. The process of putting it in created some discomfort, so I assumed taking it out would be the same.

I kept waiting and waiting for it to hurt as he un-wrapped the tape, but it never did. Not before long, a Band-Aid was being placed over the wound site, and I never felt any pain.

At last, I was sitting in the examining chair, resting my head on the chin rest. Dr. Rosenthal had to pry my right eye open because of the swelling. He examined my eye, searching for any complications, such as hemorrhaging, infection, or leaking. Thankfully, he reported no such problems.

The visual examination had been completed, and now it was time for the real test, the moment of truth to see if the procedure had done anything to reduce the pressure. Dr. Rosenthal was going to measure, or at least attempt to measure, my inner ocular pressure. I had some doubts about how successful this test would be due to my eye's present condition. My first concern was whether my eyelids would open wide enough so the tonometer would be able to come in contact with the cornea. Secondly, the actual eyeball was probably swollen, so I was wondering if the reading would be reliable. Finally, the idea of having something forced into my surgically-traumatized eye did not appeal to me.

I knew Dr. Rosenthal would not give up easily. He would continue to poke and probe until he received the information that he was looking for. I tilted my head back, while Dr. Rosenthal tugged on my lower lid, so he could administer a drop of Alkane. Usually, I was able to see the eye dropper being held over my eye, but this time my vision was much too fuzzy.

I could not see the eye drop being released into my eye, but I felt it when it hit. It burned like it had never burned before. The raw wound site in my eye felt like someone had just added salt to it. Luckily, the intense burning only lasted a few seconds. The medication absorbed into my eye, and the numbing reaction began to kick in. After a minute or so, while Dr. Rosenthal was busy attaching the tonometer instrument to the Slit Lamp/Microscope, the eye had become quite numb. As a matter of fact, it felt better now than it did before the medicine was administered. I no longer felt any roughness from the sutures.

Dr. Rosenthal grasped my eyelids firmly and pried them apart. The all-to-familiar blue ring of light was brought in contact with the front of my eye.

"Hold still," Dr. Rosenthal ordered.

I was contracting my muscles so tightly, trying not to move, that they were beginning to ache from the built-up tension. Dr. Rosenthal left the Meyers instrument in contact with the front of my eye for an unusually long period of time. The eye was difficult to measure, so the test was repeated several times to ensure accuracy. The eye was tearing quite a bit and that further complicated the test.

Dr. Rosenthal was shaking his head in disbelief as he pulled away from the microscope.

Immediately, I began fearing the worst, wondering what was wrong.

"This is unbelievable," he said. "Your pressure is down to 25 mm (from 40 mm the day before). Who would have ever guessed that a goniotomy procedure would reduce the pressure?" Dr. Rosenthal exclaimed.

Before the good news even had time to sink in, Dr. Rosenthal spoiled it by saying we need to schedule the left eye for surgery as soon as possible. Now I did not know whether to be happy or sad. The procedure on the right eye appeared to be successful, but now he wanted to send me right back to the OR. I had not even had time to get over the last surgery ordeal, and here Dr. Rosenthal was talking about sending me back to that place.

Physically, things appeared to be going well, but emotionally, I was a mess. I was still recovering from the first surgery just 24 hours ago. It was a great deal of mental stress for anyone to go through, especially a young teenager.

Dr. Rosenthal said I would be able to go home tomorrow, but that he would be scheduling my left eye for surgery next Friday. My parents tried to comfort me by saying we should be happy that the surgery seemed to work and now the left eye was going to be fixed too. I understood what my parents were saying, but I could not process the apparent success. The only thing I could think about was the fact that surgery was inevitable again.

Sunday came and I was leaving the hospital, but in the back of my mind, I knew I would be back ever so soon.

I had managed to put myself a little at ease. After all, I had survived this surgery thing once, and now I knew what to expect. The week flew by and I even managed to attend school one day that week.

CHAPTER 14:
MORE SURGERY & MEDICATION MIX-UP

Thursday came, and once again, my mom and I found we were driving the all-too- familiar route on Highway 17, over the Santa Cruz Mountains, through the west side of the Silicon Valley to Interstate 280. From there, it was a relatively short trip up the peninsula to the Alpine Road exit and Stanford Hospital. My mom and I used to joke about how the car could probably drive itself, since it had made the trip so many times by now, and we would continue making this drive for many years to come. Most kids hate long trips in the car, but I remember on many occasions not wanting to get there anytime too soon. Sometimes the 50-to-60-minute trip seemed to end much too soon, particularly on surgery days, which would become more and more necessary.

The fastest trip to Stanford Hospital is 39 minutes, and as far as I know, is a record that still holds today. I remember that trip, it is not what you might think (an emergency trip to see Dr. Rosenthal). My brother Mike was driving me, which was unusual, and my long-time best-friend John was accompanying me on the trip. I do not know what influenced my brother; perhaps he was attempting to bring some excitement into the all-too-frequent Stanford trips, but he declared that he would set a record today. I was not too sure what he meant, but it became quite apparent. He asked my buddy John what time it was, as we backed out of the driveway, and from then on, he began flying down the road toward Highway 17. My brother was a little frustrated because it took too long in his mind to cross onto Highway 17 from the Glen Wood cut-off. From then on, though, it was a racetrack, and my brother weaved in and out of the traffic through the Santa Cruz Mountains, as we made our journey toward

Stanford. John was either really focused on keeping track of time or scared to death because he did not say much of anything on the ride. Fortunately for me, my failing vision did not allow me to see in detail the maneuvers my brother was making—out of sight, out of mind, for me. Obviously, we survived the trip, because I am here to write about it. If memory serves, my check-up that day was positive, and I guess the pressure was scared right out of me.

Second surgery: We arrived at the hospital and found ourselves sitting in the all-too-familiar Eye Clinic. Today, my strategy, where I bypass the initial waiting room and go directly to the second waiting room, did not seem to speed things up. The pre-op appointment was with a resident doctor, who did not know me well, and it probably would not have mattered if he had. My mom and I sat for over an hour waiting to be seen. We did not talk much. Before appointments, my mom would pass the time by reading the various magazines available in the waiting room. The magazines were quite old and outdated. My mom would amuse me by reading the publishing dates of the various magazines that she was browsing. Most of the magazines dated back eight to 12 years and we even found one published in the 1950s. We always wondered why the magazines were so old. We rationalized that it was because Stanford focused on providing quality health care, not on updating their periodicals.

Finally, my name was called, and I headed down the hallway to the examining room. The resident doctor was familiar to me, as he had performed the work-up for my surgery last week. Dr. Bryant was a new resident in training, and you could tell he still was not fully confident with this pre-op routine. When we entered the exam room, he was shuffling papers and flipping through my file, which was beginning to grow rather thick. Dr. Bryant asked me to place my chin and forehead into the Slit Lamp fixture, which was very familiar to me by now.

I spent the better part of two hours in that examining position, having numerous lights shined into my eyes and various topical medications administered. One of these medications was used to dilate my eyes. After my eyes were dilated, Dr. Bryant shined a high-intensity handheld examining light into my eyes, which was so intense, I could feel my eyes heating up, because the light was so close to my face. Procedures like this never made much sense to me. Why dilate the eyes when you are going to shine a bright light into them? Is not this sending a mixed message to your eyes? I guess it is all about the doctors' ability to see into the back of your eye.

Dr. Bryant measured my pressure and began writing several notes in my medical records. Finally, after a long period of silence, my mom asked how the pressure was.

Dr. Bryant said it was fine and continued writing. Dr. Bryant's words seemed to put a calming feeling into the already quiet room. At some point, Dr. Egbert entered the examining room, and as always, went over and shook my mom's hand, and then my hand. Dr. Egbert proceeded to examine my eyes. Several of the tests that Dr. Bryant had performed were being repeated. However, the exam was going much quicker, due to Dr. Egbert's experience and because he did not need to pause to complete the pre-op documentation. Dr. Egbert measured my pressure and his readings were much different then Dr. Bryant's.

My pressure was in the 40s in both eyes. This was a case of wanting to believe Dr. Bryant, because his news was better, but deep down, I knew Dr. Egbert was right.

It was like having the rug pulled out right from under you. I had been reassured that everything was fine with my pressure just a few minutes earlier. Now I was being told my pressure was not good. Compounding things was the fact that this was totally unexpected. I did not know or even consider the possibility that my pressure could rise in an eye that had been operated on only six days previously. As far as I knew, the surgery had fixed my right eye, and now we just needed to fix the left eye.

Dr. Rosenthal was consulted, and he concurred with Dr. Egbert's findings. The two doctors discussed strategy and it was agreed that I would undergo a trabeculotomy procedure on my left eye tomorrow.

I had enough trouble just pronouncing the name of the procedure and had no idea what it meant. Later that night, when I was pronounced, "settled in," by the nurses, my parents thought it would be nice to call my brother and sister; this "settling-in" process involves answering a series of questions concerning various medical conditions, signing surgical consent forms, and, of course, changing into the hospital-provided gown. This process, I must admit, never made me feel too settled in, but rather anxious. Further adding to this anxious feeling was the fact that my parents had been required to sign a surgical-release form, stating I could die from known or unknown causes.

I talked to my brother and sister and explained that I was going to have what I called a trecka-becka-lectomy officially known as a trabeculotomy. Somehow I had managed to add several syllables to the procedures name, I guess trying to make the procedure sound more impressive. I explained this procedure involves cutting a tiny hole in my eye that will act as a drain and allow this built-up fluid to escape my eye. When I explain glaucoma to the school kids, I tell them to picture a balloon as it gets bigger and bigger when it fills with air. When you have glaucoma, your eye is like a balloon filling with air, and the surgery that is performed involves creating a hole, like when a balloon is popped. The concept behind this surgery seems straightforward; however, getting everything to work long-term is another matter.

Once again, I found myself being wheeled into the operating room. Even though I had visited this place before, a week ago, it did not make me feel any more comfortable. I certainly understood the routine, i.e., blood-pressure cup, EKG attachments, intravenous line, etc., but this time the surgical procedure was different. I did not know what to expect. I knew the procedure was more evasive and traumatic to the eye. Rather than clearing a natural channel, which was performed previously, this surgery would be cutting a new channel through the eye to reduce the pressure.

I was kept in the hospital for five days post-op to monitor my eye's recovery. Unlike the goniotomy procedure, when doctors do not necessarily expect the eye pressure to lower, a trabeculotomy procedure will lower the eye pressure. The question is "how long will the pressure maintain at an acceptable level?" The success of this procedure cannot be determined for several months and is based on how the eye heals. This small hole or channel that is created by the surgeon will scar. The hope is it will scar open, which means the channel will remain functioning, allowing excess fluid to escape. If the eye heals too aggressively, then the surgically-created channel will scar closed, leaving no way for the fluid to drain out of the eye. This will cause the eye pressure to rise again, which will continue to destroy the optic nerve.

The population over the age of 40 typically is the group diagnosed with glaucoma, and when surgery is indicated, it is usually more effective. One of the reasons for this success is because older people do not heal as fast or as aggressively. Unfortunately, younger people, like I was, do tend to heal more thoroughly. This was a case of being one in a million, as it is rare for a child to be diagnosed with glaucoma.

One of the complications that can happen after a trabeculotomy procedure when the eye pressure is too low is that the anterior chamber of the eye can flatten—there needs to be enough pressure in the eye to maintain its shape and structures. When the anterior chamber of the eye flattens, the interior of the eye collapses. Think of an airplane that loses pressure; things will certainly become displaced. If this happens to an eye that has been operated on, where a drainage hole has been created, then it is likely the surgically-created hole will cave in and be dysfunctional.

The time I spent in the hospital was some of the most unpleasant memories that I had—as a patient, things are out of your control. You are told when you will eat, you are told what to wear, your vital signs are checked at the hospital's convenience, your movement is restricted to the bed, the bathroom, or the pediatric recreation room, and you should accept that the nurses know what is best for you.

I understand you must have structure in a hospital setting and that patients are there to convalesce, but you also need to have some flexibility. I remember once having the nurse come into my room saying she was going to check my vital signs, which was nothing unusual, as it happened every four to six hours. I was taking a drink of something, as the nurse walked in.

"Jeffrey," she said almost accusatorily. "You shouldn't have had that drink," she said, acting as though I should have known. "Now you will need to leave this thermometer in your mouth for several minutes," she said rather matter-of-factly, as she slipped it into my mouth without warning. Medical professionals are so good at doing things to you without first explaining what is going to happen. It is so routine for these professionals, but they forget that their patient does not know what is going to happen. I think the reason why I was more surprised than other patients was due to my poor vision. Most people can see that a thermometer is coming toward their mouth, but often I could not see these types of things happening. One does not know from casual observation that someone has low vision.

Now I had no idea, nor did I even consider the fact that drinking something prior to having your temperature taken was a bad thing to do. It seems to me that the nurse could have come back several minutes later and taken my temperature after my mouth had an opportunity to warm back up, but that I guess would have interfered with her routine. Instead, I got to sit with a thermometer in my mouth for several minutes.

Another frustrating and frightening experience occurred while I was in the hospital after this most recent eye surgery. The swing shift of nurses had just started. My nurse had brought in the evening doses of eye medications that were to be administered. The nurse had removed the shield and patch from my surgically-operated eye and was proceeding to administer various topical medications. When I questioned the nurse about the name of the medicine that she was planning to put in my left eye, she said it was Timoctic. I spoke up immediately and said that I did not think that was correct.

The nurse, without hesitating, proceeded to put a drop of Timoctic into my left eye, saying she was pretty sure that was right.

Now why couldn't the nurse have stopped at that point to review the order in my medical records? The nurse did not even consider what I had said, I guess because of my age, thinking I was too young to understand. I believe even if the nurse had known, with 100 percent accuracy concerning the medication, it was still her duty to verify it with my medical records. Perhaps this would have taken more of her time, but it would have eased my concerns. Instead, the nurse used the term *pretty sure,* and that was not reassuring.

I certainly understand that we are human, and humans make mistakes. But what angered me most about this event was the fact that I had questioned the nurse concerning the medication, yet she ignored me.

Not only did the nurse put Timoctic into my left eye, but she also put Epinephrine and Pilocarpine, which were also glaucoma medications. The nurse also put Atropine, Pred Forte, and Polysporin into my left eye, which were post-surgical medications. At that time, nothing was administered into the right eye. I guess the nurse assumed that the surgery eye with the patch was the only one needing treatment.

Shortly after the nurse left my room, as I lay in my hospital bed, feeling uneasy about this last round of medication, the nurse returned, saying some of the medicine was supposed to go in my right eye. I do not remember the nurse saying anything about the wrong medicine being put into my left eye. Once she had finished putting the glaucoma medicine in my right eye and left the room, I immediately called home.

My mom answered and could tell that I was upset. Once I had explained what had happened with my eye medication, my mom hung up from me and immediately called the nursing station.

The nurse explained to my mom that she had already spoken with the on-call ophthalmologist, Dr. Bachman. Dr. Bachman had said nothing serious would happen because of the medication mix-up. It would make my pressure low in the left eye for a couple of days, but that's all. I knew my pressure was probably quite low in the left eye, because of surgery, and wondered how much lower it could go. According to the nurse, Dr. Bachman had said everything would be fine.

In our " sue

happy" society, Dr. Bachman was probably required to say everything would be fine. For him to say anything else would be putting the hospital in jeopardy. As I would learn later (when I battled too-low pressure), there was really no treatment and you cannot easily reverse the effects of medicine that has already been administered.

Now my surgically-traumatized left eye had received the entire regiment of powerful drugs to combat high pressure, but that was not the problem at this time, particularly less than 24 hours after surgery. At that time, the concept of the medicine making my pressure too low did not even compute. I had heard only about glaucoma and how permanently damaging high pressure can be if it is not treated.

When I had awakened from my first glaucoma procedure, I remember the eye felt pretty good, burning just a little. This time, the eye felt like it was on fire and the natural reaction was to blink. When I did so, it felt like there was a piece of sandpaper rubbing against the inside of my lid. This rough feeling, I learned later, was sutures, which were used to cover the surgical-wound site in my eye.

Dr. Egbert explained the stitches would be irritating for a few days, but then they would dissolve on their own. The surgical procedure, I was told by my parents, had gone well and there were no complications. As a matter of fact, when I had returned to the Eye Clinic for a thorough examination a couple of days after surgery, my eye pressure was under 8 in the left eye; however, the right-eye pressure was in the 40s. The too extremes of eye pressure, one being quite low and one being quite high, made for a complicated treatment.

The Diamox tablets, which were considered the most effective medication for treating glaucoma, are taken orally. It interacted with both eyes, lowering the pressure. The left eye's pressure post-surgery was on the borderline of being too low, so the Diamox would not help that situation. Eye pressure is a lot like blood pressure, meaning you do not want it to be too high or too low. Prolonged periods of very low eye pressure can be harmful as well.

Without the Diamox, the right eye's pressure would climb to an even more harmful level. Because of my history of glaucoma, Dr. Rosenthal opted to keep me on the Diamox, feeling it was better to have my pressure low than high.

The following morning after this second surgery, I found several doctors huddling around my hospital bed, all waiting their turn to examine my eye and Dr. Egbert's handy work. Once again, not much was said, until Dr. Egbert had finished his exam. Although the silence was stressful, as the other resident doctors took their turns, I was holding my breath, waiting for Dr. Egbert's assessment. After what had happened with my eye-pressure readings the day before (with one doctor saying they were fine and Dr. Egbert saying they were high), I did not relax, until Dr. Egbert said everything looked good at this point.

These examinations that were performed at my bedside did not allow the doctors to see in detail what was going on inside my eyes. The exams performed at my bedside were done with the doctors' naked eye, without the use of microscopes. My eye pressure was never measured during these visits, as the portable devices available were not as accurate and could be dangerous to a newly operated eye. I believe these examinations were performed more for the comfort of the patient and probably because I was a child. If Dr. Rosenthal had been around on that Saturday, I am sure I would have been taking a wheelchair ride to the Eye Clinic for a thorough examination.

CHAPTER 15:
LIMITING ACTIVITIES
& THE LOW-
VISION OPTOMETRIST

This would be the beginning of my longest consecutive stay in the hospital. Usually, once I woke up from surgery, my energy would be focused on getting out as soon as possible.

However, being that my right eye was still suffering from glaucoma, it needed treatment, as the previous goniotomy procedure had only served to lower my pressure for a short time.

As Monday rolled around, I found myself visiting with Dr. Rosenthal in the Eye Clinic and I remember wanting nothing more than to get out of the hospital and back home. The good doctor (Dr. Rosenthal) had another plan, which involved operating on the right eye for a second time, as the previous surgery had done nothing to control the high eye pressure long-term. Dr. Rosenthal's agenda did not agree with my agenda. He was scheduling me for more surgery, and I was asking, when could I get out of there (the hospital)? As you can imagine, Dr. Rosenthal's agenda won out over me, and I found myself staying in the hospital waiting for yet another surgery. With all the fun I was having, I had forgotten it was May and my birthday was just around the corner. This fact did not dawn on me until a group of my friends showed up at my bedside, thanks to our family friend/neighbor, Janet New, who coordinated this special event. There was a cake, a lot of laughter, and a well-needed distraction from what was going on.

My (dominate) right eye was going to have surgery number 2. The trabeculotomy procedure planned would lower my eye pressure, but the real question was whether it would work long-term? Treating young people with glaucoma is a challenge because, putting it simply, "they just heal too well." That would be a theme that I would come to realize over and over again throughout my treatment.

My eighth-grade graduation was coming up and the class had their annual trip to the Great America Amusement Park. Unfortunately, Dr. Rosenthal was not in favor of me going on roller coasters, bumper cars, and any other rides that go upside down or cause whiplash.

I chose not to go, as I did not want to stand by watching my friends go on all the rides. As a matter of fact, Dr. Rosenthal had banned me from Physical Education (PE) class almost my entire eighth-grade year, saying it would be dangerous to my surgically vulnerable eyes. I remember requesting a letter from him, excusing me from PE, as the school needed it for their records.

Dr. Rosenthal exclaimed, "Doesn't the school realize that Jeffrey has undergone multiple glaucoma surgeries?"

His note was hastily handwritten on a prescription pad. It was short and to the point: "Jeffrey is not to participate in PE classes until further notice."

I was a young teenager, who had played sports for as long as I could remember. All my friends played sports, so being told to stay on the sidelines was difficult. I would have many conversations with the resident doctors regarding my restricted physical activity. The residents were sympathetic to my plight and told me, off the record, that they did not feel limiting my physical activity for a prolonged period was necessary, but none of us wanted to share these opinions with Dr. Rosenthal.

When I started my freshman year of high school, I had already undergone several surgeries by now and probably could have been considered legally blind, but I was in denial and never would have admitted that at the time. *Legal blindness* is a term that the government uses to determine eligibility for benefits based on degree of vision loss. If you're legally blind, your acuity is best corrected to no better than 20/200, or your field of vision is less than 20 degrees. That means if an object is 200 feet away, you have to stand 20 feet from it in order to see it. But a person with normal vision can stand 200 feet away and see the same detail.

The Great America Day at the amusement park for my classmates turned out to be a day that I had been referred to a low-vision optometrist. By the time that I had started being treated at Stanford, my vision loss was already considered significant because my central vision had been impacted. Glaucoma is known for reducing the peripheral vision first. If the condition goes undetected without treatment, the central vision will become involved. At the time that I was officially diagnosed, my visual acuity would have been close to legally blind, the point being, my glaucoma condition had progressed to where my central vision had been impacted, and whatever damage had occurred, was permanent. This meant the goal was to save my remaining vision by controlling the pressure.

Stanford doctors understood that even if they could save all the remaining vision that I had, I would still be dealing with significant sight loss. For that reason, I was referred to an optometrist who specialized in helping people who were experiencing vision loss.

Dr. McAdams was the doctor I saw, and he was affiliated with the Peninsula Center for the Blind, which was near Stanford Hospital. The appointment began by looking at my current glasses and prescription strength. He spent a lot of time adjusting my current prescription, identifying a stronger correction, which improved my overall vision. This correction involved a little bit thicker lenses then I had been wearing for as long as I could remember.

I had been wearing wire-framed glasses for the past several years, going for the cooler look. But now Dr. McAdams was adamant about having me wear thicker plastic frames, as he felt it would work much better to support the thick lenses of my prescription. This new style would be noticeable to all the kids who knew me. I was excited to hear that a new prescription was going to help my vision, but I would have preferred to keep using the wired frames. However, that was not a negotiable option, as far as Dr. McAdams was concerned.

Additionally, I was able to try out a variety of handheld magnifiers with varying strengths. Some of the devices had built-in lights, which really could illuminate what you were viewing. In general, I learned how having appropriate lighting can make such a difference. Contrast was another useful strategy that I learned about. Placing a white plate on a light-colored table was a lot harder to see as compared to placing that same plate on a darker-colored placemat or tablecloth. Finally, I remember trying on glare shields with a variety of colored tints, which could improve the viewing experience, based on the activity or location, i.e., indoor, or outdoor, and sunny versus foggy conditions.

I remember being quite anxious about the new glasses and prescription. I had high expectations that my vision would see a big improvement, but on the other hand, I was worried about how the new thicker plastic frames would look cosmetically on my face. As it turned out, the new prescription did not improve my vision, as I had expected, and my new frames were not well received from my peers.

CHAPTER 16:
PSYCHOSOMATIC SYMTOMS
& SURVIVING PE CLASS

Around this time of transitioning from middle school to high school, I remember experiencing what I can only describe as a sudden inability to speak. This condition refers to real physical symptoms that originate from emotional trauma. With my recent glaucoma diagnosis, frequent hospitalizations, multiple surgeries, progressive vision loss, and being a young teenager, moving into high school, certainly equated to extreme anxiety and fear at the time. I remember I was taking a shower when my voice cracked. I tried and tried to clear my throat, but my voice seemed to get worse and worse within a matter of a minute or two. When I called my mom in a panic, who was working at the dental office, she was having trouble understanding me. As I was talking on the phone with her, trying to explain my speaking difficulties, I became even more hysterical, causing my speech to become even more impaired.

My mom rushed home to get me and take me to the local Scotts Valley Medical Clinic. Dr. McKenzie, who had seen me a handful of times over the years, diagnosed me with a psychosomatic episode. He explained that there was nothing organically wrong with my speech or vocal cords. Hearing the doctor's reassuring words and calming demeanor allowed me to relax and my speech began improving. By the time we were leaving the medical clinic, my speech was pretty much back to normal. It just goes to show how impactful overwhelming stress can be on one's ability to function.

When I began my freshman year of high school, my schedule had Adaptive PE listed as my fourth-period class. I was thinking that was a result of Dr. Rosenthal's note banning me from Physical

Education during middle school. I was not about to show up for whatever that was. It turns out that a couple of my friends also had PE on their schedule for fourth period, so I followed them to that class.

I remember having to go up to Mr. Tompkins, who was the PE teacher and long-time varsity football coach, because my name had not been on his attendance sheet. He demanded to know, in front of the entire class, why I was enrolled in Adaptive PE, and what was wrong with me.

I was not about to admit there was anything wrong with me, so I said I did not know. I was added to the regular PE class, and not wanting to be different, did not disclose anything about my progressive vision loss.

High school students are required to complete two years of PE to graduate. I so dreaded the two years of PE, as my vision continued to decline. Every sport that was played seemed to use sight, and that was what was failing me. I so worried about embarrassing myself or letting down the team I was on. All the typical games were played, including softball, football, soccer, tennis, etc.

The one game that was particularly brutal for someone who could not see was slotter ball. This game took place in the gym usually during rainy days. A volleyball is used, and the object is to throw the ball as hard as you can at your opponent. If the ball hits any part of your opponent's body, he is out of the game. The last man standing, so to speak, wins. If you happen to be lucky enough to catch the ball that is being fired at you, then the person who threw the ball at you would be out of the game.

There was no chance that I was going to be catching any ball being thrown my way. I was unable to see the ball when it was hurled at me. I would often hear the ball when it whistled past my head or bounced off the wall behind me. And, of course, I felt it many times when the ball plastered off my torso or face.

CHAPTER 17:

AGGRESSIVE POST-SURGICAL SCARRING

& REACTIONS TO MY SIGHT LOSS

Months would pass in between surgeries, giving my eyes time to heal, which sounds good in theory. However, healing, in my case, meant pressure rising again, causing irreversible damage. The small channel that had been created was now scarring closed, causing the surgically-created drain to become non-functional, resulting in a build-up of eye pressure.

In high school, I started to receive unwanted personal attention. Teachers of the visually impaired were now suggesting interventions based on my progressive vision loss, which were directly impacting my high school experience. There was an aide assigned to my Math class, who would transcribe, in large print, information that was on the chalkboard. All tests were also transcribed in large print, using an ink pen. What this meant to me was there was always an aide sitting next to me in Math class. When I think about it now, it allowed me to complete my Math class. At the time, though, it made me stick out from all the other students, as I received undesired attention.

I remember my ninth-grade Algebra teacher was an elderly man who did not understand the monocular device that had been given to me, which would allow me to see what was on the chalkboard. I am sure I looked conspicuous holding a device up to my eye. Mr. Merkel demanded me to give him the monocular device that I was holding up to my eye to see. Being a teenager, I refused, and was kicked out of the class for the day. My best friend John was later also kicked out of the class during the same day, trying to defend my use of the device. I heard later from my mom, after a phone call from Mr. Merkel, that my teacher thought I was using the device to "look at nudy girls"—another breakdown in communication between the school system and my needs.

And then there was Mrs. Alumbaugh, who decided that because I had sight loss, my hearing must also be impaired, so she announced to the class that we needed to speak louder and clearer to help Jeff learn, as he is blind. My friends in the class took great pleasure in yelling at me, explaining that they were just following the teacher's instructions. I did not like that my English teacher had announced to the entire class concerning my vision loss. Also, the use of the word *blind* was not something I wanted to hear or was ready to accept.

And then there was my freshman-year History teacher, Mr. Payne. At the beginning of the semester, he was approached by my teacher, Connie. Connie was a teacher of the visually impaired (VI.) and the high school Resource Specialist. This was fifth period, and the class started right after lunch break. Probably attempting to discuss the needs of a student with sight loss, right when class was scheduled to begin, was not the best timing. Connie was responsible, though, for supporting children with visual impairments throughout the county, so she had to meet with teachers of her students when she could.

I was able to hear most of the discussion between the three of them. Basically, the message that I got was Mr. Payne did not want me in his class and felt I would be better served at a special school for the blind. Connie attempted to convince Mr. Payne that I could be supported, given materials in alternative formats, and be successful in his History class.

My sister, who was a senior at my same high school, got wind about Mr. Payne's reluctance to have me attend his class. My sister does not put up with injustice when it comes to people she loves. She confronted Mr. Payne and demanded that I be allowed to take the class. As it turned out, Mr. Payne really did not have any authority over who could or could not attend his classes. Mr. Payne apparently went out of his way, toward the end of the semester, to let my sister know that he passed me in History class, announcing that I had received a D, acting as though I had not even earned that poor grade. It turned out that there had been a couple of tests that I had taken with a proctor that had not even been recorded in his grade book, because it had been left in his box in the main office. Those missing points moved my grade up to a B.

During my senior year, I remember being enrolled in a U.S. Government class, and Mr. Thompson was my teacher. It was my first-period class of the day, and I was getting rides to school with friends by now. I did not have control over what time they would pick me up and drive me to school. I was so appreciative of getting a ride, so I would always be at the pick-up location at the predetermined time. There were a few occasions when my ride was running late, so we got to school right when the bell would be ringing. Of course, Mr. Thompson's classroom happened to be furthest from the student parking lot in Building 3. And there were a couple of times when I arrived late for class. I remember racing down the hallway of the school, trying to beat the second bell, so as to not be officially late.

On one occasion, I ran into a classmate of mine who was also running late to Mr. Thompson's class. He said, "Let me do the talking," as we entered the room.

I did not know what he meant at that moment, but I did keep my mouth shut, as we entered the classroom together. My classmate had placed his hand on my back in a comforting manner.

Without prompting, my classmate explained the reason for our tardiness to Mr. Thompson: "I saw Jeff walking down the hallway in

Building 2, and he was heading into the wrong classroom. I took the time to go assist Jeff, and guide him to the correct classroom."

Mr. Thompson then questioned me directly as to the truthfulness of the story that he had just heard. The whole thing had happened so quick for me. I said it sounded like a really believable story, and it very well could have been true, but it might have been just a little exaggerated. Fortunately, for the creative story that my classmate had come up with, we were not penalized that day for being late.

CHAPTER 18:
STEROIDS, PRESSURE PATCHES & ROOMMATES

The eye pressure was elevating to unsafe levels once again, and intervention was needed, as I was at risk for losing more vision. Dr. Rosenthal felt that a more aggressive post-surgery steroid regiment be implemented during the next procedure. Steroids are used to reduce the impact of scarring after surgery.

This time, Dr. Rosenthal planned to make sure the eye was exposed to a considerable amount of steroid treatment, which translated to frequent visits to my bedside from the nursing staff post-surgery.

Dr. Rosenthal had an order in my chart for Prednisone eye-drop medication to be given to my newly-operated-on-eye every two hours. When I awoke from this most recent surgery, and was informed that drops were going to be placed in my eye frequently for the next week or two. I didn't really know what the term *frequently* meant, but the idea of anything being put into a raw eye, with an open surgical wound, did not thrill me. The first round of drops was going into my eye, and the anticipation of how much it would burn or hurt, along with the prep time it took to remove all the tape from my face, including the shield and patch, actually was way worse than receiving the drop itself. I can best describe the drop as a thick milky substance, which was very soothing to my traumatized eye. My eye felt less on fire, and the sandy gravelly feeling in my eye was lubricated with the medication. Fortunately, every two-hour routine was only enforced during my waking hours, so my sleep cycle was not going to be interrupted by this.

Of course, there are many other factors in the hospital that interfere with a good night's sleep. There was the boy in the ward room lying right next to me. He was playing his boom box at a loud level, especially if you consider there were several pediatric patients sharing the same large room. He was asked to turn down the volume on his boom box, and his answer to that suggestion was to close the curtain and turn up the volume. Curtains around the patient's bed do nothing to reduce the sound, and they do nothing to reduce the smell either. This same patient, who I said was bunked next to me, had his leg in a full cast, from his toes to his hip. It was in traction, meaning there were cords coming from the ceiling supporting his leg as it hung in the air. When nature called for my roommate, #1 was no problem, as far as I was concerned. But #2 was an entirely different experience for the entire room's occupants. This included patients who could not escape or possibly family members, friends, and whoever else happened to be visiting when nature called.

Those patients who had been around long enough, who included me, at this point, knew when nature was soon to call. The nurse would arrive, asking if my roommate was ready to have a "BM." Then I would hear the clang of the bed pan as it got pulled out of the closet and positioned under my roommate's posterior. The nurses, as this point, were free to go, telling my roommate they would be back to check on him in a few minutes. I felt like these nurses knew the routine and gave themselves a very timely break. These were the few minutes that I would have loved for Dr. Rosenthal to have called for me in the Eye Clinic.

Let us just say that there were sounds, breathing patterns, and most smells that should have been reserved for a private bathroom experience.

My most recent surgically-involved eye had been exposed to a lot of steroids this time and things were looking good for the time being.

My other eye, however, was once again experiencing high pressure, so further intervention was going to be needed.

The next surgery was being put on the schedule during the Christmas holiday, as this would not make me miss more school time. This was one of the last procedures that required me to stay in the hospital for post-surgical care. It was the week of Christmas; my surgery had been completed, and I was passing the time just waiting to be discharged. One of the nurses had started to tell me a story about a large bicycle company approaching the hospital wanting to donate bikes to all the children who were unfortunately hospitalized during the holidays.

I was just starting to imagine how cool it would be to bring home a brand-new bike, when the nurse went on to say, "The hospital could not accept the donation because not every child would be able to ride a bike."

Whenever I had a reprieve from surgeries, I was more than willing to get away from Stanford Hospital and return to regular high school life as a teenager.

I continued to travel to Stanford pretty much on a weekly basis because by now it was clear that my condition was very unpredictable. My eye pressure could change from week to week or even day to day.

A resident doctor had come up with an idea of operating in a different quadrant of my eye for the next procedure. When surgery is indicated for your eye, it is looked at as though it is a clock. The 12:00-clock position is considered the top of your eye, whereas the 6:00 position is considered the bottom of your eye. Each time surgery is performed, a certain quadrant of the eye will be indicated for the procedure. So far, the 12:00 position had been the quadrant chosen for each of my procedures. This meant the initial procedures had been performed at the 12:00 quadrant, and to date, any repeated procedures had also been performed at this quadrant.

Now a brand-new 6:00 quadrant was being proposed. This meant that surgery was going to be performed in a brand-new area of my eye, hoping that the long-term healing would be more favorable.

Multiple surgeries meant dealing with multiple doctors, particularly since Stanford is a teaching hospital. Each time surgery was indicated, it meant not only did I have what was called a work-up in the Ophthalmology Department, with a resident doctor, but also a work-up was required at the Anesthesia Department. This was also performed by a resident doctor in training. I pretty much had this routine down by now, which involved answering numerous questions about illnesses (most of which I had never heard of before), reviewing my extensive dental history, with particular focus on any and all crown and filling work, peeing into a cup, blood work, and a chest X-ray.

Before you are rolled into the operating room, they like to establish an intravenous (IV) line into your vein. On many occasions, this proved to be a bigger ordeal than I wanted. Either my veins were not cooperating with having a needle poked into them or the person manipulating the needle was inexperienced with a poor aim. On many occasions, it took multiple attempts before the needle was positioned correctly and taped down into place. Each attempt of starting an IV involved applying a tourniquet to my upper arm, which made the available veins more visible to the doctor. Once a suitable vein was selected, an alcohol pad was used to clean the area, and then there was the insertion of the needle into the selected vein. Rarely were the resident doctors successful on their first or even second attempts. If the IV was not successful, the subcutaneous area would often swell up from the saline solution coming from the IV bag. Then the procedure would need to be repeated in a different location, typically along the dorsal surface of my hand or forearm.

Usually, these procedures would be performed in the pre-op patient room, where my family was permitted to be with me prior to surgery. There were several occasions when attempts to start the IV were made in this pre-op room, but I would be moved to the hallway outside of the operating room, so my parents did not have to witness the continued difficulties with getting the IV started on me.

The attending physician would often intervene if the resident doctor was struggling with the procedure, delaying my arrival to the operating room.

When I awoke from this most recent surgery, my operated eye felt different from past surgeries. There was external pressure on the eye. It felt like a brick was lying on top of my eye. There was a lot of pressure in my eye socket, and moving my eye at all, including blinking, was difficult. The next morning, when the parade of doctors entered my hospital room, to examine the work that was performed the day before, I learned that Dr. Rosenthal had ordered a pressure patch be applied to my eye.

My understanding of this type of patch is to make your eye immobile, which could help with healing. These types of patches are uncomfortable, to say the least, and having it applied to your face is not an enjoyable experience. Try to imagine several eye patches and many pieces of tape. The patches were folded and placed snuggly in my eye socket. Tape was applied generously and firmly over the patches to hold them in place. To top things off, a metal shield was taped over the pressure patch for additional protection. It was a relief to have medication dropped into my eye because that meant the pressure patch had to come off for a few minutes. The post-surgical medication was always soothing to my eye, usually a milky eye-drop substance, along with a Polysporin ointment. This was a complete opposite of how glaucoma medication felt when being dropped into your eye. It would always burn and blur your vision for a period.

I was on a roller-coaster ride. The pressure of one of my eyes would be in normal limits, because of the recent surgery it had undergone, whereas the other eye's pressure was on its way back up, because it had been several months since its last surgical procedure.

A continued complication was balancing both eyes' needs regarding the Diamox medication. Diamox is taken orally, so it affected both eyes. The newly operated eye did not need the lowering effect of the Diamox, but the other eye always did. Dr. Rosenthal never wavered, believing high pressure was way more damaging then low pressure, so that meant I never stopped taking the Diamox.

CHAPTER 19:
DIAMOX SIDE EFFECTS & EMERGENCY TREATMENT

I was taking the maximum dosage, and unfortunately, Diamox has some uncomfortable side effects, including intestinal issues. I usually did not feel like eating breakfast, figuring anything I ate would just go right through me. At lunchtime, I would force down a burrito from the school cafeteria and wash it down with a half-pint carton of milk. Not the most nutritious diet. Probably should have focused more on eating a healthy breakfast, but when your stomach is upset, adding anything to it just does not sound good.

In the mornings, the Diamox would do a number on my gastrointestinal system, cleaning it out. I spent a lot of time in the bathrooms. High school bathrooms were the place most students tried to avoid because they were frankly disgusting. Since I had started taking Diamox, it had a way of coming back up, if you know what I mean. My brother had a name for this coming-back-up thing that the Diamox caused. He said that I was good at burping up farts.

I was so paranoid about how my system and breath were affected by the Diamox that I was known as the Binaca Man in high school. My friends always knew they could freshen up their breath by asking me for a blast. You would have thought I was the local drug dealer, handing out fixes to my friends, but it was only a breath freshener meant to disguise the effects of how the Diamox so messed with my system.

We lived in the Santa Cruz Mountains and attended high school in Soquel, which meant it was a 25-minute ride by car. None of the kids in the neighborhood wanted to take the bus because it was a 50-to-60-minute ride. The kids who did not have a license or car were always looking for rides to school from those kids who were driving.

My freshman year, I was lucky because my sister was a senior at the same high school, so I was able to get rides to school. Many of the neighborhood kids would also want a ride to the high school, so there were many mornings when the Ford Fiesta had six people crammed into it, three in the front (where there were only two bucket seats), and three in the backseat. I know there were only five seatbelts available in the car, but this was before seatbelts were required, and your minor-aged friends could ride with you.

Anyway, the idea was that the car was packed with people. My stomach would begin reacting to the Diamox pill that was taken less than an hour ago, and I would begin to strain, holding back the abdominal cramping that was building up. Usually, I would not be able to hold back what I would describe as the toxic gas needing release from my gastrointestinal system. Usually, I was unable to hold back the increasing build-up of pressure for the entire commute to school. Out of necessity, I would need to let one of my ends go, to relieve the excessive pressure building up in my stomach. I would release the gas tension through the plumbing of least resistance. If the Diamox had only just began to digest, then the associated gas would come right back up the same tube. If it had a little longer to digest, then it would result in gas coming out the other end. Either way, as far as my brother was concerned, it resulted in a toxic discharge.

Sometimes I would decide to release the gas pressure early in the ride to school, and I remember my fellow passengers making a negative comment about the failing septic system of whatever neighbors we were passing at the time that the offensive odor took over. It was nearly impossible to control the build-up of pain in my stomach, and my only option was to release—sorry to all the family and friends who got to live this with me.

The other side effect I remember about Diamox was numbness and tingling in my hands. One boring afternoon, I remember telling my friend, John: "I cannot really feel my hands right now."

John, not believing me, took the opportunity to test if I was bluffing or not. He claims he pinched the skin on the back of my hands very hard and was amazed when I did not respond, because I did not feel it.

The post-surgery pressure patch routine was continued through the next several surgical procedures, while Dr. Rosenthal was still running my treatment protocol. In addition, I was also prescribed Prednisone orally. The idea behind increasing my steroid intake, to include both drops and pills, was for my body to heal more favorably in terms of the surgically-created channels remaining open.

Dr. Rosenthal's back issues did not allow him to perform surgery, but all my pre- and post-surgical care was controlled by him.

There were a couple of emergency experiences when my pressure had risen to the point where my eye was reported to be pulsating. This meant the pressure was so high that the blood supply to the optic nerve was being impeded, and if something was not done quickly, this could result in sudden sight loss.

Dr. Rosenthal had requested that Dr. Egbert perform what is called a paracentesis. This is when a needle is used to extract fluid from an eye. This was performed in the exam chair at the Eye Clinic.

There was no time for me to change into one of those fashionable gowns and be sent to the OR. My eye needed the pressure reduced immediately. I was given a topical anesthetic to numb my eye. The anesthetic made it so I would not feel the needle penetrating my eye, but it did nothing to blur the image of a needle approaching my eye. Of course, I needed to hold still, so Dr. Egbert could place the needle where it needed to go. The instinct when you see a needle coming toward your eye is to blink and pull away. Remember, I had not been given anything for relaxation or sedation, so it took all my will power to hold still and let the doctor complete the procedure.

Dr. Egbert was focused on looking through the Slit Lamp/Microscope and positioning and manipulating the needle to extract fluid from my eye. Dr. Egbert was unable to see how much fluid was being extracted, so Dr. Rosenthal was monitoring that part of the procedure. He announced that one-tenth of a cc was in the syringe. That sounded like such a little amount of fluid being removed, but that would serve at least for the time being as a relief to my eye. Unfortunately, Dr. Rosenthal had accidentally mistaken an air bubble in the syringe for actual fluid that had been extracted. What that meant was the needle was going to make an immediate return trip into my eye to extract actual fluid. That was a huge let down for me at the time. I thought I had just survived the biggest nightmare of my life, but now I realized it was not yet over. Fortunately, I did not have really any time to stress about the anticipation of a second go-around with extracting fluid. Fortunately, this time, the procedure was considered a success, as fluid had been removed, reducing the pressure, eliminating the emergency for now.

I remember being given what I will call a Glycerin Cocktail.

This was another emergency treatment for elevated intraocular pressure. It involved me drinking a cup of glycerin, which is a very sweet syrup-like substance that, in my case, was diluted with grapefruit juice to make it more tolerable to digest. The medication was designed to lower eye pressure quickly, but the lowering pressure effect only lasted for a few hours. In my case, the reduced pressure effect was not significant, and I would still experience elevated harmful pressure.

To this day, the memories of those cocktails make me gag when I think about or smell grapefruit juice.

CHAPTER 20:
THE PAIN OF COMPETING
& THE IDEA OF COACHING

My friends, brother, sister, and parents were continuing to compete in different sporting activities, including Colt League, softball and slow pitch. I was no longer seeing well enough to participate in organized sports.

I remember a pick-up basketball game which I participated in with my older brother and our friends. The game was operating at a pace well beyond what I could see and keep up with. Passes would come out of nowhere and bounce off of my chest or head. I would improvise my game by not looking back at the person dribbling the ball, so I would not be a target for receiving a pass. While on the court, my focus truly became survival. I did not care about scoring baskets, but rather avoidance of being pummeled by a high-velocity pass, which would come out of nowhere and bounce off of whatever part of my body that happens to be in the ball's path. After receiving what must have been a behind-the-back, bullet-speed pass that made direct contact with the middle of my face, resulting in a bloody nose, my pick-up basketball career was over.

Then there were the ski trips with my friends. They were all good skiers and keeping up with them on the slopes involved moving down the hill at a pretty rapid pace. Think of driving through ground-level fog. Everything was white and recognizing detail on the actual ski slope was not possible. I could see the darker blur of the tree line on either side of the run, so I always aimed for staying in the middle of the slope between the blurry darker edges. I was aware of the chair-lift poles which were typically positioned in the middle of the slope, and as I approached them I knew to avoid them. The hazards that I could not make out, such as bamboo poles in the X formation, meant to warn skiers about an upcoming danger, would not register in my visual field. Those were the worst experiences on the slopes, as I would be skiing through my white blurry world, and without any warning or knowledge to prepare for impact, I would smash into the hazards at full speed. This would often result in the wind being knocked out of me, being separated from my skies, and my goggles and glasses flying off my face. I would need a moment to catch my breath, assess my body for injury, and then the search for my skies, goggles, and glasses would begin. Without my glasses, my already-limited vision was even more compromised.

My parents had often volunteered to coach whatever team I or my brother or sister was playing on. That gave me and idea. Why don't I coach girls' softball? Number one, the softball is larger and easier for me to see, and if I coach a younger group, the overall game speed will be much slower. So, that is what I did for the next four years, during high school. Even though I had missed Pony League and was not going to be able to participate in Colt League baseball with all my friends, being able to coach softball seemed to fill a void for me. I learned from my dad that one of the most important elements of having a competitive team, especially a younger team, was to have a player who could pitch strikes. These girls were in the 8-to-10-year-old range. Many of the girls at this age would not even swing at a pitch, as they were too frightened when they came to home plate to bat. If the pitcher could not throw a strike, then the batter would be granted first base based on a walk. On the other hand, if you had a pitcher who could throw strikes, then you were in a much better position to compete. I always dedicated some portion of my teams' practice to pitchers just pitching. Without having a player who can throw strikes, the entire game becomes a walk fest, meaning every player who comes to bat just waits for balls to be pitched out of the strike zone, and then they are granted first base.

Usually, games like this were controlled by a run limit or time. If enough batters were walked during an inning, then the maximum number of runs and/or batters for an inning would be reached. That would result in a change of sides and the team that was batting would defend the field. If the defending team did not have a pitcher who could throw strikes, then the pattern would be repeated.

For the first year of my coaching, I was unable to develop a consistent player who could throw strikes. That year, the team probably only won like two games, losing 10. The next year, which was my sophomore year of high school, I started my softball practices by focusing on developing a pitcher or two.

I also enjoyed pitching batting practice to my team and leading infield drills by hitting grounders to my position players. I was back on the field, not competing with my friends/peers, but at least participating in sports at some level. I remember a time or two when my survival skills must have kicked in. A few of my players were very good hitters, and they launched the ball on a line drive right past my head at the pitcher's mound. Somehow my instincts told me to duck, or there was just enough of my vision remaining, telling me to hit the dirt. And that is exactly what I did. That technique worked most of the time, but there was the occasion when one of the girls would connect with my pitch, and the resulting line drive would end up right in my back or stomach if I was unable to react. I remember walking off from leading batting practice on a couple of occasions, because frankly, I was in too much pain. I always acted like I was just taking a break, because I was not about to admit to my players that I was in pain and needed a time-out.

For the four years that I coached, two of the years were not so good, but the other two years resulted in championships. The first year, as I said, was 2 wins and 10 losses. The second year, the team won the championship with like a 10-and-2 record, and as an award, we were tasked with playing the all-stars from all the other teams combined. Let's just say that we were not able to compete against all stars. My third year of coaching, which was my junior year of high school, the team was undefeated, with a perfect 12-and-0 record. We once again played all stars from all the other teams, and this time, we won easily, if I recall. It was all about the pitching.

My fourth and final year of coaching resulted in another 2-win 10-loss season. I do have fond memories of coaching those girls, and later hearing about their high school softball accomplishments.

CHAPTER 21:
THE BLINDNESS BOMB SHELL
& SEEKING A SECOND OPINION

My continued need for treatment meant weekly trips to Stanford. I was missing many days of school, missing my friends, and missing the whole growing-up-as-a teenager thing. The pattern was for my pressure to yo-yo, meaning it would be too high, then surgery, then too low, and it would slowly creep up to too high again.

Dr. Rosenthal preferred that my regular follow-up appointments with him be scheduled as his last patient of the day. He said he needed that time to ponder my case and try and make sense of it. Having the last-scheduled appointment of the day also worked well for me and my mom (who was usually the driver), because it gave me an opportunity to attend pretty much the entire day at school, and my mom was able to work most of the day as well.

Dr. Rosenthal would present my case during ophthalmology conferences, seeking the opinions of other eye specialists. I remember coming to an appointment with Dr. Rosenthal when there was an eye convention taking place at Stanford. That day, the Eye Clinic was closed to regular operations, but it was crowded with many gentlemen in suits and ties. It turned out these people were ophthalmologists from all over the world. Dr. Rosenthal was pushing me from behind, through the pack of doctors, guiding me to an examination room. He summoned several of his colleagues to the room to examine my eyes. I remember one of the ophthalmologists was Dr. Winter. Dr. Winter was the doctor responsible for developing the trabeculotomy procedure that had been performed on me many times by now. I remember Dr. Winter expressing the opinion that the trabeculotomy procedure(s) appeared to be functioning at some level in my eyes. Of course, not to the degree I needed to control my pressure. Not sure why, but it was reassuring to hear that these surgeries seemed to be sort of working for me—perhaps it was just a matter of time before the combination effect of undergoing multiple surgeries, or one specific surgery, that would finally maintain my pressure at an acceptable level.

It was truly an honor to be examined by these highly regarded eye doctors, and I felt like a VIP. I felt fortunate to have had the opportunity to be examined by these experts in the field of ophthalmology.

Before leaving that day, Dr. Rosenthal gestured for one of the nurses to bring over the hors d'oeuvre platter that was being circulated during the pre-conference gathering. He gave us an opportunity to select from all the snacks being served, so we would have something to eat during the drive home.

Whether I wanted to admit it or not, the huge sways in my eye pressure were taking their toll over time, destroying my optic nerves. Glaucoma was slowly stealing my eye sight away. The changes to one's sight are relentless and difficult to detect on a day-by-day basis.

Moving forward, surgery would be done on a same-day basis, meaning I would go to the hospital in the morning, have the procedure completed, and be home by evening that day. Not sure if this change was because of all my surgical experience or the insurance companies' way of saving money.

I clearly remember a traumatic visit to Dr. Rosenthal in the middle of my sophomore year. I was several months' post-surgery from the most recent procedure. My eye pressure was measured, and it was beginning to rise again. Dr. Rosenthal, without any hesitation, or softening of his message, announced that I was going blind. This was a shock to me, and I am sure a shock to my parents. With tears falling down my face from what I had just heard from my doctor, I remember my mom asking what other ophthalmologists we could consult. Dr. Rosenthal also announced that he would be leaving his position at Stanford for one in England.

We were given the names of several eye doctors and clinics. My parents wrote to a few of these glaucoma specialists and I was fortunate that one of these specialists was at UC San Francisco, which was not too much farther than Stanford was from my home.

My parents would send my medical records, along with a check, to several ophthalmologists throughout the country, asking for their opinion regarding my case, treatment approach, and prognosis. The response from these highly regarded ophthalmologists was consistent: My treatment at Stanford was of the highest level.

I went in person for a second opinion to see the specialist in San Francisco, Dr. Shaffer. This doctor did not impress me or my parents initially. When he came into the examination room to meet me, he was convinced that I was some congenital cataract case that he had remembered receiving notes about. Medical professionals sometimes forget that the patients who they are treating are not just a diagnosis but a human being with a serious eye condition. Once he realized I was the child glaucoma case referred from Stanford, he really warmed up to me. Unfortunately, he also thought that everything medically that could be done had already been done by Stanford. He was unable to offer us any new approaches to controlling my glaucoma. I think he gave his opinion regarding the suture technique that had been used during my most recent surgery, because there had been an excess of blood visible in my eye post-surgery. Unfortunately, this was not magical advice that would help me long-term with my glaucoma battle.

With Stanford's assistance, my parents and I had learned about experimental surgery that was being introduced in New Zealand for glaucoma patients. It had to do with a Molteno valve implant (more on this procedure later).

CHAPTER 22:
A FRESH APPROACH TO
MY COMPLICATED CASE

Dr. Rosenthal had left Stanford and was no longer managing my case. Dr. Egbert would become my primary physician for all my ongoing eye care. He had been with me from day one in terms of my surgical treatment, but the rest of my care was driven by Dr. Rosenthal. I am sure that Dr. Egbert was aware of the opinion that Dr. Rosenthal had expressed to me and my family concerning my prognosis of continued sight loss. Dr. Egbert said the battle against my glaucoma was not over and we still had a few tricks up our sleeve. This gave me a renewed level of optimism, knowing that I was not going to be given up on by my doctor. I could still see and wanted to save the remaining vision that I had.

Dr. Egbert performed a few more mainstream trabeculotomy procedures, choosing not to implement the extreme post-surgery regimen of steroids and pressure patches. Unfortunately, Dr. Egbert's surgical results were no better with this less intense treatment approach. But it was at least more tolerable for me as the patient to endure.

Dr. Egbert had come to understand that my eye pressure could spike up and down within a matter of days or even hours. He wanted a method where we (meaning, my family and I) could measure the pressure more regularly at home without the need of traveling to Stanford. We were introduced to a device called a Schiotz tonometer. This device rests on the surface of the cornea, and it is calibrated to produce a measurement based on how hard or soft the eyeball is. If, for example, the tonometer was placed on the surface of a marble, the measurement would come back as zero, because the device did not indent the marble. At first, it was difficult for me to understand that the higher the number from the tonometer meant my pressure was lower. Another way to understand this system of measuring pressure was to understand that the softer the eyeball meant a higher tonometer reading, equating to lower eye pressure.

Dr. Egbert trained my parents to operate the Schiotz tonometer, which involved making sure it was calibrated prior to placing it in my eye. Operating the device involved centering the device over my opened eye and lowering it until the tip of the instrument meets the cornea. Being sure that only the weight of the tonometer is resting on my eye, I was given a prescription of a topical anesthetic that needed to be dropped into each of my eyes prior to testing.

My dad used the computer to create a line-graph representation for plotting my eye pressures. This was a great way for Dr. Egbert to see what my pressures were doing in between my actual appointments at Stanford. I knew my medications well and would be proactive in adjusting dosages as my pressures changed based on the readings we got at home.

My eyes had gone through so much by now, but another approach was needed, because it was obvious by now that conventional treatment was not effective long-term for me.

Cryo Therapy was presented as the next treatment intervention for controlling the pressure in my eyes. This involved freezing ciliary bodies in my eyes, which are responsible for producing aqueous fluid. This procedure is designed to lower the pressure by destroying the ciliary body. This surgical procedure focused on reducing the amount of fluid production, rather than creating a drain. Another analogy of glaucoma is to picture a sink that is backing up with water. To fix this, one needs to either clear the drain, so the water can leave the sink—this is what the trabeculotomy procedure attempted to accomplish, but it was never effective long term—or, the second approach, reduce the amount of water coming from the faucet, which is what cryotherapy is designed to do.

For me, the unknown was often the worst fear. There were always new ideas being proposed to combat my glaucoma. These proposals would quickly evolve into actual procedures being scheduled for my "benefit." The problem was, from my perspective, was that I would be the one being poked and probed. In other words, if these new procedures were going to be uncomfortable, I would be the lucky one to experience that.

Dr. Egbert did not often prescribe pain medication or sedation prior to any procedure, but I think he could sense my anxiety toward this new thing called cryotherapy. I had shown up at the Eye Clinic in preparation for my first go-around with this new treatment. I was given a Valium pill for relaxation and told to sit and wait.

I remember a bit of time had passed, as I sat in the Eye Clinic, waiting for the next step. I guess Dr. Egbert's secretary had glanced at me, as she passed by the waiting room. Her report back to Dr. Egbert was, "Jeff has a smile on his face, I think he is ready."

I cannot think of any reason why there would have been a grin on my face, as I sat in the Eye Clinic waiting room. I was about to undergo yet another procedure for lowering my pressure, so this was definitely not a happy time for me. I remember asking my mom if she felt I was acting strangely or more relaxed. Neither one of us felt like the medication had done anything to change my anxiety.

Dr. Egbert, taking the advice of his secretary, determined that I was properly medicated and ready for the procedure. I was summoned into the treatment room at the Eye Clinic. This room was a little bit bigger than the standard examination room that I was used to. It did not have a Slit Lamp Microscope examination chair for patients. Instead, it had a gurney bed in the middle of the room. That bed was meant for the patient, and since that was me, I was asked to assume the supine position and lie on this narrow bed. This was right around the time I wished that the Valium had done something to relax me.

This was the first of my eye procedures that I was awake for. As I walked from the waiting room and lay down on the gurney, I just wanted to be put to sleep, in terms of anesthesia. These types of procedures, though, did not call for full sedation. That meant the patient, who was me, would be awake.

The nurse, trying to be gentle, let me know that it would be a soft needle—that clued me in that a shot was soon to come. Again, I smelled the aroma of alcohol. The lower quadrant of my eye socket was being wiped down in preparation for an injection. Next thing I felt was a needle being pressed into my lower eye socket. It did not feel great, and as the medication took effect, my vision also went away, along with having a numb eye. It was scary, because I did not understand that my vision would be affected by the anesthetic, as well. Next thing I remember some sort of a metal paper-clip-like gadget was being positioned under my top and bottom eyelids. This gadget's job was to make it so I could not blink. The technical name for it was a Wired Speculum. Even though your unconscious mind is telling you to blink, the speculum is preventing that from naturally happening.

The cryo machine itself was turned on at this point. If memory serves, there was a rubber tube running from the machine out to a probe that I think looked like a pencil. The freezing substance from the cryo machine was carried through this tube to the tip of the pencil probe. The probe was placed on my eye surface in a specific location. The cryo machine was activated, and the freezing reaction was transferred through the tube to the surface of my eye. The probe needs to remain in contact with my eye for 60 seconds for the first round to be complete. Sixty seconds of having a probe with a freezing substance applied to the eye surface can seem like an eternity. After the 60 seconds of -112 degrees, the probe was still attached to my eye surface. I remember some sort of a liquid substance being dropped into my eye, which worked to release the probe from the surface of my eye. Remember the movie, *A Christmas Story*. There was the boy who licked the frozen pole. His 98.6-degree tongue was put in contact with a freezing pole. Let's just say that is the best way I can describe what happened to my eye during cryotherapy, where the freezing probe tip was put in contact with my eye. I also experienced the classic ice headache, when you drink something that is very cold too fast, and it gives that freezing experience throughout your entire head.

Cryotherapy is not just administered once during a treatment session, but rather, in several spots on the eye surface, to make sure enough of the fluid-producing cells were eliminated.

Dr. Egbert had always been conservative when it came to treating my eyes. He seemed to really understand that my eyes were small and underdeveloped. My eye's pressure could change rather suddenly and drastically on many occasions, after what would be considered minor interventions. Therefore, his approach was of the mindset that less was better. My eyes' response to treatment was unpredictable. This meant that he was not going to expose my eyes to more cryotherapy than was necessary. His thinking was, if more treatment was indicated, then it would be performed.

Cryotherapy is usually a procedure that is performed in multiple locations of someone's eyes. This meant that the probe with freezing consequences would be placed in several locations of one's eye. My first cryotherapy treatment regiment resulted in three separate areas of my eye being exposed to the freezing therapy. I learned later that treating three locations during a cryotherapy session would be considered conservative.

Cryotherapy, I would also learn later, was not a great treatment for controlling one's eye pressure long-term. The cells that were destroyed during cryotherapy would eventually reproduce, and the eye-fluid production would return to normal, which meant high pressure again.

It would have been nice if optic nerve cells could also have this ability to re-generate after being damaged from glaucoma. Then potentially my vision could be restored, but this is not the way human bodies respond to central nerve trauma. This is the same issue that prevents people who have experienced a spinal-cord injury from having the ability to heal.

Cryotherapy also has undesirable side effects because the freezing procedure's effects cannot be limited to just the ciliary body, but rather the entire eye. I am pretty sure the overall effects of cryotherapy, in my case, led to the development of cataracts. When an eye receives a trauma, and in the case of cryotherapy, severe trauma, often it causes scarring—in my case, the lens of my eye would eventually scar over, requiring surgical removal. My need for cataract surgery would not occur for a couple of years. It was kind of ironic that the cataract surgery would do nothing to help my glaucoma, but the need for it would be directly caused by my glaucoma treatment.

Often after cryotherapy, I would return to high school with quite the shiner, aka, a black eye. Hearing some of the comments from those I passed by at school was amusing. I think they thought of me as the fighter kid. "Wow!" I would hear, as I walked by, "that dude has quite a black eye. I wonder how the other guy is doing."

I had cryotherapy performed a few times on each of my eyes over a period of a couple of years. The pressure would be under control for a while, but true to my pattern, the pressure would once again begin to rise to harmful levels. I had mentioned to Dr. Egbert that I was not overly thrilled with the numbing injection that was administered prior to every cryotherapy treatment. He offered to attempt to perform the treatments with topical anesthetic. What I heard was no more shots in my eye, which sounded great to me. What I did not hear was the word *attempt*.

I am pretty sure the conventional approach with patients undergoing cryotherapy is an injectable anesthetic prior to the procedure. Dr. Egbert understood all the treatment that I was enduring and he wanted to do anything to make the experience more tolerable for me.

The next go-around with cryotherapy was completed with a topical anesthetic. The actual numbing process took several minutes to administer. It involved repeatedly placing Q-tips that had been soaked in Alkane topical numbing solution onto the surface of my eye, where the cryotherapy would be focused. I remember my eye becoming quite numb, and even areas of my nose and throat were affected. As the procedure was being performed, my eye was definitely not as numb, and those 60-second intervals of the freezing probe being in contact with my eye were significantly more painful.

It was a trade-off; not having the numbing injection meant not having a black eye visible for a week or more, but it also meant more discomfort during the actual treatment.

CHAPTER 23:
FUNCTIONING WITH LOW VISION

My sophomore year was coming to an end. Most of my friends had or were in the process of getting their driver's license. Up until now, our means of transportation had been by walking, bicycling, or the occasional ride from an older classmate or sibling. I was still functioning at what I would consider a high level in spite of my progressive sight loss.

At this point, I would have been categorized as legally blind, for sure. When I looked at trees, for example, there was no distinguishing of branches or leaves, just a blurry blob. When I looked at peoples' faces, I could not see their eyes or other features. I might see dark spots where their eyes were located, but nothing else. Whatever the main color of an object was is the blur that I would see. If there was other color or patterns intermixed, the primary color was the blur that I would see. If I looked at grass, it would be a green blur, the sky was a blue blur, or on those foggy days, a gray blur.

I was good about pretending to see what others were seeing. When there was a discussion about those girls in the distance, I would be right in on the conversation, acting as though I could see what was happening. I could bullshit my way through most of these conversations. Being partially sighted could also create a lot of problems. Anyone you would interact with assumed that you could see things just like them. There is no way for the casual observer to know or understand that you have sight loss and to what degree. And, of course, I was in denial about my vision loss, so I was not about to share that information with those around me.

People would observe me walking independently around campus, running when it came to Physical Education class, and I regularly rode my bike around town with friends. I would hear from people, asking me why I did not wave back at them. I am sure there were a lot of times that people would wave or smile at me. Of course, I never responded because most of the time I would not even know there was someone near me, and if I did, I would never have seen the gestures. For those who did not know me very well, they probably thought I was some sort of a stuck-up asshole.

Around this same time period, occasional signs of my failing vision would present themselves.

Case in point, when I was walking within the hospital to the Eye Clinic, the usual plan when reaching the hospital was for my mom to drop me off in front. This gave her time to search for a parking space, and still allowed me to get to my appointment on time. On this particular trip, when I had been traveling to Stanford for several years by now, my mom arrived at the Eye Clinic before me, even though I had a good 10-minute lead on her.

I remember being dropped off at the hospital's main entrance. I knew the route from here up to the Eye Clinic, relying more on my memory than my vision to get me there. I went through the automatic doors, somehow managing to avoid all the poles that held up the awning that protected you from the elements as you entered the hospital. I proceeded to turn left immediately after going through the doorway. I continued down the main hallway until reaching the gift shop, where I turned right. Beyond the gift shop on the left was an alcove where I could catch the elevator. The Eye Clinic was on the second floor, so I needed to board one of two elevators, which materialize out of the same wall next to each other. I had trouble finding the up-button on the wall, so I would just stand there until I heard one of the elevator doors open. It was an usually a short wait. Someone was always going up or coming down. The elevator door slightly to my left opened, and a woman exited. I knew it was a woman because of the sound that her high-heeled shoes made when they echoed off the floor. I entered the elevator that had just been vacated. Surprisingly, no one else entered the elevator with me.

The doors closed and nothing happened. I mean the elevator was motionless with me in it. I started to realize right then that I was in trouble. I waited a few more seconds and still nothing was happening. Never had I faced this dilemma. Always in the past, someone else riding with me or someone on another floor would trigger the elevator. This elevator is not going to move, I thought, unless I do something. I began making my way toward the blur that I knew must be the control panel. Arriving at what I determined was the control panel, I began feeling around, and sure enough, there were several buttons to choose from. Which one would make this damn thing move? Since I had no idea, I just pushed one of the buttons and waited to see what would happen. The elevator lunged upwards, and I was relieved to be moving. The elevator slowed and came to a halt. The doors opened and I exited, thinking I was on the second floor. Do not ask me why, but I assumed that the elevator would stop at each floor. After all, that is the way the elevator had always operated in the past, but not today. And this was before there were audio cues for each time a new floor is encountered.

Apparently, I had pushed the #3 button, so the elevator shot straight there, bypassing #2. Unfortunately, I was not aware of this fact at the time. Upon exiting the elevator, I did a 180-degree turn to the left. Immediately, I encountered a closed door, which was not familiar to me on this route. I just figured it was later in the afternoon and the doors had been shut for some unknown reason. I went through the doorway and proceeded down the hallway.

It was uncharacteristically quiet, as I wandered down the hall. The surroundings that I could partially make out were unfamiliar. As I approached another closed door, I began getting concerned, thinking I had missed the right turn, which leads to the Eye Clinic. I back-tracked a few feet, but did not locate the hallway. The turn had to be just beyond this door, I thought, so I proceeded through. The sound of machines buzzing and beeping, and the cry of babies, overwhelmed me. Right away realizing I was on the Pediatric Floor in the Maternity Ward, I did an abrupt about-face and scrambled back to the elevator. I remembered that wing of the hospital from the many days and nights I had spent on the Pediatric Floor as a patient.

Coming toward the elevator was an orderly pushing a cart full of what I thought sounded like breakfast dishes. As I stood there facing the wall, where the elevators are, I heard the wall open behind me, and an elevator materialized from a place where I did not know one existed. The orderly pushed his cart into the elevator. Now I had a split decision to make. I could either follow the orderly into this elevator I knew nothing about or I could take my chances that someone else would happen to trigger one of the other two elevators. Being that I had little patience, was now running late for my appointment and was eager to get off this floor, I opted to follow the orderly.

These elevators in the hospital operate so smoothly that it is difficult to sense that you are moving. It makes it difficult to judge what floor you are on. The elevator made an initial surge downward, and then I did not sense the movement for several seconds, but figured we must be going down slowly. The doors to the elevator opened, and I did not know for sure what floor I was on, but assumed that it must be the second. I could have asked for help, but that would mean I was admitting that I had a problem.

When I exited the elevator, an uneasy feeling came over me. Things still did not seem quite right to me, but I figured I was letting paranoia interfere with my better judgment. I began traveling down the hallway, which if I had been on the second floor, would have led me to the Eye Clinic.

Upon opening the door, I heard a stern voice from across the room say, "May I help you?"

"I am trying to find the Eye Clinic," I said, startled.

The man's voice became softer. I think, realizing from my thick glasses and destination, that I had some sort of visual impairment. He explained that I was on the basement floor. The gentleman was kind enough to escort me back to the second floor, where I was able to proceed to the Eye Clinic, without any further problems.

The inaccessibility of elevators for someone with sight loss taught me an important life lesson. My plan moving forward was to avoid elevators whenever possible and find the stairs, which would keep you oriented within the building.

CHAPTER 24:

NEEDING MORE THAN LARGE PRINT

& OFFERED THE DRIVER'S SEAT BY MY FRIEND

Many of my teachers did not understand nor were they given information concerning my vision loss. What they saw was me independently entering their classroom and finding a seat. When I would ask for assistance with reading information, whether it was presented on the board, on a handout, or in a book, they really did not know why or how to assist me. I would utilize the students around me if they were willing to help.

As my vision continued to decline, I had a teacher of the visually impaired (VI.) Connie, who took a bigger and bigger role in supporting my academic needs. The large-print books that I would use when they were available were becoming more and more difficult for me to see. All tests that I took were now being read to me out loud. I started to get other materials on tape, and in some cases, like my Math classes, there would be some adult aide sitting next to me providing me with handwritten large-print notes of what was being presented. Usually, a felt pen would be used to create ½- to ¾-inch-high letters, numbers, and symbols.

I remember being tested for braille sensitivity, meaning could I distinguish tactilely between different bump patterns presented on a sheet of paper. I remember performing well with this exercise, but ultimately, it was determined by Connie that was not recommended for someone with functional remaining vision. This was not just her opinion but the consensus of the VI teaching professionals in the early 1980s. If a student had remaining functional vision, the thought was to develop an instructional approach, using the vision. In my case, and with other visually impaired students, looking at one's prognosis would have been important. If one's vision loss was progressive, then non-visual approaches to learning should be considered.

Other academic assistance that I was receiving started to come from my peers or upper-class people. This had some advantages, as several of those who volunteered to assist me with reading tasks were very cute and kind girls. This was confirmed by their sweet voices and friendly personality, but also by my friends, who always seemed to make a point to come visit when I was working with one of these girls. They would tell me later how cute they were.

Then there were some of the awkward times. All high school, students were required to take Health class. This also meant a section covering Human Sexuality/Reproduction. There was a very nice student in that class who was selected to read handouts and other materials out loud to me. I do not think he volunteered for this position, but rather was appointed to it by the teacher, Mr. Meyers. At least, the Health classroom itself had adjoining unoccupied rooms that were available. So, my appointed aide and I were able to seek out this space when asked to review the current content. I have so much respect for my student aide who was responsible for reading out loud to me some graphic content. I must say though that the handouts with visual illustrations of the reproductive anatomy are completely incomprehensible to someone with sight loss.

My friends were getting cars, and I knew that was out of the question for me, but I did begin my lobbying for a moped. A moped, put simply, is a bicycle with a 2.5 horsepower motor. There are even peddles to assist the motor if necessary. I think top speed was like 25 mph on the flats. I wanted something that would be able to carry me up to my house in the mountains, so I would not have to manually peddle myself up hill. I think also I was looking for my own independence, as well. I pleaded with my parents for several months, saying that I had and was still riding a bike without difficulty. A moped, in my mind, was no different from a bicycle.

My junior year of high school had started, and I was now getting rides to school from my friends. They all understood how much I wanted to be driving just like them. After school one day, Dave and I were taking a couple of hits off of his marijuana pipe and were contemplating this idea of me taking the wheel. Dave thought he would make that a reality for me on this particular day.

Ever since my glaucoma diagnosis, my friends would regularly remind me that marijuana was a known treatment for lowering eye pressure and I could take it legally. So, of course, for medicinal purposes, we had an excuse to get high.

On our way home, when we were getting close to my home, Dave suddenly stopped the truck and announced that I was going to drive.

"You're kidding, right?" I questioned him.

Dave simply responded with "Nope."

I found myself in the driver's seat of a full-sized truck. So glad it was an automatic transmission. My buddy, Dave, climbed into the passenger seat, and I released the emergency break, shifted the big truck into drive, and gave it a little gas; my nose was touching the windshield, as I leaned forward, as far as I could, struggling to see what was ahead of me. We slowly nudged our way forward. I do not remember Dave cluing me in about where to go. I knew the route from here to home from memory, as I had grown up in these hills. We were on Glen Wood Drive. I slowly drove the truck over the cement bridge crossing Bean Creek, following what I saw as the edge of the road. It is the grayish blur of the roadway surface versus the darker blur of dirt, which I interpret to be the shoulder. I had no actual driving experience and could not see where I was going. Not a favorable combination. Somehow I managed to drive past

Stonewood Drive and make the right turn onto Northridge Drive, which was the road I lived on. From here, it was a ½ mile up-hill trek to reach my home. The transition from Glen Wood Drive to Northridge Drive meant that the road had narrowed slightly. My strategy of following the contrast in blurs, which I assumed was the edge of the road, had worked up to now, so that is what I continued to do. According to Dave, as I passed the first driveway in the neighborhood, I was within inches of taking out their mailbox, because it happened to be placed right on the edge that I was following. Next, I heard a car coming down the road in the opposite direction. Not knowing what else to do, I just stopped, hoping the car would go around or by me. It turned out that the car was full of other friends of mine, and they broke into total laughter when they realized who was behind the wheel. Now they thought that they had seen it all. Here was their half-blind friend, Jeff, driving a truck up the road. The fact that I made it to my home without damaging the truck, or property, or other people was a bit of a miracle.

I had kind of given up and forgotten about my desire for a moped. I am sure the idea to my parents was truly terrifying, but at the same time, they were trying to honor my need for independence, while balancing the need for safety.

One weekend morning, they said let us go look at mopeds. Many of the motorcycle shops that we visited offered real high-end machines meant for the open road and even highway. This was not the type of machine for me. We did eventually find a moped that had just enough power to take me up the road to my house without the need for peddling. I do think its top speed was right around 25 mph. The motor ran on a mixture of gasoline with oil. I think I could go like 80 miles on a gallon of gas.

By the end of my junior year, I was the proud owner of a moped. I so enjoyed riding up and down the road that I lived on. I used the moped to get me to and from the softball practices that I coached, and eventually, it would take me to and from work.

The softball field and, later, my workplace were both a 3.5-mile ride from my house in the mountains. The windy country road that I traveled on was a bit challenging. When I think back to those few years of piloting the moped, it was insanity. I truly appreciated foggy days, because the blurry road that I followed was a consistent gray blur. On sunny days, the trip was much more grueling, because of all the shadows the tree branches would cast over the roadway. Those days, I was following a mixed blur of light and dark blurs. Truth be told, I could not really see the road, with all the shadows, and drove more by intuition. I think some higher power was watching over me during these trips.

CHAPTER 25:
THE ELECTRONIC VIDEO MAGNIFIER
& TAKING THE SAT TEST

My senior year of high school had begun. Although my vision had continued to deteriorate, I was still doing a good job of faking it. I was still walking around and driving the moped. Reading was becoming more and more difficult. My VI teacher was able to get me a device called a CCTV, which is now referred to as an electronic video magnifier. This device has a built-in camera with an attached monitor. You place hard-copy print or images under the camera and the content will be displayed on the screen magnified. There was a knob that could be turned to adjust the magnification level and a switch that could be pressed that would change the print from black on white to white on black. Color monitors were not available in the mid 1980s. I remember being totally amazed by this machine that allowed me to see and read again. One of the first things I remember using the CCTV for was looking at my class yearbook. I was able to view images of my friends, and more importantly, many of the girls' pictures in my class. I was able to see facial characteristics like eyes, noses, and teeth. Even though things were not in color, I was seeing details of people who I had not seen for years.

When you first get to use a device like this, and it allows you to see things that you have not been able to, you start to think this device could be the answer to all of your reading difficulties. It was true that I could read my textbooks again, and initially, I spent a lot of time using this magnification machine, but what I began to realize is that reading like this was very slow. When a page of text is magnified, only a portion of it will fit on the screen at any given time.

The tray that the book is on needs to be manipulated back and forth to view all the text on a line. It would easily take me five minutes to read a single page. Additionally, my eyes were already poor, so trying to read for a prolonged period was painful. The CCTV worked well for spot reading or viewing pictures.

Going away for college had been an ongoing discussion, and to be eligible, you needed to take the SAT Test. I received special permission to take the test at my home, utilizing the CCTV. The test would be proctored by my VI teacher Connie. The standard SAT is a timed test that takes several hours to complete. I am sure I must have been granted extended time due to the circumstances. I am not sure how much additional time was approved and how that was even determined. I can tell you that it would not have mattered if I had been given unlimited time. As I had said, trying to read with the CCTV for any length was exhausting. The math portion of the test was particularly difficult, as many of the questions ask you to compare relationships between angles and illustrations on the page. I was not able to magnify the entire picture at once, so I might see one portion of the illustration, but then I would need to move the test booklet to see other parts of the illustration. I could never see the entire illustration all at once. Finally, I would need to move the test booklet to the area where the answers were presented. Again, I was only able to see parts of any given answer at a time. I would use my #2 pencil to shade in the oval that represented the answer that I had chosen.

To be perfectly honest, the test was way too exhausting to be taken under a magnifier. I absolutely gave up on the test shortly after I had started. I would focus on just shading in answers, as that was difficult enough. I did not actually read more than half of the questions because I just wanted to be done with it.

CHAPTER 26:
DIFFERENT DOCTORS, DIFFERENT HOSPITAL
& AN EXPARIMENTAL SURGERY

It was strike 2 with finding surgical solutions for controlling my eye pressure long-term. The trabeculotomy and cryotherapy procedures would work to control my pressures for a little while, but they would need repeating several times a year. To keep with the baseball analogy, all these surgeries were keeping me in the game, but I was still losing in the late innings, when it came to closing out and permanently defeating this thing called glaucoma.

Yet another approach was being discussed, which involved implanting an artificial tube into my eye. There was a doctor with a last name of Molteno from New Zealand. This doctor had been doing a lot of research with silicone implants for controlling glaucoma.

Dr. Egbert had been reviewing this new treatment approach and thought it might be a good option for someone like me with "End-Stage Glaucoma." I did not really know or pay attention to terms like that at the time, but now I understand it to mean we are desperate to find any effective treatment to work for this patient. Dr. Egbert had reported to my family and me, promising results from a doctor abroad (Dr. Molteno), doing work with glaucoma patients.

He was developing an experimental procedure, which involved implanting a silicon-based tube into an eye to control pressure. The procedure was simply described as a drain placed in your eye. The procedure did not have a fancy name and was simply called the Molteno Valve. The valve would act as a pipe creating an alternative means for releasing excessive fluid from the eye. With this surgical treatment, the goal was to keep the beginning and end of the tube clear of scarring. Scarring around the valve was fine if the entry and exit points of the pipe remained open, allowing for fluid to pass. This procedure had been invented by a doctor in New Zealand, so to be a patient for receiving this, what I will call experimental treatment, meant you would most likely need to travel to New Zealand.

My parents were prepared to take me on a trip to New Zealand if there was a chance it could save my remaining vision. Right around this same time, Dr. Baerveldt, who had trained with Dr. Molteno, had recently returned from New Zealand, joining the faculty at the Doheny Eye Institute. This practice was located in Los Angeles. Dr. George Baerveldt, by chance, had just begun practicing in my backyard, if you compare it to New Zealand. He was only an area code away as compared to a country code.

Soon plans were being made for me and my parents to travel to Southern California. My family had a smaller truck with a camper shell and that is what we used to travel to the Doheny Eye Clinic. It was approximately 350 miles away from my home in Northern California.

The Doheny Eye Clinic is located on the campus of University of Southern California (USC). It was a self-contained clinic without hospital services. Doheny had a partnership with Alhambra Community Hospital, which was near the clinic. Any patients requiring hospitalization or surgical intervention for their eye conditions would be admitted to this community hospital.

All my medical records from Stanford had been forwarded to Doheny. I do not think Doheny having all my medical records, which were quite extensive by now, did anything to cut down on the number of tests that would be performed. It seems that every independent clinic has their own protocol and series of tests that they insist the patient completes. Obviously, it does not matter that all these tests that I went through had been performed by Stanford several times. There was the basic eye examination, measuring of my pressure, dilation of my eyes, ultrasound, visual field testing, photographs, and probably several other procedures that I have forgotten.

I arrived in the early morning and finished up in the Eye Clinic by mid-afternoon, after having a final consultation with Dr. Baerveldt and the glaucoma specialist, Dr. Minckler. It was agreed that I would undergo the Molteno Valve Implant surgery in the morning. The other concern at the time was the elevated pressure occurring in the eye that was not having the valve procedure. The plan was to perform cryotherapy in that eye to assist with controlling the pressure, while we would wait for results from this newest surgery.

This would be the first time surgery was going to be performed on both eyes at the same time. This was a new experimental surgery, being performed on me, by doctors whom I had just met, at a hospital that was unfamiliar to me. I recalled hearing that I would be the third patient in the United States to have this procedure. This was truly going to be uncharted territory. To say that I was a bit terrified would be an understatement.

Since surgery was scheduled for the next day, I still needed to travel to the hospital to complete the pre-op screening process. This community hospital setting was so different from Stanford. You would think a new experimental surgery should be performed at a prestigious facility, but that was not the case. The smaller size gave an overall calm to the place. The pre-op routine took the remainder of the afternoon to complete, and finally I was able to leave the hospital in the early evening. I was scheduled to be back at 6:00 in the morning. My restrictions were always the same: nothing to eat or drink beyond midnight.

It had been a long day for all, and my parents suggested that we go out to dinner prior to checking into the hotel. They were probably hungry, and I would usually be starving by now, but with all the uncertainty, I was not feeling too hungry. My parents suggested Mexican, which they know is one of my favorites. That sounded like a really good choice. But really nothing sounded good, as my stomach was in knots. I did order a tostada, knowing I would not be able to eat anything for like 24 hours. I managed to eat a few chips, dipped in salsa, and some of my taco salad. The food just seemed to stick in my throat and was not moving.

My body had a way of expressing itself regarding surgery. Many surgery days, I would spike a low-grade fever. I believe it was my body's way of saying I do not want to do this. The fever would always cause an alarm with one of the doctors. Usually, it would be the resident anesthesiologist who had never treated me before. Dr. Egbert and the other ophthalmologist in the department knew my MO by now and gave it little attention or concern.

I checked in for surgery early the next morning. Even though this was a different place, with different people in charge, the routine was very familiar. When I was rolled into the operating room, I was full of anxiety and stress regarding all the unknowns.

I would be receiving general anesthesia again, because the surgery was new, and the duration would be much longer, as both of my eyes were going to be worked on. I just wanted to be put under as soon as possible, to get me out of misery.

The next thing I recall was a lady shaking my shoulders and speaking rather sternly: "Wake up, wake up." Then I was asked to cough. This lady, who was accosting me, I learned later, was my anesthesiologist.

I was in the operating room, in a drug-induced sleep. Apparently, all the tension in my body had finally released and I had thrown up during surgery. Because I had been asleep, my body's natural reflexes had been turned off. This could have been a life-threatening situation, due to easily chocking or aspirating into my lungs. I think it was a very scary moment for medical personnel in the operating room. I really was not fazed by the experience, because I had slept through most of it. The doctors were convinced I had eaten breakfast even though my parents and I swore that I had not eaten anything that morning. My body had a way of rebelling when it was not happy.

The next morning, Dr. Baerveldt and Dr. Minckler showed up at my bedside. They performed a quick exam with their pin lights, and then a wheelchair was rolled up to my bed. I was asked to transfer into it, and I was pushed down the hallway to a small closet-like room. There was the all-too-familiar Eye Clinic examination chair with the chin rest and Slit Lamp/Microscope.

I was examined by both doctors, and they were not completely satisfied with the current position of the valve that had been implanted. It was decided that I needed to return to the operating room, so the valve could be nudged into a more favorable position. My heart began racing, as I dreaded yet another visit to the operating room. This too would be a first. Never had I returned to the operating room less than 24 hours since my last visit. I did learn that no anesthesia would be necessary. Air was going to be pushed into my eye.

At Stanford, returning to the operating room, without having it pre-scheduled, just would not have been possible. Having been a patient for so many surgeries, my parents and I knew the routine. If your surgery was scheduled for 7:00 a.m., then that meant Stanford wanted you to check in by 4:00 a.m., which meant we would need to leave our house by 3:00 a.m. After a handful of surgeries, when I would arrive at the designated time, I would spend hours waiting for my turn to be rolled into the operating room. Usually, things would be running behind, so surgery scheduled for 7:00 could often not get going until 8:00 or even 9:00. Since we knew the hospital's protocol when it came to surgery day, we would modify it based on the reality that we had experienced. The pre-op instructions are not designed for the convenience of the patient. The surgeon's time and maintaining the hospital's schedule are the priorities. As a patient, it often felt like the roles were reversed. Who was serving who anyway? You (the patient), it seemed, was there to serve the hospital. You were expected to follow their instructions, show up at their convenience, and, of course, pay the bill.

We liked to cut our waiting time by like one-third. That meant if surgery was scheduled for 7:00, then we would arrive at 5:00. This strategy worked almost 100 percent of the time and reduced slightly our hospital waiting-around time. As one could imagine, my teenage years had been consumed by doctors, hospitals, medications, and surgeries. Just being able to exert a small bit of control by deciding the actual time that I deemed it necessary to arrive gave me a little bit of autonomy over the medical establishment that was running most of my life at this point.

There was one time that I recall arriving at Stanford later than I was instructed for surgery, and I was reprimanded the moment I did show up in the Admitting Office for being late. From the reaction that I received, you would have thought I had broken the 11th Commandment, "Thou shalt not be late to the hospital on surgery day."

The band identifying me as the patient along with my doctor's name was attached to my wrist. Next, I needed to wait for an orderly to bring a wheelchair, so I could be transported to the pre-op nursing station. This is the launching point that will get you to the operating room. I must interject here and state, if I had been allowed to walk to the Same Day Surgery Ward independently, I would have arrived many minutes earlier. Now the wheelchair stopped at the Same Day Surgery Unit, and the breaks were set. I heard the disappointed tone of the nurse demanding to know where I had been and why I was late.

I had been to this nurses' station 20-plus times by now and so badly wanted to fire back with the same tone, asking her why things were on time for the first time ever, but decided that probably would not have helped the situation. This did not help to put me at ease, as I was once again being prepared for surgery. We were put on the defensive when relaxation should have been the focus. My parents and I made up some excuse about oversleeping or foggy conditions on the drive to the hospital that delayed our arrival.

I changed out of my street clothes into the fashionable hospital gown in a matter of a minute or two. There was another patient in the Same Day Surgery Ward whose case had been moved up since I had been "late." I remember that patient being taken to surgery after I had arrived in the Pre-Op Ward, so I am thinking my scheduled case time really didn't need to be changed, but I am sure the hospital staff has protocol that they must follow, and since I was expressing my autonomy and did not follow the rules, I had screwed up the day's schedule.

Returning to Alhambra Hospital and the operating room for a second time within 24 hours to reposition the Molteno Valve that had been implanted yesterday, this time, all the prep duties took longer than the actual procedure. I moved from the gurney to the operating table, and then my head was positioned where the doctors wanted it. The speculum was manipulated under my lids, which prevented me from blinking. Some sort of a device was used to blow air into my eye. Having air blown into your eye was not painful, but I would describe it as irritating. There I was with my eye forced open and air being pushed into my eye. The valve was moved enough for the doctor's satisfaction, so I was being moved out of the operating room almost as soon as I had gotten there.

The doctors indicated that I could most likely leave the hospital tomorrow, but they would like me to stay in town for one additional night after my discharge, so I could be seen one final time before heading home to Northern California. My parents had mentioned how they had been sleeping in the truck's camper in the parking lot.

Dr. Minchler, upon hearing this, immediately, offered to arrange for my parents to shower in the surgical lounge at the hospital. This doctor, who really did not know us, I am sure thought that financially, the family was short on funds from the burden of covering the costs of my ongoing eye care. Fortunately, my dad had a good job at IBM, with excellent healthcare coverage for his family. My parents thanked Dr. Minchler for his offer of utilizing the hospital's facilities but assured him that they would be getting a hotel. My parents stayed in the parking lot to be as close to me as possible and honestly knowing they were there, was reassuring.

I was released from the hospital and I was given the green light to go home during the follow-up examination. My eye pressure in both eyes for a change was low together. The eye that had received the cryotherapy was bordering on being too low. The drive trip home was uneventful and having the camper to lie down in during the long trip was a bonus. I did worry a bit about how to lie so as not to negatively influence how the new valve was settling in my eye. I knew that it had already needed to be repositioned once, so I did not want to do anything to mess that up anymore. I do remember almost being home and stopping in Castroville, which was known as the Artichoke Capital of the World. We purchased a couple of orders of deep-fried artichoke hearts. Let us just say my appetite was back and the artichokes tasted great.

CHAPTER 27:
AN IMPLANT, A CATARACT & PRESSURE TOO LOW

I know my optometrist, Dr. Anthony Giannotti, was totally amazed the first time he examined me after the valve implant. As a matter of fact, he was so excited that he rounded up his receptionist, medical assistant, and I think anyone else who was in the office that day to show them the unusual piece of hardware that had been implanted in my eye. Dr. Giannotti was not only my optometrist, but also a true supporter of me and my journey into sight loss. He was responsible for all my glasses prescriptions throughout high school and college. He assisted with my transition into contact lenses during my sophomore and junior years, and part of my senior year. Dr. Giannotti thought contact lenses might help to make my vision a bit clearer. I think most patients getting contact lenses for the first time might experience sharper vision, but I was not your traditional patient. Due to my progressive vision loss during this transition to contact lenses, I really did not experience any improvement, but who knows, maybe the lenses made what I could see a little better.

I had worn glasses my entire life, so having the opportunity to change to contact lenses for my high school years felt liberating. Perhaps it was good for my ego as well. I hopefully would not be considered the nerdy guy with glasses anymore. As a matter of fact, I had contact lenses when my senior pictures were taken, so that is the lasting image my classmates will have of me.

Learning to manage contact lenses when you are legally blind did prove to be a bit of a challenge. I had different prescriptions for each eye, so it was imperative that I develop a system for tracking each of my lenses. I had the type of lenses that needed to be removed each evening, and they were put through a cleaning process. The container that the lenses were placed in for the sanitation had separate attached identical compartments for each lens. Each separate compartment had a small round screw lid. I had one of the screw lids colored a bright red, so I could identify it, and always use that one for my right lens. This system worked well for me, but the problem came if one of the lenses was dropped during transfer to and from my eye. Trying to find a clear tiny contact lens with perfect vision is difficult. Now try and find that same contact lens with significant sight loss. Let us just say it took a great deal of searching, more with my fingers, rather than my eyes, to have occasional success. The fastest way to find the missing lens was to ask for help from my family.

As soon as we had rolled into the driveway back at home, I was being scheduled to return to Stanford for follow-up care. I think it was fair to say that the Stanford Eye Clinic doctors were anxious to examine me after my treatment at the Doheny Eye Institute. I guess none of the ophthalmologists at Stanford had ever examined a patient with a Molteno Valve implant, as it was such a new procedure at the time. I am sure they had read about experimental valve surgeries, but now I would be a real-life patient for them all to see. I figured this was my contribution to medical science and hoped that they could all learn a lot from my case.

There was a line-up of doctors wanting to look at the new plumbing that had been installed in my eye. Because Stanford is a teaching hospital, there were always several doctors taking their turn examining me. I was now the patient who carried the most interest because of the unique procedure I had just undergone.

The feedback from Dr. Egbert and his colleagues was that the Molteno Valve appeared to be functioning as designed. My other eye, which had received cryotherapy, on the other hand, was not doing so well. My whole battle up until now was to reduce the pressure. But this time the eye did not bounce back, meaning the eye pressure had been running too low. Dr. Egbert and others had difficulty measuring positive pressure in the eye. It was running under 5 mm. This equated to the pressure being too low, affecting the structural integrity of the eye, as well as the reduced fluid flow not providing adequate nutrition to the innards of my eye.

There is no real treatment for pressure that is too low. You can stop taking any medications that are designed to lower eye pressure like the Diamox drug I had been taking orally for several years now or the topical drops. Since the surgery in Southern California, I had stopped taking all glaucoma medications in both eyes, which was a first. Usually, one of my eyes would need lowering of the pressure, while the other eye most likely was recovering from a surgery and did not need medication.

My eyes had been through many wars by now for controlling pressure, and the one eye might just be saying I have had enough. Also, the amount of cryotherapy that my eye received at Doheny was more than I had ever received before in a single session.

That eye did basically shut down for a couple of months, and the vision in that eye paid a price because of having pressure too low.

Eventually, my eye began to show signs of life again. The pressure was rising to a normal level. This prolonged period of pressure being too low had also caused vision loss. For optimal eye health, your eyes needed to stay within a certain range. Unfortunately, my eye pressure was mainly recorded to be above the acceptable level, and on a few rare occasions, the pressure would fall below the acceptable level.

Dr. Egbert was having trouble seeing into this eye now during examinations because of cataract growth. All the surgical trauma that my eye had undergone had caused progressive scarring on the lens—if there was trouble seeing in, then my ability to see out was also impaired. It was decided the cataract would need to be removed.

By removing the scarred lens, it was hoped that my vision might improve in that eye.

I was being scheduled for yet another surgery. Ironically, this surgery would have nothing to do with glaucoma. When the lens of your eye is removed, it needs to be replaced with an artificial lens, which is usually implanted into the patient's eye. At this stage of my treatment, putting additional things into my eye could cause more harm than good. My artificial lens would be accommodated through wearing glasses again. My time with contact lenses was also coming to an end for the same reason.

This would be a same-day surgery, meaning there would be no hospitalization. The surgery would also be performed with local anesthesia, meaning just my eye would be anesthetized. You are usually sedated, but you can hear noises, smell odors, and recall some of the experience. Your job is to lie very still, and your wish is to not feel any discomfort.

The cataract surgery was completed, and I think considered a success, since the scarred lens of my eye was removed. I was hoping I would experience improvement in my vision now that the scarring had been removed. When I received the updated glasses prescription and was given the opportunity to try them on, unfortunately, I did not experience any kind of dramatic improvement. Because my expectations had been to see better, it was a bit of a letdown. I should have been appreciative of the fact that I could at least still see out of the eye, but my focus had been on better acuity, rather than simply maintaining acuity.

My left eye had continued to recover from the cryotherapy trauma, and eventually, the pressure had begun to rise once again to an unacceptable level. Glaucoma had returned with a vengeance, attacking my remaining vision, and the fight was back on. I found myself needing medication again, and the discussion of more surgery was in the back of everyone's mind. I was close to graduating with my high school class, and glaucoma was looking to take over the limelight. A new plan of action was being considered, which once again involved surgery. I did not want to undergo anymore procedures prior to my graduation from high school. I felt like I was controlling what and when would occur next with my intervention. That was a first for me. It is really amazing how the medical establishment can pretty much take over your life, and if you don't advocate for yourself, you will become a sheep in the flock, feeling like you need to follow the leader, without questioning the leader, just blindly following.

I was present for my high school graduation, and we were going to be the first class that would need to sit in the bleachers, along with all our family members and friends. We can thank the previous graduating classes' disruptive behavior for this change. It meant that our backs were to the audience that had come to recognize this rite of passage. I remember staying up all night with my friends, Dave, John, and Tim, and in the morning, we drove back to our high school to pick up our diploma. My eyes' needs were put on hold for the first time, and there was no medical interference with my graduation festivities.

Now that summer had officially begun, my eyes needed attention again. The all-too-familiar eye aches and blurry vision that always seemed to accompany my rising pressure had returned. That would once again involve some type of surgical intervention.

After getting this latest round of glaucoma under control, my plan was to find summer employment and my fall college plans were to attend the local junior college.

Dr. Egbert and the team of doctors at Stanford were not ready to subject my other eye to the Molteno Valve implant. The procedure was so new and had only been in my eye for a few months. The jury was still out on whether this was an effective and safe treatment for the long-term. They opted to move forward with another trabeculotomy procedure. They were going to focus on a different quadrant of my eye. A lot of work had been done at the 12:00 and 6:00 positions. Now they were planning to work in the 3:00 location.

This was one surgical procedure that is still vivid in my mind. There I was lying on the table in the operating room. Suddenly, my sedation level was clearing, and I became aware of where I was and what was happening to me. Further, I began hearing Dr. Egbert's voice, as he was asking for different instruments, as he worked on my eye. Next, I remember hearing drill-like noises coming from a device that was in my eye. I was also experiencing vibration sensations in my eye. My conscious level was continuing to clear, and I was starting to worry about feeling more discomfort, as I continued to wake up during this surgery. I had no idea how much longer Dr. Egbert was going to be working on me, but I was aware enough to know that I did not want to sit back and just wait for things to run their course. I knew the doctors did not know that I was awake enough to know and feel what was going on, but I needed to somehow let them know this fact. The muscle relaxers were doing their job making me essentially paralyzed, so I was in a body that was mentally waking up, but my muscles and voice were still in a heavy fog. I needed to somehow communicate with Dr. Egbert, but it was a struggle to get any type of words out. I remember hearing background conversation with chuckling and laughter. It felt like there was a party going on, and I and my eye were the center of this celebration.

I heard Dr. Egbert ask for assistance to have someone hold the flap, whatever that meant.

I managed to muffle out a couple of words about "starting to feel it." Not sure if my words were understandable, but the fact that I was responsive at all, I am sure was a concern to Dr. Egbert.

PRESSURE

The last thing I remember hearing from my doctor was "I have done what I can with the local; can you do something?" which must have been a question to the anesthesiologist.

I remember nothing after that, and I am sure medication was injected into my IV line, which shut me right up.

CHAPTER 28:
A JOB, A GIRL FRIEND & STARTING COLLEGE

Due to my legal-blindness status, I qualified for a county employment program for underrepresented youth. I was able to choose from a list of jobs working at different public agencies. My goal was to find something in my local town of Scotts Valley, so I would be able to drive my moped to and from work. This hiring process was not like any standard job interview. Instead of interviewing for a position, you were pretty much able to point to the job that you wanted, and it would be yours. I remember jumping at the opportunity to work for Scotts Valley City Hall performing grounds-keeping tasks. I was already pretty much accepting this position because it was close to my home and the job sounded very doable with less than perfect vision. The representative from the jobs program encouraged me to read through the entire list of opportunities before making a final decision.

That piece of advice turned out to be great on several levels. Farther down the list of job opportunities was one for a summer recreation leader at Vine Hill Elementary School. This was the same school that I had attended as a child. This job was even closer to my home, the school grounds were very familiar to me, and the job involved playing games with kids. What more could a guy ask for? Unknown to me at the time, this job would also allow me to meet my future wife.

Mr. Edwards was the PE teacher at Vine Hill School, and he was the one who ran the summer recreation program. There were probably 50 to 75 kids enrolled in the summer camp. Along with me, there were several others who worked staggered shifts to cover the camp hours, including Todd, Jeff, Mike, Belinda, Amy, and Jeff's sister, Stephanie. We all worked various overlapping shifts to make sure the proper ratio of kids to staff was maintained throughout the day.

Fortunately, Mr. Edwards liked the way I worked with the kids, so I was offered a permanent position to continue working in the program during the fall. A new teenage girl also started in the fall, and this was not a child enrolling in the after-school recreation program. She was a friend of Belinda's who had been hired. Her name was Amy. She was a tall 16-year-old brunette with long legs and brown eyes. This girl had it together. When I talked to her, she had her plan figured out. After high school, she would attend Cabrillo College and complete her general education (GE) requirements, along with any prerequisites for her major. After that, she would transfer to San Jose State University (SJSU) and complete her major in Occupational Therapy.

I had never even heard of Occupational Therapy, so I asked her about it. Amy's mom Molly had a cousin named Elaine who was a physical therapist. The Physical Therapy degree had more math and science requirements, which did not interest Amy. Elaine suggested Occupational Therapy (OT). Amy researched this career choice, and by her junior year of high school, her mind was made up. There is no changing Amy's mind. When she decides about what she wants to do, it will happen.

The idea of assisting people who have experienced disabling conditions is what drew her to OT. Amy also has an artsy creative side, which traditionally was part of the OT practice. Historically, training and education for OT practitioners had included learning crafts for use as therapeutic interventions. Early course work in OT included training with specific mediums, such as needlepoint, weaving, leatherwork, etc. Sadly, many of these modalities are no longer being utilized by therapists. There have been so many changes with Medicare and other-third party insurers and what services are reimbursable.

Amy had started working in the after-school recreation program with me in September of 1984. It took me until November of that year to gather up the courage to ask her out. I had checked in with her friend, Belinda, on a few occasions, asking if she thought Amy might go out with me.

Belinda was direct with me and said, "I think you should ask her out."

I do not think she would have encouraged me unless she knew Amy would most likely say yes.

When I had finally built up the confidence to ask her out, Amy did say yes.

I told her I did not drive and asked if she would be okay with doing that. Amy, of course, already knew this fact, so when she had said yes to going out, she knew she would be the driver. I still was not disclosing information about what I could or could not see. I would go on faking it for a while, but I think Amy caught on to my deception pretty much right away. Amy picked me up at my house for our first date.

Of course, I had no plan for what we were going to do. We ended up at Carl's Jr. Restaurant. The big spender that I was, I told Amy to order whatever she wanted. She ordered a Diet Coke and wedge-cut fries. I was not a regular customer of Carl's Jr., so I did not know the menu from memory and could not see it well enough to read it. Of course, I was not going to ask Amy to read it for me. I thought I was so sly when I simply ordered what she had. Truth be told, at that time, I did not even like Diet Coke.

Attending Cabrillo College and being able to stay at home made a lot of sense to my situation. My eyes had continued to be unstable, so being close to Stanford was important. My SAT scores (where I had just arbitrarily shaded in the ovals on the test sheet) most likely would not have qualified me to attend a four-year school anyway. And attending a state college right out of high school without knowing what I wanted to major in felt like a waste.

This is when I began learning to advocate for myself. I no longer had a VI teacher who was going to support my academic needs, and if I needed help, it was going to be up to me. I was now a legal-age adult, who needed to take responsibility. As I transitioned from high school to college, I became a consumer at the State Department of Rehabilitation. This was a program that provided counseling and financial support to people with disabilities. It was a vocational-based program whose goal was for consumers to ultimately find employment. As part of this support, my books and tuition were paid for.

I learned that the college had a Disabled Student Services (DSS) Department, and they could assist with my academic needs. There was funding available for me to hire note-takers, but it was up to me to find someone for this job. At first, I would awkwardly just ask students around me if they would be a note-taker for me. I would go on to tell them that it paid $100 for the semester. Most folks I asked did not understand why I needed assistance or thought I was somehow scamming them. I quickly learned the best way to find a responsible classmate was to utilize the course professor. By speaking to the professor ahead of time, I was able to make him/her aware of my needs, and they were usually more than willing to make an announcement to the class. It also gave the professor time to prepare course materials and schedule proctors for upcoming examinations.

Another benefit of attending the junior college was the smaller campus size and fewer numbers of students as compared to a university. The resources available to me as a disabled student were abundant. The other big issue for me was keeping up with the reading demands of college. Even though my parents had purchased a video magnifier machine for me, which now had the capability of enlarging material in color, having this newer video magnifier was useful, but it was not possible for me to independently keep up with the reading demands of college. Getting academic books on cassette tapes was virtually impossible. Most books were not available on tape, and in the rare occasions that one was available, and you requested it, it would not be delivered until the semester was half over. This meant I would be depending on human assistance to get my reading done. This also meant I needed to find people willing to read out loud to me. That proved to be an ongoing challenge, because the person needed to be willing to meet with me outside of class time and read out loud. It also takes longer to go through the material when it is being read out loud.

Once again, I did try to recruit fellow students who were in the same class as me, figuring they also needed to read the same material. I could offer them a way to be paid, as they did their homework. This was an effective method for me to get support, but I still needed more help than I could find on my own. Fortunately, the DSS had several people, both volunteer and paid, who could provide further support to me. It turned out the volunteer readers were the best and most reliable for my needs.

It was a lot of work to just manage the supportive services that I needed so I would have access to the course material. Then there was the chore of completing the assignments. All my tests were taken one-on-one with a proctor usually in the DSS Office. If it was an essay examination, I would need to write my answers with a black ink pen. My writing, by now, was very large, would fill up the test booklet quickly, and honestly did not look too scholarly. I found printing to be easier for me to read back what I had written as opposed to cursive writing. I was once asked by a fellow student why I wrote like a child in kindergarten. I thought the reason was pretty obvious, but it just goes to show that some people are clueless.

Once I wrote my essay answers, I could have it transcribed by the proctor, but they did not always understand my large writing. This meant I would need to read back to them what I had written, and that was a blurry strain of words to sort out.

When I needed to complete a formal written report, which was required to be typed in a certain format, my mom came to the rescue. She could read, understand, and make edits to my large-print handwritten text. I knew how to type from the classes I had taken in middle school and high school, but I could not see the letters that the typewriter produced. My mom would turn my handwritten manuscript into a formal typewritten paper that I could turn in. She did this over and over again for me during college, and truly earned an honorary degree.

CHAPTER 29:
CONSULTATION WITH DOHENY & A SECOND VALVE IMPLANT

The eye that had not undergone the initial valve surgery was continuing to have elevated-pressure issues. Stanford referred me back to Doheny in Southern California. It would be an opportunity for Dr. Baerveldt and Dr. Minckler to evaluate the initial valve implant that they had performed. Stanford also wanted an opinion from Doheny concerning the idea of a Molteno Valve for my other eye.

The date I made a return trip to Doheny was Tuesday January 28, 1986. It was one of those historic days that you never forget. Unfortunately, it was a tragic day for the United States and NASA, as the Space Shuttle *Challenger* exploded shortly after taking off, resulting in the death of seven astronauts. This time, my mom and I flew to Southern California because this was going to be a day trip, fly down in the morning, be examined at Doheny, and return home that same evening. I also remember having a root canal the previous day and being advised that flying after a root canal can cause uncomfortable pressure changes in the recently treated tooth—a different context, but there was that word *pressure* coming up again in my life.

The ophthalmologists at Doheny were in favor of a Molteno Valve implant for my other eye. They felt like the initial procedure was doing well. They were ready to schedule the procedure while I was there for my follow-up appointment. I had a decision to make, because it had been a couple of years, and Stanford was now performing the Molteno Valve implant surgery. It was my decision and it did not take me long to decide. I would return home and have any additional surgery performed by Dr. Egbert.

In the winter of 1986, I had undergone a second Molteno Valve implant surgery, so now both eyes were equipped with this new type of plumbing.

CHAPTER 30:
EUROPEAN VACATION

In the summer of 1986, my childhood friend, Chris, was an exchange student in Austria. At the same time, his parents and sister were living temporarily in Rome, as Chris's dad was working as a consultant for the Italian government. During the previous summer, Amy had traveled to Holland to meet her cousin, Liesbeth, where she got to stay with the family for a couple of weeks. Liesbeth then traveled with Amy back to the United States, where she also stayed for a couple of weeks. I was dating Amy at the time, so I got to know Liesbeth well. I told Liesbeth that a friend and I were talking about traveling to Europe during the following summer.

My buddy, Dave, and I agreed we would travel to Europe. The timing was right, since we would have several options for staying with people we knew in different countries. Additionally, we would take backpacks, camp, and stay in youth hostels. Amy was graduating in June, but our reservations had us leaving in late May for our six-week adventure to Europe. I was the bad boyfriend, since I would not be at my girlfriend's high school graduation ceremony. I sent my sister instead to the post-graduation party, which was at the Dream Inn Hotel, right on the beach next to the wharf and boardwalk. I heard that Amy and all of her classmates had a great time celebrating this rite of passage.

Dave and I had purchased an Eurail Pass in advance of our trip, which would entitle us to 30 consecutive days of unlimited rail travel on the European continent. Our trip would start and end through London.

As it turned out, making this trip while still having some vision was so fortunate, not that I was thinking about, or even considering, the possibility that I would not have vision at some point in the future.

Chris met us at Heathrow Airport right outside of the customs department. To clear customs, you needed to present your passport and answer questions about the purpose of your visit to England. Dave was ahead of me in line and was directed to a specific booth number by the customs agent. When it was my turn, I was also directed to a specific booth number, but the problem was I could not see any of the numbers. Not knowing what else to do and afraid to ask for help, I headed out in the same direction that Dave had gone in. That was obviously the wrong choice, because I was immediately reprimanded and redirected. I ended up being directed to the same agent who Dave was interacting with.

I remember chuckling when I heard Dave's answer to the agent's question, "What are your plans here in England?"

"To get to Belgium."

It was very cool of Chris to meet us at the airport. Dave and I were two young novice travelers with no international experience. Chris was a seasoned traveler who had been to many countries by now. He could also speak German. I could not see any of the signs, and even if I could have, the only language I spoke was English.

Chris had found us a place to stay that first night. It turned out that I knew the guy, a neighbor of mine and a teammate from Little League, Jeff. He was attending college in London and had an apartment with roommates that he let us crash at.

Chris was the leader, Dave was the co-pilot, and I was the follower, who stuck with my friends for guidance. We did quickly discover that Chris had no money. If we wanted to keep Chris as our tour guide, then we were going to need to cover his costs for the time being.

Dave and I headed to the English coast and camping. Chris had things to do in London, and we planned to meet up in Spain in a few days. We left England after a night and took the Hovercraft to Belgium. This was a high-speed jet boat that just glided across the surface of the ocean.

From there, we headed to Paris, where we found a campground near downtown adjacent to the Seine River. I always remember what my seventh-grade Social Studies teacher said. "You would have to be insane to swim in the Seine." Apparently, there were some serious pollution issues.

France was the place where we had the most difficulty with ordering food and communicating. It was just Dave and I at this point. There we were at a bakery. Dave could see the menu, but was unable to read the French words. I could not see any of it and asked if there were any pictures that we could just point to, as I recalled the expression that a picture is worth a thousand words. Unfortunately, that was not an option. The café worker ended up playing the game of charades with us. She would grab a bread roll and then point to various condiments that could be added. Again, I could not see the items that she was pointing at, and Dave did not know what many of the items even were, so we ended up nodding yes to most things that she pointed at. We were hungry travelers, so we had no trouble consuming the sandwich that had been created from the nonverbal communication.

I remember climbing the Eiffel Tower while we were there, and I am sure we visited other tourist attractions, but we were ready to leave France and head to more affordable Spain.

We took the train into Barcelona, where Chris met up with us. There, we found a cheap room to rent for the three of us and learned firsthand why you get what you pay for. The next morning, I headed to the bathroom for a shower. No matter what lever I twisted or turned, there was no hot water. That was one of the quickest showers I had ever taken. I reported back to Dave and Chris concerning the lack of hot water, and they dismissed my warning. I was sure thinking

I just could not see how to work this foreign plumbing. I was pleased to observe each of them returning to the room after spending very little time in the shower. It turned out that it was not my lack of vision in operating the shower, there was truly no hot water.

I remember the Spanish gentleman who had rented us the room returning the next day to check in on us. I mimicked taking a shower and shivering to him. I think he understood me because he took out a lighter from his pocket and flicked it on. Later, our landlord and Chris had some sort of a conversation. Chris did not speak his native language of Spanish, and the landlord did not speak Chris's native language of English. Somehow, they figured out that they both could speak German. Chris communicated our need for hot water, and we were assured there would be some tomorrow. Chris also asked about nightlife and where we should go in town.

We were directed to what I am sure was the Red-light district. That night, we ended up at a strip bar, where we paid for a show, which included two drinks. Not being too experienced with the bar scene, I ordered whiskey. There I was with my two shots, when the show began. I was told there were women on the stage wearing very little clothing, and as the show progressed, I was told the clothing was removed. This was not fair to a guy who could not see well. What I saw was dots or blurs that represented women on a stage. I had a device in my pocket that might help to remedy this situation. I remember when my freshman-year Math teacher accused me of looking at nudy girls through my monocular telescope. Well, I had traveled to Europe with this same type of device, thinking it might come in handy to see the sights. I had not had an opportunity to use the telescoping device yet on my trip, but figured this would be a great opportunity to try it out. Now I could make my high school Math teacher's accusation come true by using the device to actually view naked women on stage.

Blurs and dots on the stage were not satisfactory. I was looking for detail. I must have looked conspicuous, as I sat in the audience, with a miniature telescope up to my eye. I knew that the show's MC decided to make these three young American boys (Chris, Dave, and I) the comedy part of the show. He came right up to our table, speaking into a microphone with a rapid Spanish dialog, mimicking looking through a telescope with his hand. We could not understand what was being said about us, but the bar crowd erupted with laughter, so everyone present must have been told about the monocular device that I was using.

From Spain, we headed to the Netherlands, with a plan to stay with Liesbeth's family for a few days. First though, we had heard all about Amsterdam. We found the well-known Bulldog Coffee Café. Their menu had a lot more than just coffee. We got to choose from a variety of cannabis products from chocolates, gummies, oils, capsules, and the traditional pipes and joints. Even though all this stuff was legal, we justified our purchase of Afghani Black, saying it would be good for my eye pressure. There we were, just sitting in a café in Amsterdam, lighting up a joint, getting high.

There was a period when Dr. Egbert took a sabbatical in the late 1980s and I was placed in the care of Dr. Lieberman. I had never asked my doctors about marijuana as a treatment for my glaucoma. By now, nothing had worked long-term to control my eye pressure. It had never been prescribed to me, I am sure, because it was not officially legal. I was desperate and had a new temporary doctor, who I barely knew, so I decided to ask the question about marijuana. Dr. Lieberman was very honest and direct with his answer to me. Marijuana did lower eye pressure, but the lowering effects only lasted if you were high. I took this to mean marijuana would provide temporary relief of my eye pressure, but for sustained results, one would need to remain high pretty much all the time. He went on to say that using a water bong was the healthiest method to ingest THC.

It was so nice of Liesbeth's family to not only put me up in their home, but they also let two of my friends stay at their home. For the several days that we stayed with them, they fed us and acted as our tour guide, showing us the sights of Holland. There was one moment I remember when we were all sitting around the table, having a tasty meal, when I had reached out for more of the fried potatoes. Had I been able to see that the bowl was empty, I would never have reached out. Of course, my action prompted Liesbeth's mom Margaret to get up from the table, return to the kitchen, and prepare more food. I felt so bad and tried to stop her, but she insisted on making more food for me.

From the Netherlands, we headed to Switzerland. We decided to go snow skiing in the Alps. Apparently, this resort was on a glacier, which allowed you to ski year-round. I remember how, on one of the runs, we skied through a tunnel in the mountain and ended up on the other side of the glacier. I had never skied through a tunnel before, and I remember it being dark because we went from bright sunshine into a dark tunnel. My eyes had not had time to adjust to the extreme lighting change, so navigating through the tunnel was more accomplished by sound, following the noise of my friend's skis ahead of me.

The next country on our itinerary was Austria. We stayed with Chris's exchange family in Salzburg. These people were well to do. Their house was more like a mansion with multiple rooms. Each of us had our own room and bathroom. Chris was very familiar with the town, as he had been living there and taking classes. He took us to the local pub, and we learned all about drinking and sharing beer. I remember hearing about some huge stein of beer that could be ordered. I was young and stupid, and decided that more would be better. Apparently, it was tradition when this large volume of beer is ordered and the stein is passed through the pub, allowing any patrons to help themselves to a drink. When the stein finally made it back to me, it had been drained, but there was still plenty of beer to consume. Drinking out of this huge glass vessel required both hands to manage it. There were handles coming off each side of the mug, and I used both of my hands to hoist it up to my mouth.

Being simply drunk is one thing, but being drunk when you're half blind can create additional issues. When I reached for my glass of beer—normally I would move my hand slowly across the table until I contacted what I was seeking—well, due to my impaired coordination, in combination with my impaired vision, meant that my hands were moving at a faster uncontrolled rate. Within a span of five minutes, I knocked over not one, not two, but three glasses that crashed and shattered all over the floor of the pub. Each time, I would break a glass, my friend, Chris, would make sure that we paid for the broken glass. By the third time this had happened, I was starting to feel ill. My friends escorted me to the bathroom. Unfortunately, the stall was occupied, so I threw up in the sink.

The pub worker demanded that we clean up the sink where I had become ill. Chris said that was not our job. He pointed out that we had paid for the glasses that had been broken, and we were going to be leaving. As we walked out of the pub, more words were being exchanged between Chris and I and the pub worker. The pub worker was attempting to physically restrain us, threatening to call the police. By now, the patrons in the pub had come outside and formed a circle around the three of us, thinking they were going to witness some type of a brawl. There I was stumbling around inside this circle of humanity, trying to put myself between the pub worker and Chris. We managed to break away from this crowd without any physical altercation occurring.

Now that we had overstayed our welcome in Austria, the next morning, we decided to get out of town and catch a train to Italy, where Chris's family was living temporarily. It was a long overnight ride from Salzburg to Rome. To break up the long trip and to stretch our legs, we took a walk through the length of the train. As we reached each connecting car, we had to slide a door open to proceed. When we reached the last rail car, which we discovered rather suddenly when we slid open what we thought would be another connecting door, instead, we were greeted with open air, as we stared out the back of the train, as it moved down the tracks. I was glad Dave had been leading our walk through the train when the door leading to nowhere was encountered.

Another memory about the rail system that was disturbing concerned the onboard toilets. When they were flushed, Chris and Dave informed me that you could see the railroad tracks appear through the bottom of the toilet, so that is where the contents of the toilet were deposited when flushed.

In a couple of the European cities that we visited, there were single-stall public restrooms that could be utilized right from the street. The funny thing about these stalls was the fact that your head stuck out above the enclosure and your legs were visible below the enclosure. At least, where you did your business was covered. Sometimes when accessing indoor bathrooms, the layout could be quite different from what I was familiar with. In place of an actual commode, there would simply be a hole in the ground with grab bars mounted on either side that I guess could be utilized while you squatted. The other thing you needed to know was to supply yourself with toilet paper prior to entering the stall because there was no paper available once you were in the stall. There was often an attendant in the bathroom expecting a financial contribution from those using the facilities.

Public restrooms in general are unpleasant for people with sight loss to navigate. Every bathroom's design seems to be different and the larger the venue, the more complicated the restroom is. When you cannot see, finding the urinal or stall door is a big enough challenge, and once you find the correct facility for your use, then the fun really starts. Feeling around to find the location of the commode, toilet paper, or the flushing lever is not what you really want to be doing in a public restroom. Sometimes after searching for a flushing mechanism, you will discover that the system has automatic flushing. Being that I am in a family with two girls, I will often have Amy or Megan go into the women's bathroom first to conduct surveillance. It will not tell me specifically about the Men's Room, but at least I might learn about the plumbing system being used. I always prefer single-stall public bathrooms, because they are much easier to navigate, and Amy can perform a preliminary visual inspection, which is invaluable information for me to receive.

Rome was a city full of history. The highlights we visited while there included Vatican City and the Roman Coliseum. The Voris family were also wonderful hosts, allowing us to stay in their Italian home, feeding Dave and I, and showing us around the local sights.

We were pretty much out of traveler checks by the time we made it to Rome. Chris's dad settled with us regarding costs that we had acquired while the three of us had traveled together. Our Eurail Pass was going to expire in a couple of days, so we wanted to leave Italy and get as close to London as possible, since that is where we would be flying out of to return home.

Originally, we had planned to stay in Europe for six weeks. We were back in London now, approaching five weeks that we had been traveling, our Eurail Pass had expired, and our funds were running low, so we were considering coming home a week early. My parents had provided me with a credit card in case of an emergency. When I attempted to take an advance of some money using this card, I was asked to sign my name to verify the transaction. The receipt that I needed to sign was a small piece of paper with a tiny area for my signature. I leaned over, bringing my nose as close to the receipt as

I could, trying to figure out where the area to sign was—when I completed the task and presented the receipt back to the cashier, he arbitrarily decided that I took too long to sign the receipt and refused to process the transaction. I was speechless from the cashier's reaction. I had signed my name as best as I could, but it was not good enough for this guy. Not knowing what to do, I just walked away from the money-exchange booth, and Dave and I decided this was a sign telling us it was time to come home from this European adventure.

CHAPTER 31:
PREREQUISITE COURSES, IMPLANT REMOVAL & MOPED ACCIDENT

After returning from our European adventure, it was time for me to get serious and figure out what my plan was going to be. During my first two years at the junior college, I had been taking GE classes, focusing on earning my Liberal Arts degree. I was still undecided concerning a major, but Amy's idea of Occupational Therapy sounded good to me. I liked the idea of helping people with disabling conditions. And as a bonus, pursuing an OT degree would mean I could see Amy more.

It took me three years to earn my AA degree, which included completing prerequisite courses to make me eligible to apply for entry into the Occupational Therapy Program. Prospective OT students also needed to complete several observation hours as part of the application process.

In the fall of 1986, Amy joined me at Cabrillo College. One of the prerequisite requirements for the OT major was an Anatomy/Physiology course. The junior college did not offer a combination course, which would have been acceptable. There was such a course at San Jose State, but we were not yet enrolled there as students. We needed to take a separate Anatomy course and then a Physiology course. We also learned that a Chemistry course was required before you could take Physiology.

For me to qualify to begin the OT major next year, I was going to need to double up on sciences during this third year at the junior college. Fortunately, Amy was now at the junior college and she needed to complete the same classes, so we would be doing this

"

together. This first semester of my final year meant I would need to take Anatomy along with Chemistry. Anatomy consisted of a weekly one-hour lecture, along with a three-hour lab. During that semester, we were required to dissect a cat and worked on a real human cadaver.

I have one clear memory from the Anatomy Lab. Small groups of students wearing surgical gloves would take their turn going into the refrigerated room at the back of the classroom. This is where the human cadaver was stored. When it was my turn to gather around the gurney where the body was lying, our professor was also present and was pointing out various anatomical structures to the students. I was standing across from my professor with this dead body between us, when all of the sudden, without any warning, she reached into the cadaver and grabbed some appendage that was part of the body. This appendage was thrust toward my face positioned close to my eyes. My professor let me know she was holding a vessel and asked me if I could see the two tiny holes.

I was in shock as I stood there with this body part from a dead person inches from my face. I responded quickly, saying, "Yes," thinking that would be the right answer and fastest way to get this part placed back in the body where it came from, and away from my face.

My professor went on to tell me one of the holes was an artery and the other hole was a vein. That was TMI for me that day.

By the fall semester of 1986, my eye that had undergone the initial Molteno Valve implant was beginning to ache. The pain in the eye continued to be more and more painful as the semester progressed. Physiology was the most demanding class during this semester. It was a five-unit course that had an hour lecture and six hours of lab each week. It was not a class that you wanted to miss. There were a couple of times, though, that the eye pain was such that staying in the car and lying down was the best option for coping.

Dr. Egbert suspected that my eye was rejecting the valve that had been implanted, and this foreign object was being forced out of my eye, causing a lot of discomfort. The tissue around the implant site was breaking down, and medications were administered to promote regeneration. The medication regimen was given for several weeks in the hopes for a positive response. It was fair to say at this point they were attempting to treat a condition that they have no experience with. The area in my eye did not improve, and the tissue continued to break down. The longer this went on, the risk for infection would go up.

Surgery was scheduled to remove the implant. This was a case where my eye was aching when I went into the operating room, the valve was removed, and the pain was gone by the time I made it to the recovery room. Was this an omen though of what was to come for my eye that had just undergone the valve implant? The initial implant had lasted approximately three years, before needing to be removed. I was still hoping this would be a permanent solution.

Not experiencing eye pain anymore was truly a relief. I completed my final semester at Cabrillo.

When the school year ended in the spring of 1987, working for our very cool boss, Mr. Edwards, was coming to an end. We (Jeff, Todd, Amy, Stephanie, and I) had been told that Santa Cruz County Parks and Recreation was taking over the program at Vine Hill School. We had all worked together for the past three years, but we were told if we wanted a summer recreation leader position, we would need to apply through Santa Cruz County Parks and Recreation. The independent recreation program that Mr. Edwards had led for many years was being pushed out.

We all had to apply individually for a position as a recreation leader through Santa Cruz County. Fortunately, we were all hired, but we were separated and placed at different recreation programs throughout the county. They were accommodating to me and placed me back at Vine Hill School, which was familiar to me, but it would be without my friends and coworkers.

Behind the scene, Mr. Edwards had made a deal with the city of Scotts Valley to offer a summer recreation program at the local park, which happened to be adjacent to Vine Hill School, so this program would be in direct competition with the new county offering. Mr. Edwards asked me to come work for him in a supervisory role. I had just turned 21, so I was of legal age to run the program. Mr. Edwards also wanted all his previous staff to join him at this new city recreation program, but they were younger than me and needed a job through the county during the upcoming school year. I, on the other hand, would be leaving the area to attend SJSU, so I would not need a county position during the upcoming school year.

I, without hesitation, agreed to come work for Mr. Edwards. It was more like working with him because we did a job share, where he covered part of the day and I covered part of the day. We needed to hire additional teenage staff to work as recreation aides. I was able to hire Amy's brother, Mark, as a recreation leader.

I usually covered the morning shift, which started at 7:30. Being that I was still driving my moped to and from work, I appreciated the early-morning time because it usually meant it would be foggy and there would not be shadows on the road. The moped was different from a bicycle in a couple of ways. First, it had a tail pipe that would get extremely hot from the running motor. In the summer, I would often ride the moped wearing shorts, and if my leg happened to meet the pipe, it would burn my skin instantly. Unfortunately, I experienced the effects of the tail pipe torch more times than I care to remember. The noise of the motor also created additional challenges for me. With a bicycle, I could hear cars that were passing me or approaching me from behind. My hearing awareness was a critical tool used to compensate for my lack of vision. When the moped motor was running, the audio cues that I relied on were drowned out. Unfortunately, this meant that I had to use more of my vision, which was not a good option for me.

There was one day when I was riding the moped to work on the 3.5-mile country road. I was probably two-thirds of the way through my commute. It was a typical foggy morning, which I considered a good-visibility day for me. I rounded a corner probably moving at a whopping 20 mph. As I was coming out of the turn, my front wheel hit something, and I ended up flying over the handlebars. The next thing I remember was striking the pavement, sliding to a stop in the middle of the road. The left side of my body was burning covered in a bright red rash where the skin had been torn up. The fact that I could walk away after this accident was a good sign in my mind. I retrieved my moped that was lying in the road. I discovered the cause of the wreck. There was one piece of firewood lying next to my moped in the middle of the road. I suspect that it must have fallen off someone's truck, landing in the road, blending in with the gray asphalt. I can say that I never saw the log. This was another sign of my failing vision, and a message telling me it might be time to give up riding the moped.

A Good Samaritan had even come out of her driveway shortly after the accident and brought me back to her home for some first aid. I had a ripped-up shirt and bloody scrapes along my arm and side. The cuts were cleaned up and several band aids were applied, and I was back on the moped, riding to work, hoping not to be too late.

CHAPTER 32:
STORIES WHILE DATING

Amy and I would often double-date with friends. I remember one particular date when we had decided to go to the Surf Bowl with our friends, Billy and Ingrid. As the name suggests, we decided to bowl a couple of games. I had bowled plenty of times in my life, but as I lined up to throw my ball down the lane, it was fair to say that all the lanes were a blur. I could not really distinguish one lane from another. For the first few frames, I managed to walk a pretty straight line, and send my ball down the lane that was assigned to our group. There was a guy next to us bowling by himself, and for all I knew, probably had a perfect game going. I managed to mess with his score by mistakenly using his lane during one of my frames. On this particular throw, my line-up was not good. Instead of releasing my ball down my lane, it ended up in the lane next to me. Of course, no one in my group had told me what happened. I went back to the ball return, preparing for my second throw of the frame. I waited and waited for my ball to pop out of the ball return, but it did not come.

The next thing that happened was my buddy, Billy, handing me my bowling ball. I really did not process why he had my ball, but just figured I must have missed it coming out of the machine. I continued playing through the frames, just trying to get the game over with, and try not to make a complete fool of myself. But I had already done that.

I had noticed the guy bowling next to us actually moved down several lanes away from us. I remember thinking how much easier it was having more space. It was a concern not being able to see clearly who was next to me and determining whether it was my turn or not.

I was so embarrassed and upset when I had heard later about what my bowling actions had done. Everyone in my group had known; if they had told me at the time, I would have immediately walked out of the bowling alley. I have not bowled an actual frame since.

During another double date with friends, there was an Italian restaurant that we were eating out at, and upon exiting the establishment, I maneuvered myself right in the middle of the two swinging doors, thinking this would give me the best clearance path when leaving. This restaurant had glass doors that could be pushed or pulled on the left side, as well as a duplicate door on the right side, and when both doors were closed, they met in the middle. What I could not see, and painfully discovered, was that there was a stationary doorway frame right in the middle where the two doors met. And, of course, that is right where I was walking, as I pushed the door on my right away from me, as I attempted to exit. I was grateful that I was only moving at a walking pace, but the resulting whiplash to my body from being stopped abruptly when crashing into the unseen door's steel framing definitely got my attention.

Waitresses' reactions to my sight loss have been some of the most entertaining experiences. The classic question regularly asked and directed to Amy or any other person joining me at the table is "What does he want to eat?"

Amy's response to this question is to simply look at me, which seems to be an effective method for focusing the servers' attention on me, allowing me to articulate what I would like to order.

Some of the servers who actually do speak directly to me will noticeably increase their volume level and occasionally even speak slower to me. So it must be assumed, along with my vision loss, I must also have hearing and comprehension issues.

Having drinks delivered to me at the table can also be a surprising experience, particularly if I am unaware that water or some other item has been placed or moved from in front of me. When I first sit down at a table in a restaurant, I make a conscious effort to explore the place setting in front of me with my fingers to determine the location of specific items. Once I have that mental picture of how things are laid out, I feel more comfortable. The fun begins when, unknown to me, a drink is placed in front of me or moved to make room for something else, but these harmless actions, if not communicated to me, can result in embarrassing accidents. Discovering that my beverage is being filled up right as I am reaching for it or that my drink has been filled up without my knowledge creates opportunities for spills, complete knock-overs, or my hand finding the mashed potatoes on the plate that I did not know was now in front of me.

Even eating the meal that you know was just placed in front of you can be an adventure. Often the plate is garnished with things that are not meant for consumption, but if you cannot see what you just stabbed your fork into, chances are it will end up in your mouth, and by then, it might be too late. I have had the pleasure of chewing on aluminum-wrapped servings of butter, the peal of a sliced orange, parsley, toothpicks, the tail of a shrimp, and spicy peppers that can ruin your meal, to name a few.

I am an advocate for finger food and absolutely appreciate when a waitress describes what is on my plate, using a clock-face method, i.e., your spaghetti is at 6 o'clock, your bread is at 12 o'clock, your drink is at 1 o'clock, etc.

Amy and I had taken a trip up to the family cabin in Arnold. I woke up early one of the mornings, and decided it would be a good time for a run. Amy was sleeping, so I put on my shorts & socks, double knotted my laces and set out for what I thought would be 30 minutes of uneventful aerobic exercise. Definitely no sidewalks in the mountains, but I always found following the gray blur of what I considered was the road compared to the darker blur which I figured was the forest edge helped me to navigate.

I did not have any visual memory of this area to pull from, so I was relying on my vision for guidance. I knew the cabin was on a main road and that there was an intersecting road that went below the cabin and reconnected with the main road closer to the highway turn off. My plan was to run from the cabin to the intersecting road, and travel along that road below the cabin and reconnect to the main road. That plan actually worked and when I reconnected to the main road, I knew the cabin's driveway would come up on my left eventually. I continued down the main road, when I realized I was in trouble. Every blur on my left that I thought could be a driveway looked the same to me. There was no way I was going to be able to determine which blur was the correct one for the cabin. I figured Amy was still sleeping, plus she had no idea that I was now lost, so I knew any kind of rescue was not going to happen. There were no other pedestrians out at that early hour and only an occasional car that would pass by. It was evident that I was going to need to find my own way back to the cabin. This was the type of experience that really illustrated how impaired my acuity was getting. I was not ready to accept my severe lack of vision, and situations like this were becoming more & more frequent. To say that I was scared and worried about my progressive vision loss would have been an understatement.

I did end up wandering up several different driveways along the main road, but I could not make out enough detail to satisfy that it was the correct one for the cabin, so I would always turn back. I finally made it back, to what I was pretty sure, was the intersecting road that I had jogged on at the beginning of the run. I remembered that the cabin's driveway was not too far from this intersecting road, so I only needed to reverse my direction for a short distance and I should find the blur that would represent the cabin's driveway. I did find a driveway and this time I forced myself to continue walking forward, and I was never happier to find the familiar yellow dasher parked there.

CHAPTER 33:
SJSU & THE OT MAJOR

In the fall of 1987, I was accepted at San Jose State University, where I would major in Occupational Therapy (OT). I had also applied for on-campus housing and was approved to move into the Joe West tower, which was a 12-story dormitory, located right on the SJSU campus. Being within walking distance to everything I would need academically was important, as I was beginning to accept my low vision and adjust to the accompanying mobility challenges.

My roommate was Sergio. He was also a transfer student and a Nursing major. He was focused on his studies like me, so we got along well. My needs as a visually impaired student were unique. I needed a private place where material could be read out loud to me and where I could record notes. This did not work well when you had a roommate, because he would be disturbed by the verbal conversation that I was having or the task that he was engaged in, which could have been anything from watching TV, to talking on the phone, to listening to music, etc., which would be disruptive to my studies.

The recruiting work that I needed to do at the junior college for readers and note-takers was a thing of the past. The OT major gave me access to a department full of students primed to help people, which equated to a large pool of willing students to assist me. It was great that a stipend was available for the students who read and took notes for me, but I know they would have helped me no matter what. Showing their true OT adaptability, many times my readers, Chris, Diane, Doreen, Cyndi, and others, found ourselves sitting in the staircase at the dorm, as they read out loud to me the current assignment, so as not to disturb any other students.

During my first semester at SJSU, I was enrolled in the Nero Anatomy course, consisting of a one-hour lecture and a three-hour lab each week. The lab started at 7:30 a.m. I connected with a graduate student (Cyndi), who was in the OT master's program. There were a few courses that both the graduate and undergraduate students took together, and this was one of them. Cyndi was a fellow OT student taking the class alongside me, but outside of class, she was a personal tutor. We spent many hours together, working in the dorm room or later in the off-campus house where she rented a room. She would swing by in her truck and pick me up in front of the dorm. I remember learning all the cranial nerves and the commonly used acronym to memorize each of them: On Old Olympus's Towering Top a Fin and German Viewed Some Hops.

Cyndi had a way of presenting the material non-visually to me, and whenever possible, we would use tactile models. I remember the professor allowed me to take the lab tests, one on one, with Cyndi. The lab test was very visual, as there would be pins stuck in different locations of the brain, and it was the student's job to identify the structure in question. Sometimes we would be asked to write down the function of the structure, as well. Cyndi would describe the surrounding structures, and it was up to me to recall the answer from the studying that we had done. If required, I would also articulate the function/purpose of the structure.

For my second year at SJSU, I requested and was approved for a single-occupancy dorm room at West Hall. This meant I would no longer have issues with roommates and the reading and recording that I needed to do.

I must share the story about how the university brokered a deal with a local San Jose cable company, though, to bring TV service to each student. For a week or two, all the students living in the dorm were overwhelmed by the noise of coaxial cabling being installed in every floor of the 12-story dormitory. There was nonstop drilling going on all day long, the sounds reverberating throughout the entire building. And to top things off, once the wiring had been completed, they gave each student an opportunity to "purchase" service with the promotion that there would be no installation fee.

Please tell me that this project to bring cable TV service into every dorm room was not an academic priority for the university. The level of noise generated by this project made it impossible for students to study in their rooms. And for me, having a quiet space for my readers and I to work and having access to the desktop video magnifier in my dorm room was critical to my academic success. I remember recording the extreme noise that was generated by this installation project. I figured I could use it as evidence of how to not foster a positive learning environment.

Attending SJSU did mean I was closer to Stanford, so when I needed treatment, it made for a quicker trip for me. The challenge was scheduling the visit to minimize the impact to my academics. The OT Program was a very demanding major for all enrolled students. Having sight loss was an added complication, and needing to schedule regular visits to the ophthalmologist amplified the entire experience.

I remember when I had first arrived at the university just prior to the semester starting and met with the academic advisor (Professor Eyler). My goal was to make her aware of my visual impairment and see if there were things I could do to better prepare for the upcoming semester. The message that stuck in my mind from that initial meeting with Professor Eyler was that she would not be making the major any easier for me. She was a no-nonsense older ex-military woman who probably felt I needed OT intervention rather than supporting me in becoming an OT.

CHAPTER 34:
DANGLING STICHES
& THE LOMA PRIETA
EARTHQUAKE

My eye that no longer had the valve was once again experiencing damaging levels of pressure, and the limited amount of remaining vision that I had was being jeopardized. Several times a year, I would undergo visual field testing in each eye to determine the effects of the ongoing glaucoma. This is where you place your head inside a circular dome, place your chin on the provided rest, and stare straight ahead at a bull's-eye light. Other lights will be brought in from the periphery, and my job was to tap when I saw the light. You were required to keep your eye staring straight ahead while you waited for the light to appear. If you did not see the light after a short period, your natural reaction was to look around for it. This is when the test examiner would reprimand you for moving your eye. I was just trying to find that damn light, but I was not following the rules. The results of these visual field tests usually confirmed some degree of vision loss. It was a gradual thing, so it was difficult for me to consciously detect any change, and quite honestly, I did not want to admit that I was losing vision.

This was the time that Dr. Egbert had taken a sabbatical from his active practice, and I was placed in the care of Dr. Lieberman, who had been added to the Ophthalmology staff at Stanford. I was being prepared for another surgery, and Dr. Lieberman had a slightly different approach to operating on my eye. It would be the same standard trabeculotomy procedure, but Dr. Lieberman wanted to find a quadrant of my eye that had not been exposed to multiple prior surgeries and with minimal residual scar tissue. In my case, that was easier said than found. The area in the 9:00 position, closest to my nose, was determined to be the best option. Because of the location adjacent to my nose, it made the surgery more technical. Initially, the IBM health insurance that was responsible for covering all my medical care denied the increased cost for this surgery, as charges were higher than previous surgeries.

My mom needed to write a letter to the insurance company explaining the reason for the increased charges. Fortunately, the insurance company agreed to pay the full amount for this more technical surgery. I think my office visits to Stanford were 80 percent covered and my hospitalizations were 100 percent covered. Within the first year or two of me being a patient at Stanford, Dr. Rosenthal, and later Dr. Egbert, had agreed to accept whatever the insurance paid for my care, and any additional fees were written off.

After this most recent surgery by Dr. Lieberman, I was probably back in the dorm taking classes within a day or two. I do remember waking up a few days after this surgery, feeling like there was a build-up of what I thought was crusted sleep in the corner of my eye. When I went to wipe the discharge away, it remained. I proceeded to be a bit more aggressive with removing the irritation. I wrapped my fingers around what felt like a piece of dental floss, hanging from my eye, and gave it a little tug, thinking things just needed to be loosened up. The tug resulted in resistance from the other end, and it felt like my eyeball was going to pop out. It turned out what I was pulling on was a suture from the most recent surgery. It was a concern at the time thinking what I might have done to my eye by pulling on this string that was dangling, but a quick trip to Stanford and a trim down of the suture by Dr. Lieberman was all that were needed. I was told the remaining portion of this suture, and any other sutures that I happened to feel, in my eye would dissolve over time.

Each time I would undergo surgery, it would buy me a few months of controlled pressure, but it was always a temporary fix. The permanent solution that I had been seeking just kept eluding me. Things would be so promising right after surgery, but time seemed to be my enemy. After my eyes had adequate time to heal, the newest drain that had been created would become dysfunctional, causing the pressure to elevate. It was that vicious cycle that repeated time and time again. The other reality that was lingering in the back of my mind was how much surgery could an eye take before just shutting down? I think I was starting to realize subconsciously that the battle with this disease called glaucoma was coming to an end, and the outcome was not what I had been fighting for.

Certainly one of the most memorable events of this final semester at SJSU was the Loma Prieta earthquake that occurred on October 17 of 1989. I remember it well. I was in my eight-stories-high dorm room and I had just turned on the TV to watch Game 3 of what was being called the Bay Bridge World Series. My San Francisco Giants were trailing the Oakland Athletics 2 games to 0. Amy had just left for her evening class, and later that night, we were scheduled to pick up Amy's parents at the airport. All of a sudden, there was a rumbling noise, the building began swaying back and forth, the lights went out, students were screaming, and people began running outside of my room in a panic, trying to get out of the building. The elevators were non-functioning due to the power outage. The Residential advisors (Ras) were beginning to come around, announcing that everyone would need to evacuate the dorm through the staircase. The staircase was dark due to the lack of lights, and some students were complaining about having trouble seeing. I did not have any difficulty walking down the darkened staircase. By now, I had learned to find the steps by feeling ahead with my feet as well as following the metal handrail. Also, remember, I almost always traveled the stairs, rather than taking the elevator, after my adventures of getting lost traveling to the second-floor Eye Clinic at Stanford Hospital.

I remember meeting up with Amy outside of the dormitory, as she had been evacuated from her class, as well. I had grabbed my wallet and rushed out with just the clothes on my back. Amy thankfully had her school bag, which included her purse and keys. The dorms were locked and all evacuated students were being directed to the college gymnasium. Amy and I still needed to find out the status of her parents' flight from the East Coast. There were several people lined up at a payphone waiting their turn to make a call. I think we must have waited in line for an hour or so before we had our chance to contact the airline. After many attempts and being transferred to different extensions, we learned that the airport had been closed. Highway 17 connected San Jose to Santa Cruz, winding its way through the mountains. It was the route that got us to our homes in Scotts Valley, but it was closed due to the earthquake damage. That night we ended up at Amy's aunt and uncle's house in San Jose.

CHAPTER 35:
INTERNSHIP PLACEMENT & POST-SURGICAL EYE INJECTIONS

It was my final academic semester in the OT Department. The focus for students currently was completing their clinical course and applying for their field-work placement.

The clinical course involved being assigned a patient who you would evaluate and treat throughout the semester. My patient was Archie. Archie was an 80-year-old gentleman who experienced a stroke with hemiparesis. He could walk with a support cane, but there were deficits on his right side, particularly the upper extremity. There was a lot of spasticity in the arm and hand, causing flexor tone, which inhibited Archie from performing functional tasks. A big focus of my treatment was using modalities to decrease the muscle tone. I remember using an air splint on the involved extremity and at other times submerging the arm/hand into a bucket of ice water. His unaffected extremity would often be used to guide the affected extremity through normal tasks and movement patterns. I had him doing activities such as sawing wood, swinging a bat at a nerf ball, and making a batch of cookies through measuring and stirring ingredients.

Once OT students complete the required academic work, they then need to complete six months of internships, typically three months in a mental health setting and three months in a physical disability setting. We were provided a list of many possible internship opportunities, but it was the students' responsibility to pursue specific placements by scheduling interviews with the supervising therapist at the given facility. By mid-semester, many of my fellow classmates were talking about their internship placements that they had been approved for.

I had been on a handful of interviews, with no offers and very little follow-up from the given supervisor at the facility. Getting concerned about my inability to land an internship placement, I met with Professor Stills, the OT faculty member overseeing students' field-work assignments. She said she would investigate the matter. Later, I had a meeting with my Clinical Professor, Dr. Burton, and Professor Stills concerning my internship placement. The professors cut to the chase and were brutally honest with me.

The intern supervisors who I had met with said they did not want to be the person who failed the blind guy. So rather than being given a chance to pass or fail based on my performance, it was assumed that I would fail due to my vision loss. I deserved the same opportunity as any other OT student would have.

Around this same time my elevated eye pressure needed attention again. Dr. Lieberman was still in charge of my case. Healing and scarring had always been the underlying issue that caused the surgeries to fail. The surgeon would cut a channel, which would act as a drain, allowing the excess fluid to leave my eye. Within a few months, the scar tissue would begin to grow, closing off the channel, making the drain dysfunctional.

Dr. Lieberman had an idea that involved using chemo medication to inhibit the development of scar tissue post-surgery. Much like traditional chemotherapy that is used to eliminate cancerous tumors, there was a medication called 5FU used in small focused dosages that was reported to impede the development of scar tissue so the drain that is created during surgery remains open.

Dr. Lieberman was once again planning to perform a trabeculotomy procedure. However, this time, I would receive daily 5FU injections into my eye for seven days post-surgery. I underwent the standard trabeculotomy procedure and was in and out of the hospital the same day. My follow-up exam was the next day, and usually that consisted of several doctors shining bright lights into my eye to visually inspect the surgical site. Sometimes my pressure would be measured, but that was the extent of the intrusiveness. Now I knew that the post-surgical exam would include an injection. The anticipation of having a shot in my eye was unsettling. I had experienced shots in my arm, in my butt, and even in my mouth, but the idea of having a shot in my eye was truly frightening, and it was not going to be a one-time thing.

I arrived for the post-surgical follow-up exam. My eye was visually inspected, as usual, but then it was time for the injection. I do not remember receiving any kind of anesthetic, but I do remember seeing Dr. Lieberman bringing what I knew was the shot toward my eye. I was asked to hold still, which was always difficult to do when you see something coming into your eye. When the needle was pressed into my eye, there was a sharp pain, followed by a burning sensation, but fortunately, it was short-lived.

I had endured the first round, but in the back of my mind was the knowledge that there were six more rounds to go. I also needed to juggle my school schedule with the everyday trips to Stanford. My mom and I made the daily trips to see Dr. Lieberman so that I could receive the injection of chemo medication that we were hoping would allow the trabeculotomy procedure to be a long-term solution for controlling my pressure. The seven days of injections into my eye were certainly not enjoyable, but worth it if my remaining limited vision could be saved.

Professor Stills took a more active role in my field-work assignment. She understood that my situation was unique and that I was dealing with medical issues with my eyes. She worked out a placement for me at the Veteran's Hospital in Palo Alto, which was an area familiar to me, as it was close to Stanford. It was reassuring to know that I had an internship now lined up for January of 1990.

I still needed to finish out the semester, and then we would have a commencement ceremony for the OT class of 1989.

My return visits to Stanford late that semester were disappointing. The pressure in the most recently operated eye had plummeted to virtually nothing. This condition of no pressure was probably more damaging than glaucoma because there is really nothing that can be done medically to raise the pressure.

My vision was deteriorating at a level where I was noticing it. I remember I would take off my glasses and wipe down the lenses, thinking they were dirty and blurring my vision. No matter how much I cleaned those lenses, my vision never seemed to clear. A few times I remember straining to see something that I had seen before. Convinced that I must not be wearing my glasses, I would reach to my face and realize my glasses were there, but my vision just would not come into focus.

CHAPTER 36:
OT COMMENCEMENT &
FIRST & LAST DAY OF MY INTERNSHIP

The commencement ceremony took place in December of 1989 in a building that was unfamiliar to me. I was very familiar with the Central Classroom Building at SJSU, as it was the home of the OT Department, where many of our courses were held. At this point, I was moving around campus, relying on visual memory rather than actual vision. Case and point, I was walking through the Student Union area of campus, which I had passed through many times during the past two-and-a-half years of attending SJSU. All of a sudden, my head smashed into a metal object. When I reached out, I discovered the object was a backhoe from a tractor that had been apparently parked there. I had no memory of there ever being a tractor in the SJSU Student Union; therefore, having the knowledge to avoid this obstacle was not part of my history.

The 37 OT students (35 women and two men) from the Fall class of 1989 were assembled in chairs on the stage in a building that was completely unfamiliar to me. I had no memory that I could reference regarding the layout of this room. There was a podium where the department chair (Dr. Llorens) acted as the master of ceremonies. She welcomed all our family members and friends in the audience and congratulated our class for their accomplishment in completing the academic portion of the Occupational Therapy degree. Each individual student was introduced and asked to come to the stage, where they were presented with a certificate, and as they exited the stage, they were presented with a rose from our class advisor, Professor Eyler. When my name was called to approach the stage, I realized how blurry things really were. I managed to make it to the podium following audio cues, but after that, seeing where to go was out of the question. My professor, Dr. Swortz, sensing my hesitation, leaving the podium area, came up to rescue me. She acted as if she was congratulating me, but more importantly, escorted me off the stage. I was presented a rose from Professor Eyler, who I am sure never expected to see me on this stage after our initial meeting over two years ago when I entered the OT program.

In January of 1990, Amy and I took a drive to the Palo Alto VA Medical Center so I could orient to the facility prior to starting my internship. The hospital was a large campus, consisting of many multistory buildings representing different medical units. There were the Neuro, Ortho, and Mental Health units, along with a Western Regional Blind Center. I was learning the military lingo, i.e., canteen, latrine, commissary, etc. I was trying my best to be prepared for my internship experience. What I could not prepare for was my lack of vision or blindness. I had not fully accepted this new label of being blind and up to now had done nothing to adapt to this new role as a blind person/therapist.

The first and last day of this internship was a huge reality check for me. The experience of simply finding the OT Department and my supervisor, Cathy, proved to be a challenge. I was unable to actually see where I was going in the hospital, so arriving at the OT Department was somewhat of a miracle. Cathy, my supervisor, had given me a schedule for the day (which I could not see), but I remember from the conversation with Cathy. My first patient who I was scheduled to shadow was on 2 West in the Ortho Unit. Even for someone with no vision issues navigating this new hospital environment was overwhelming. Now if you add blindness to the equation, there is a real problem, especially if the blind person has had no training.

As I walked down the hospital hallway, I was actually a danger to anyone around me. I could not see to avoid patients who were walking or rolling in a wheelchair. I bumped what I thought was a patient's IV Pole and ran right into a patient in a wheelchair. At that moment, I realized that before I could help others, I needed to get help for myself. I managed to fake it for most of the day, trying to keep myself out of the way of patients, family members, and the medical personnel who were doing their job. I was so frightened of bumping into some piece of equipment, or worse, some patient, that I fell back into the background, keeping my distance.

I was glad that I had hung in there for the day because it turns out my afternoon was scheduled at the Western Regional Blind Center, which was an entire facility dedicated to assisting veterans throughout the United States with vision loss. I was given a tour of the facility and each of the departments available to assist with sight loss. There was Orientation and Mobility, focusing on travel skills, there was the Independent Living Skills, focusing on self-care and homemaking tasks, there was the Assistive Technology, focusing on using computers and other devices, and there was Manual Skills, focusing on developing fine motor dexterity, using instruments and power tools.

For me, learning about these resources designed to assist people with sight loss gave me a renewed optimism, but I also must admit this was a true low point for me. My vision was gone, and I could not perform my internship. I was failing, I was angry, and I was depressed. Had the last five-plus years in college just been a total waste of my efforts? I doubted whether I would be able to complete my field work and earn my bachelors degree in Occupational Therapy.

Significant doubt entered my psyche concerning my ability to function without sight. Perhaps those prospective intern supervisors who did not want to give me a chance to perform as an OT were right to deny me that opportunity. From their frame of reference, they could not comprehend how someone without eyesight could be an OT.

If my vision loss prevented me from successfully completing this final academic requirement for OT, could all the college credits that I had earned be for nothing, or could they be transferred into some other modified degree?

I had reached a very low point in my life and was looking to find someone to blame for my blindness. Someone needed to pay for my loss of sight, and the one person I could think of was my original ophthalmologist, Dr. Wand. He was the one I decided was responsible for what had happened to me. I went as far as contacting a lawyer to see if I had a case. I was told the jurisdiction for malpractice suits is one year. Since the malpractice that I was alleging actually occurred when I was a minor, I would have had until I was 19 to file a case.

As I look back at this sad time in my life, what was I actually accusing Dr. Wand of? It might have been true that he did not diagnose my glaucoma condition immediately when I had come to see him complaining of blurry vision, but the final outcome resulting in blindness would not have changed.

CHAPTER 37:
LEARNING TO LIVE WITHOUT SIGHT

My internship was placed on hold so that I could obtain necessary training to regain my confidence and independence. It was also time for me to open my mind to learning to live with blindness. I realized how much of my energy was focused on trying to see in this visual world we all live in. Once I began accepting that I could not see things, and did not need to spend time trying, I felt myself relaxing and beginning to adapt to my new circumstances.

My immediate perception to improving my mobility was a guide dog. In my mind, the sooner I could get a guide dog, the sooner I could solve my travel difficulties. In theory, the guide dog would take me wherever I wanted to go; what I did not understand at the time, though, is that it was my job to know where we were going, and how to get there.

My mom tells stories about my early-on vision loss, and when the topic of a guide dog came up in the conversation, I wanted nothing to do with it. I must have blocked out those ideas of using a dog to assist me. I am sure I was in complete denial at the time.

Now I had a true need for mobility assistance and figured a guide dog could fulfill this need. I applied to Guide Dogs for the Blind (GDB). Fortunately, GDB has a very thorough application screening process. Part of the screening involves a home visit from an instructor at the school. They want to make sure that there is a safe environment for this highly trained dog to work and live in. They also want to make sure that you, as the handler, have the necessary Orientation and Mobility skills to direct the dog. They will ask you to walk a familiar route in your neighborhood to show that you can travel independently. What I would soon learn is that a successful guide dog team meant that both the dog and visually impaired human had responsibilities to make the partnership a safe and productive one.

It became very clear to me that I was not yet prepared for a guide dog in my life. I needed training in order to become the navigator that the dog would look to for direction. This meant I needed white cane training. I would need to learn to orient myself in space, understand cardinal directions, use audio cues, identify tactile changes, and have knowledge about streets I wished to travel on.

My Department of Rehabilitation Counselor, Marilyn Mendoza, who had approved me for financial support that had covered my books, tuition, readers, and tutoring throughout college, was now involved with facilitating this training that I needed. The main resource that the state of California had for offering these types of services was the Orientation Center for the Blind (OCB). This center was located in Albany, which was over an hour's drive from my home in Scotts Valley, and with the recent highway damage from the Loma Prieta earthquake, getting there was more like a two-hour trip.

OCB was a dormitory setting where students were expected to stay from three months up to a year in order to receive the necessary training where they would learn to live with their vision loss. Students of OCB needed to have an active case with the Department of Rehabilitation (DOR) in order to be eligible to attend the school free of charge. Being a DOR client meant that you had an agreed-upon vocational goal that would eventually lead to employment.

Marilyn Mendoza, who I had not really known very well up to now, stepped in with the guidance that I now needed. Before this, she was simply a voice on the phone who authorized my financial support during college and provided encouragement as I studied toward my goal to be an occupational therapist. She drove me to

OCB, where I was given a tour of the school. It was similar to the Western Regional Blind Center that I had toured during my first day of OT internship.

The school offered comprehensive services from instruction, to independent living skills, to assistive technology and Orientation and Mobility training.

I was focused on getting a guide dog, as my priority was mobility and learning to travel with sight loss. I also wanted to get going on my internships as soon as possible. The idea of living in a dormitory for several months was not the approach that felt best for me at the time.

I was an occupational therapist now, and I believed that this background, along with my personal experience, would allow me to adapt to this new role as a person with sight loss. As I look back at the curriculum that OT students cover during their academic course work, sight loss and vision therapy was not a topic area covered with any great detail.

Marilyn Mendoza was really good about listening to my thoughts and did not pressure me one way or another. I decided to pursue cane training through an independent contractor. It was up to me, though, to find an Orientation and Mobility Specialist willing to provide me with this critical training. DOR's answer to this question was OCB, but since that was not my plan, I would need to find the right person willing to assist me.

Not knowing anywhere better to turn, I reached out to the Santa Cruz County Office of Education, specifically the Visually Impaired (VI) instructors. I updated Connie, who had been my VI teacher supporting me throughout high school, concerning my new blindness status and need for training.

I was introduced to Jill Tardive, who was another VI teacher working in the county. I am sure she knew of me when I was a student at Soquel High School, but I do not remember formally working with her at the time. At the time, Jill was not really looking for more work outside of her regular job through the county office of education. Somehow my story and motivation to learn how to travel touched Jill in such a way that she agreed to take on my case and the extra work that it would entail.

Jill's willingness to assist me was my first big step out of this darkness and my chance to literally start moving forward. I was measured for a white cane. Typically, the distance between your sternum and the ground is the length that your cane should be. For faster walkers, having a little bit longer cane was the standard recommendation.

The idea of using a white cane had always made me feel self-conscious because in my mind it placed a bull's-eye on you. You were definitely going to stick out in a crowd, whether you liked it or not. I used to not like the attention the cane caused, but now I realized the cane identified me as a person with sight loss to those around me. It was also the tool that was going to give me back my mobility and independence.

I remember our first lessons were at Dominican Hospital in Santa Cruz. The floors were a smooth tile-like surface that allowed the cane tip to easily glide over it. Proper grip and hand positioning was emphasized. I was taught the proper sequence for tapping my cane on one side while stepping forward with my foot on the opposite side. This was a constant back-and-forth pattern, where the cane would swing to one side, as your foot was moving forward on the other side. The more this technique was practiced, the faster you could learn to travel.

Of course, the lessons became more technical as the environments that we traveled became more challenging. We had moved to outdoor travel, and walking on a sidewalk is not a smooth surface, so the cane tip naturally gets caught up in cracks and uneven areas, which will disrupt your tapping-and-walking sequence.

Another persistent issue with travel is overhanging obstacles. Even if the white cane technique is implemented perfectly, the blind traveler will only be protected from the waist down. This means anything protruding into that zone from your waist to head height will go undetected. Many obstacles that you encounter in this unprotected zone are merely annoyances, but there can also be the occasional harmful experience.

The majority of my traveling experiences have been with a guide dog, but the issues with overhanging obstacles still persist. I have heard the claims that guide dogs can detect obstacles in that unprotected zone from the waist up. My personal experience using a guide dog is that the dogs do great avoiding obstacles from ground level to your waist and do a good job from one's waist to shoulder height. Above the shoulders is hit-and-miss, in my mind. One of the really wonderful things about using a guide dog, though, is that they are very trainable. This means when you encounter an obstacle you can teach the dog to stop at that location, so that means when you walk the route again, the guide dog has learned to stop at that given location. The cane, on the other hand, is not trainable, and is only as good as the person using it.

One of the experiences I recall with overhangs happened at my neighborhood Riley's Grocery Store. This is a location that my guide dog and I frequent. On this particular trip, the store had hung plants for sale right at head height. This meant that, as my dog and I approached the entrance door, we had to pass under these hanging plants that were not hung high enough to miss. I am only five feet 10 inches tall and my head found the plants. Fortunately, no permanent damage was done, but it did not feel great having my head come in contact with several unexpected hanging plants.

My most severe and painful overhead-obstacle experience happened with my second guide dog, Hale. Hale was a big German shepherd who never needed a leash correction and was very responsive to verbal commands. We took him out hiking in a regional park with our family. Hale and I were in the lead, moving out at a pretty fast pace. We were probably a good 30 yards ahead of our hiking group. Amy said everything happened so quickly. She saw that a tree had fallen across the trail right at head height. Amy thought Hale would stop and show me the obstacle, but before she could say anything, my nose impacted the tree trunk, causing whiplash, with my neck snapping backwards. I ended up on the ground and my nose was gushing blood. At one moment, I was moving freely through space, enjoying the sounds and smells of nature, when without any awareness or ability to brace myself, I was literally knocked out by a tree trunk—I'm. pretty sure that my nose was broken and I would have a couple of black eyes, but this time eye surgery would not be the cause.

At the same time that I was receiving Orientation and Mobility training, I visited the Doran Center for the Blind in downtown Santa Cruz. The Doran Center merged with the Vista Center in 2007. I was encouraged to learn braille, so I began taking classes. I lost interest in learning shortly after I had begun and stopped attending my one-on-one class. Even though I was a 24-year-old adult, somehow my mom was contacted by the Doran Center, letting her know that I was no longer participating in instruction. Had the Doran Center contacted me directly with their concerns about the importance of learning braille, I might have reconsidered. At the time, I just did not see the importance of learning braille. I could not see how this would assist me in my current situation. Later, I would re-visit learning braille and understand how it could help me.

One of the most difficult skills to learn when traveling with vision loss is street crossings. Orienting yourself to make a straight and safe crossing is complicated. Every intersection presents with its own unique layout. Most intersections have truncated domes for wheelchairs, walkers, and strollers. Usually, these ramps are angled such that they actually are at a diagonal, which funnels you toward the center of the intersection. The pedestrian poles need to be located in order to press the button to facilitate a pedestrian crossing. These signal poles are often placed at varying distances from the actual crosswalk, so finding them can be a challenge. And after pressing the button, one needs to get realigned at the position to make the crossing.

Once the traveler has located the pedestrian button and has reoriented to the crosswalk, then auditory skills are taught. As the blind traveler, you need to listen to your cue of the changing traffic patterns at the intersection. You need to hear when the cars are moving perpendicular in front of you as opposed to parallel next to your shoulder. You are taught that when you detect a parallel surge of traffic that is your cue to make the crossing. It is always easier said than done to make that first step into the street. It takes a certain level of guts to actually make yourself enter the crosswalk. Once in the street, moving as quickly as possible to reach the other side is the goal. You need to synchronize the sound of the parallel traffic over your shoulder in order to maintain a straight line of travel. The survival reaction is to move away from the car sounds, but if you drift too much, you will not be traveling straight and you will probably be out of the painted sidewalk markings.

Many cities have installed audible signals when the pedestrian crossing button is pressed. There is a different sound alert based on the direction of the crossing. In my hometown, a *cuckoo* noise represents a north/south crossing and a *tweet* noise represents an east/west crossing. Audible signals are very useful and reassuring to someone with vision loss. You get an audible cue to walk/start your crossing and an audible cue/beacon broadcasting from the destination corner, giving you assistance with line of travel and the end point.

Street crossings are never what I would call fun to do. You can do everything correct on a crossing, but you are always at the mercy of the drivers of the cars. You need to pay special attention to the cars making right turns in front of you, because in most cases, that maneuver can be done on a red light. Another issue that can occur is the perpendicular cars that you are crossing in front of often do not stop before the crosswalk, but rather in the crosswalk itself, as they wait for the light to turn green. It is very unsettling to be traveling across a street when you suddenly encounter a vehicle in your path of travel. At that point, you can either choose to go around the obstacle, which may or may not be safe, and you lose your straight line of travel, or you are taught to remain standing at the side of the car until it moves out of the way.

When I have experienced this situation with cars blocking the crosswalk, I try like hell to get out of the street, whenever possible, attempting to go around the vehicle. At other times, I have waited in the street for the car to move out of the crosswalk. That is a very uncomfortable feeling, as you are standing in what you know is the street, and you feel so vulnerable as you are hearing all of the traffic sounds moving around you.

There was one time when I was traveling with my first guide dog, Hoyt. We were on the sidewalk, crossing a driveway into a shopping center, when we encountered a car blocking the crosswalk. In this circumstance, I chose to stop and stay next to the side of the car until it moved out of the way. The driver of the car, I think, panicking, suddenly, placed the car into reverse, lunging backwards, hearing it smashing into the vehicle that was behind. The driver in the car behind had laid on the horn, but it was too late to stop the collision. I waited for a half of a minute or so, hoping someone might cue me that it was okay to proceed. No one said anything to me after the accident, I am sure they considered it being my fault for causing the crash. I moved on with Hoyt and got out of the shopping center driveway.

At the same time that I was building my cane skills, I also wanted to learn about technology that could assist me. I had heard about an agency called Sensory Access Foundation (SAF). Their mission was to help people experiencing sight loss build the necessary skills to become vocationally ready. It was also located in Palo Alto, and with DOR's support, I attended a week-long evaluation/training to see what assistive technology was available for people with sight loss.

Amy's grandma lived in Menlo Park, which was just north of SAF. This was my first big opportunity to use my newly acquired cane skills to travel independently. I had previously viewed the route from Grandma's house to SAF with Amy. It involved me catching a bus near Grandma's house, riding it for a couple of miles, and getting off at the Caltrain station. I needed to catch the south-bound train and ride it for two stops, getting off at the California station. From the California station, SAF was just a couple of blocks to walk.

I remember traveling the short distance from the bus drop-off point to the train station was initially confusing. The bus had dropped off passengers at a different location from what I had practiced. I did find asking strangers for help was a positive experience. You learn as a blind traveler to ask detailed questions, though, because people are so conditioned to just point and say things like, "Over there."

Once on the train, I discovered that there was another blind gentleman on board with his guide dog. He also got off the train at the California station. I remember hearing the conductor telling him as the train was slowing that we had just passed the station before coming to a complete stop. I realized how valuable that bit of information was to a blind traveler. Now he would know which way to turn when exiting the train. I was thinking this blind person was most likely heading to SAF, as well, so I figured it was my lucky day, because I would just be able to follow them. I was no match for this experienced blind traveler who was using a guide dog. They left me in the dust shortly after exiting the train, so I was very glad I had practiced the route with Amy ahead of time.

It turned out the blind traveler with his guide dog was actually my instructor at SAF. His name was Peter, and I believe he had been blind is whole life. He introduced me to the world of text-to-speech capability on a computer. At the time, computers were running the DOS Operating System, so commands needed to be typed into the system. I was using a program called Flipper with a hardware synthesizer called Accent. Text-to-speech meant any content visually displaying on the screen would be read back to me through the Accent Synthesizer. Word Perfect was the software being used at the time for word-processing tasks. I could create my own files independently, copy them to a disk, or print them out. Man, if I had this kind of technology during college, this would have made my life so much easier. This text-to-speech technology, though, was very new and probably not available a couple of years earlier.

I was so fortunate to have my dad who was an engineer at IBM. He was very familiar with DOS on the computer. I understood how to use the Flipper software to control how the Accent Synthesizer spoke information back to me, but my dad was able to teach me how to use the command-line prompts to complete tasks on the PC. My parents made sure I was set up with a computer and the assistive software and hardware needed to make the system talk for a blind user.

CHAPTER 38:
MY 4-WHEEL DRIVE CANINE GUIDE

After a couple of months of intensive Orientation and Mobility training, I reapplied to Guide Dogs. This time, I was prepared, and I was accepted into class. Guide dog classes at the time were four weeks in duration. I was part of Guide Dog class # CA490, and my fellow classmates, who were first-time guide dog students, along with me, arrived on a Sunday afternoon in August of 1990. My classmates all flew in from different cities in the United States. I was the only one who drove to campus, since the GDB School was in the Bay Area where I lived.

I was still wearing my glasses at the time, not that they did anything to assist me with seeing, but I guess it was a comfort thing, since I had been wearing them pretty much my entire life. I would actually give up wearing my glasses for good during this GDB class.

We all arrived, white canes in hand, ready to take on this new challenge of learning to work with a guide dog. Immediately, we were asked to store our canes and learn to navigate the dormitory by trailing the hallways and rooms, using our hands and audio cues to explore this new environment that would be our home for the next four weeks.

The school, the training, the guide dog, and room and board were all covered free of charge. GDB is supported all through private donations without any government funding. At the time of my first class, each student shared a room and bathroom with one other student. There was a bed, closet, desk, and chair for each student. Each student had their own sink and a floor-level sink for their dog. There was a shelf for all of your guide dog supplies. The dorm itself had a living room, where our lectures took place each morning and evening. There were laundry facilities, an exercise room, a music room, a dining room, a library with books on tape, brail typewriters, a payphone in the hallway, and even a swimming pool.

Students were well taken care of during their stay. We were fed three delicious nutritious meals each day. There was a registered nurse on staff to assist with any medical needs, food, and around-the-clock veterinary care for our dogs. There was always support staff checking in with each student to make sure all their needs were being met. GDB was really trying to make it so students could put all of their energy on learning to be a guide dog handler.

When I first arrived at the guide dogs school, I thought they would present you with a dog that was going to lead you through your life travels moving forward. What I did not understand at the time was that the guide dog was already trained and ready to go. The problem was you as the blind navigator. The dogs were highly trained canines that just needed someone to tell them where to go. The training that one undergoes is to learn how to command your dog to guide you where you want to go. That does not mean giving your dog a command to go to Safeway, because your guide dog knows a handful of commands, i.e., left, right, and forward, but Safeway will mean nothing to your dog. That is why you, as the handler, need to know and give commands based on where you are and where you are going.

For the first two-and-a-half days, you participated in simulated guide work. Your instructors performed what are called Juno Exercises with each of the students. In these exercises, students are taught how to attach and remove the harness, as well as the collar and leash. You learn how to properly grip the harness handle, foot positioning, and hand gestures. Your instructor identifies your walking pace, so that can be considered, along with your lifestyle, to make the best handler- and-dog partnership decision.

Each of the guide dogs was raised as a puppy by individuals/ families who volunteer their time to teach basic obedience, good house behavior, and attend regular meetings with puppy leaders and other raisers. The puppies are exposed to various experiences in the community, like riding on a bus or airplane, attending a sporting event, going to the grocery store, camping, etc. By the time we, as blind handlers, meet the fully trained guide dog, they have been exposed to so many experiences, so any place we might travel with them is no big deal to the dog.

During your first week in class, Wednesday is called "dog day". This is the time when you will be presented with the guide dog that has been determined to best fit into your lifestyle. Some handlers are full-time students, while others work in an office setting, and some are self-employed or a homemaker. Each dog has its optimal guiding speed, and some dogs are very content with lying at a desk most of the day, while others prefer to be more on the move. All these factors are taken under consideration when making a partnership.

My first guide dog was a one-and-a half-year-old male Golden Retriever. His name was Hoyt. It was definitely love at first pet. We were going to be traveling miles and miles together. Having a guide dog is a lot like having a child. You are responsible for taking care of this living canine, and this living canine is responsible for leading you safely in your travels. The white cane can be placed in the corner, and even folded up, if it is the collapsible style—out of sight, out of mind, so to speak.

The dog has regular requirements that need to be met, including feeding, relieving, grooming, and obedience training. Dogs, in general, and guide dogs, even more specifically, do very well with routine. Knowing when they will eat, when they will be relieved, and knowing when they might be performing guide work are all expectations the dogs get used to.

When students first start working with their guide dogs, it is performed in quiet residential neighborhoods. Our instructors will verbalize the route that we are to travel, so we can command our dogs to lead us where we want to go. Early on working with Hoyt, I discovered how different using a guide dog is from using a cane. The cane is designed to be an obstacle indicator, meaning it will alert you to obstacles in your path of travel. And, as I often say, having the cane come in contact with a fire hydrant before your leg does is much preferred. The guide dog, on the other hand, is an obstacle avoider. They have been trained to take you around things that are in your path of travel. Your walking experience with a guide dog is often much smoother and faster because all those obstacles that you might bump with a cane are avoided by the dog. The lack of obstacle indication can also make you a bit less aware of what is around you.

To place your trust in a dog that is going to lead you down the sidewalk as you hold onto a harness handle is an amazing experience. The more guide work that you perform, the more confidence you build. Hoyt had already completed all his training, and he was ready to take us anywhere. I was the one who needed the training. The method used by GDB to develop team cohesiveness between the handler and guide dog seemed to work really well. The areas that we worked in became increasingly more complicated as we went through the weeks of training.

We moved from working residential streets to working downtown San Rafael, with lighted intersections, to working Chinatown in San Francisco, with all kinds of food and pedestrian distractions. We rode on buses and BART trains, and took breaks, while we hung out with our dogs in coffee shops. We were exposed to sidewalk-less travel, where the dogs have been trained to follow the edge of the road. We were also taken on routes in Muir Woods and other trails to experience working our dogs while hiking in the wilderness.

A typical day in class at guide dog school started at 6:30 a.m. with relieving your dog. We quickly learned that our dogs had their smart end, and then there was their other end, which we focused a lot of our time on managing. We are privileged and have the right to take our guide dog pretty much anywhere in the community—with that right comes the responsibility of making sure our guide dog behaves appropriately without accidents. One really important task is to offer regular and frequent relieving opportunities for our dogs.

At 8:00 breakfast for the humans and at 8:30 breakfast for your dog was followed by relieving your dog. By 9:00, you would be heading out for the morning workout with your guide dog and instructor. Routes consisted of 20-to-30-minute walks, where you were given directions about where you would be traveling to. You would return to GDB around 11:30, where you would relieve your dog. At noon was lunch for the humans. Around 1:00, you would relieve your dog and head out for the afternoon training session. You would return around 4:30 and relieve your dog. At 5:00, your dog would have dinner and be relieved again. Around 5:30, humans would have dinner. At 6:30, there would be a lecture, covering some element of guide dog care and providing information about the next day's training routes. In the evenings, we would groom our dogs, brush their teeth, or just have some play time. We did occasionally have night routes, and for those students who had different eye conditions like Retinitis Pigmentosa, which can cause night-time blindness, traveling at night could be a very different experience. The evenings were also a time to socialize and catch up on any personal business. There was one final relieving with your dog around 9:00.

One of the final training experiences that students go through prior to graduation with their guide dog is traffic checks. This is when one of your instructors will purposely drive a car in your path of travel while you are working a route. Your dog is familiar with this game as they have played it before during their formal training, but to you as the blind handler hearing a car racing toward you can be very unsettling.

Typically, these human car encounters occur when you are crossing a street, but traveling along sidewalks crossing driveways is another potential danger zone. When you hear a car's motor approaching you or blocking your path of travel, it is a very uncomfortable feeling. You cannot make eye contact with a driver who you cannot see, so having reassurance that the driver knows you are there is really not possible. On a few rare occasions, I have had a driver roll down their car window and verbally let me know that they are waiting for me to cross.

On one occasion, I unfortunately, was backed into by a car driven by a neighbor leaving his driveway. I was walking down the sidewalk in the middle of the block when I heard a car motor start up in a driveway ahead of me. As I continued walking, being led by Lucas, the sound of the motor had not changed, so I assumed the car was still idling in the driveway. I proceeded to cross the driveway where I heard the car motor. Right at that moment the car began backing out of the driveway, I felt Lucas pull me to the left toward the street and away from this car that was coming at us. I also yelled "Stop," hoping to get the driver's attention. The car's bumper came in contact with my thigh as the car was suddenly coming to a stop after noticing Lucas and me.

No physical harm was done to Lucas or me, but the fear of what could have happened lives on in my memory. Every time I am out walking, I become very anxious when I hear a car's motor.

There is one neighbor of mine who regularly starts the car each morning, leaves it running, I am thinking, to defrost the windshield, and goes back inside the house. To make matters worse, the car is parked across the sidewalk while it is idling. I am required to encourage Lucas to take me up to this running automobile, which he has been trained to be very cautious around. Once I discover that there is no one in this running vehicle, I have to direct Lucas to lead us around it. This type of incident turns a peaceful walk into a very stressful situation.

GDB graduation ceremonies are very moving events with many tears shed. Each graduating guide dog's puppy raiser is welcomed back for the public ceremony, where they officially present your guide dog to you. There is so much thanks to go around for all the pieces put together that end up making this blind person–guide dog partnership possible, from the donors, to the volunteers, to the puppy raisers, to all the GDB staff, who take care of the dogs, train the dogs, and provide ongoing support to the graduates.

Hoyt was raised in Newcastle, California, by Alisa Clader. Alisa and her family did a great job preparing Hoyt to be a guide dog, and if you consider the statistics, only 45 percent of the dogs placed actually end up qualifying to be a guide dog. So, if your dog makes it, it is a proud moment, and you, as the puppy raiser, should give yourself a big pat on the back. It has to be so difficult for these raisers and their families to give up these dogs after caring for them, socializing them, training them, and building a huge bond, then having to give the dog back to the school for formal instruction.

CHAPTER 39:
FIELD-WORK PLACEMENT & INTERACTIONS WITH THE PUBLIC

I now was equipped with my 4-wheel drive named Hoyt. I had a talking computer system that would allow me to create reports and other correspondence independently. Also, the experience of working at the VA Hospital gave me valuable insight into the type of setting that would work best for me with vision loss, as I moved on with my internship. I knew working in an acute hospital setting was not a good choice for me. The hospital is an unpredictable environment that I have very little control over. In addition, patients are often connected to different types of machines, tubes, cords, etc.

I needed a working environment that I had more control over and that I could set up to meet my needs. I needed a placement where patients would come to a specific location for therapy services. This could be an outpatient clinic or day treatment program. I spoke with Professor Stills concerning my thoughts, and we worked together to find such placements.

There was a mental health program for older adults operated daily for at-risk seniors. The professional staff consisted of an occupational therapist, psychologist, and nurse. The Santa Clara Senior Center, where this day treatment program was offered, was in an older converted Victorian-style home. Clients were transported to and from the Senior Center each day, where they participated in group and one-on-one classes.

This ended up being an ideal setting for me to work in. Most of the group classes were held in the living room, where we worked on stress management, memory activities, social interaction with games, and cooking tasks. Having Hoyt at my side would often serve as an icebreaker for those clients who were withdrawn.

Once I was confirmed for this placement, I had moved to an apartment just a few blocks from the Senior Center. Hoyt and I could walk to and from work each day. The desktop computer that my parents had purchased for me was moved into the Senior Center, so I was able to complete all of my documentation responsibilities right on site. Fortunately, DOR had purchased a laptop computer, which I could use at my apartment, and later, it would be a great portable solution that I could travel with. I completed my three-month mental health internship and was ready to move on to my physical disability internship.

My physical disability internship placement began at San Jose State University, working in the Disabled Student Services Department. This was definitely a nontraditional placement for an occupational therapist. Students attending a university with a disability are usually what we would call high functioning and not necessarily in need of traditional OT interventions. I was able to draw on my personal experiences when it came to finding note-takers and readers and setting up test proctors. I really did not have a supervisor during this internship and definitely not an experienced occupational therapist to mentor.

I ended up sitting in on one-on-one meetings that different academic advisors would have with students. I remember speaking up during some of these meetings, offering my personal experience, advocating for the supportive services that I knew disabled students needed. I felt I needed to let students know that it was best to secure note-takers and readers at the beginning of the semester, but that there was a limited budget for alternative-formatted materials which required longer time to prepare. My willingness to provide what I thought was practical information for students was frowned upon by some of the advisors who met with the students.

Throughout this internship, I had kept in close contact with my field-work advisor, Professor Stills. As a matter of fact, the Central Classroom Building, which housed the OT Department and her office, was only a building or two away from the DSS Department. Professor Stills was aware that the SJSU DSS Department was not a traditional OT placement.

I was anxious to be done with my internship, so I could officially be done and be given my Bachelor of Science degree in Occupational Therapy. Later, I would still need to pass the National Board for Certification of Occupational Therapists, in order to practice as an OT, but completing my degree was going to take a little more time. Professor Stills convinced me that getting more experience with physical disabilities would be in my best interest.

After six weeks of interning at the SJSU DSS Department, I had pretty much reached a plateau with the experience, and it was time to move on. Professor Stills had found another promising placement for me. It was a day treatment program called the Services for Brain Injured (SBI). The program was operated out of a church in Santa Clara, and there was an occupational therapist and speech pathologist on staff. Most of the clients had experienced some type of traumatic head injury resulting in multiple physical and behavioral manifestations.

Just like my other internship placements, clients came to the facility for services, so this once again gave me the opportunity to set up the environment that would work best for me. I had continued to live in the apartment in Santa Clara, but I did need to take public transit each day to get to SJSU, and later, to this new SBI internship.

Traveling by bus and being blind was an adventure. Usually, the experience was positive, or at least, amusing. There was the rare rainy day when my fellow passengers would be so worried about Hoyt being wet. Holding an umbrella while being guided is not a real practical thing to do—one of your hands is in constant contact with the harness handle, and the other arm is needed for gestures when commanding your dog to move in a particular direction. Passengers would try and offer me napkins or some sort of a rag from their bag, so I could use it to dry him off. I really was not interested in accepting these well-meaning strangers' gifts for my guide dog. I would try and let them know that my dog was fine, and that he actually really loved water. I could not help feeling judged by these concerned passengers because I was not taking their hand-outs. I am sure they must have felt I was neglecting my dog. Never in all of my travels do I remember anyone ever offering "me," the blind guy, a towel to dry off with. It was always about the poor dog.

People are not necessarily on the look-out for a dog when it comes to loading or leaving the bus. They are often distracted by their children, the bags that they are carrying, or some conversation they are having with real or imaginary people around them. It is my job to protect Hoyt with all the comings and goings of the bus riders. I make sure that his body is not sticking out into the aisle for the passengers. The dog's tail is another one of those parts that can suddenly change position and be a target for an un-expecting foot from a passenger moving through the bus.

Many people will pet my dog without asking, and some will even try and feed him a bite of whatever they might be eating. First of all, dogs should not be offered food from strangers. Secondly, guide dogs are on a strict diet, and should not be consuming human food. Remember, guide dogs are legally allowed in restaurants, and exposing them to real food can cause upset stomachs and behavioral issues. In addition, food can also be very distracting to the guide dog, and this can become dangerous for the blind handler if the team is not focused on working. I have had people actually reach out with food when they see Hoyt working and guiding me down the sidewalk passing them. It amazes me that people think it is okay to pet or feed the dog without asking.

Other people who I would encounter while traveling around did not hold back with their opinions. Some would tell me that my dog was too heavy, while others would ask me why the dog was so skinny. They would want to know how much I fed Hoyt, and whatever my answer was, it was not the correct amount. There were even a few people who felt it was abusive to "force" my dog to perform guide work. I wish these people could simply see how enthusiastic and excited these guide dogs get when you take out the harness for a walk.

There was an unsettling incident during one of my commutes to my internship. I had exited the bus at my regular spot, and was waiting at the corner to cross the street on my way to the church, and when I heard the parallel traffic surge, I knew it was my turn to cross, so I gave the forward command to Hoyt. I might have moved one or two steps into the street, when all of the sudden, I was grabbed by a fellow pedestrian and literally pulled across the intersection. It was so unexpected, I was truly caught off guard, and once I had a second to process it, I was ready to fight, thinking I was being mugged. Why would someone attempt to accost me in broad daylight with other people around did not make sense. I remember shouting at the person: "What are you doing?!"

The response was in broken English with a heavy accent. The person let go of me once we reached the corner at the other side of the street, patting me on the arm, as she walked away. I believe this person had good attentions and was trying to assist me with crossing the street, but by suddenly grabbing me without warning, almost caused me to throw a punch in self-defense. I think there was a cultural misunderstanding, but it is always best to ask someone if they need assistance rather than forcing yourself on them.

Then there was the time I was working a summer camp for the United Cerebral Palsy organization. It was for kids ages six to 17, and we offered a week of activities for disabled children at the local community park. I was working with my second guide dog, Hale, and he would lead me to the park each day for the camp. Once I arrived at the park, Hale was placed on a tie-down with a water dish under one of the picnic benches, where we kept the supplies for the day's activities. One of the family members or acquaintances saw my guide dog, Hale, under the bench and came to the conclusion that he must have been neglected, I guess, because of the time period he was under the table. Guide Dogs was contacted by this anonymous person. The idea that Guide Dogs needed to question me about my dog's well-being felt really bad. I explained that my dog had been put on a tie-down while I was working. Hale was in a safe location, and all of his needs were met. Unfortunately, this uninformed person came to the conclusion that my dog was being mistreated because he was on a tie-down for several hours. The truth is, that guide dogs are raised/trained to be on tie-down for the majority of the day.

I realized more than ever at that point my every movement is being watched by the public because seeing a guide dog in action is a pretty amazing sight. It really becomes my job to educate those around me to avoid misunderstandings.

One of the most difficult things for me to determine is when to know that my stop is coming up. At the time that I was riding buses regularly, unfortunately, GPS technology did not yet exist. I always tried to sit up front when riding the bus. I would engage with the driver, letting him know what stop I needed. I usually knew approximately how long the trip would take to my stop, so if I had not heard from the driver when I thought my stop should be coming up, I would make another inquiry with the driver. Usually, this would result in me being dropped at my requested stop. On one occasion, however, after not hearing from my driver, and figuring I was close to my stop, I asked when my stop would be coming up. The bus quickly slowed and stopped, letting me off. I was told my actual bus stop was just a little bit behind the bus from where I was getting off. It was true that the stop that I wanted was behind the bus, but what I did not realize at the time was that there was a major intersection between where I was departing the bus and the actual bus stop that I wanted.

Hoyt guided me to the corner, where we encountered an unfamiliar intersection. It was a busy one, which I needed to study before attempting to cross it. I discovered that there were parallel and perpendicular surges of traffic as well as separate cycles for left-turners. When I deemed it safe to cross with the parallel surge, I gave Hoyt the forward command. After only a short distance, Hoyt had stopped to show me an up-curb. We had only traveled a short distance in the street, so in my mind I knew we could not have crossed the entire intersection. I stepped up onto what I learned later was a small island for vehicles turning right. In my limited travels so far with sight loss, I do not recall experiencing this type of an intersection configuration that had a separate island for right-turners. When I had encountered the island, I began to panic, and did a 180-degree turn back the way I had come, searching for the corner that I had just left. That unexpected experience had undone me. I needed time to take a deep breath, and calm down. Traveling as a blind person is certainly challenging, so I make a conscious effort to know and understand my route. When the unexpected happens, you cannot necessarily figure out what is going on at the moment. And when you have a dog that is looking to you for directions during the situation, it can definitely create a lot of stress.

At some point, I managed to gather enough courage to travel out to the right-turn island that I had found. I was able to stand out there and further analyze the intersection's traffic patterns. As I was standing on the island, and the left-turners were moving through the intersection, I had an opportunity to actually speak to the passenger of the car that was waiting at the light in front of me. I was able to confirm where I was and my plan of action for crossing the street.

I did make it across that previously untraveled intersection and had never been happier to find the corner and sidewalk on the other side. In my walks around this area , I had been at this this corner before, but had never had a reason to cross this intersection until today. I was late arriving back to my apartment.

I had forgotten that my childhood friend, John, was coming by for a visit, as he was working in Silicon Valley at the time. John could immediately tell that I was shaken up the moment he saw me. I was too upset to contact the bus company regarding my unfortunate experience. So, John took it upon himself to look up the number and spoke to a supervisor concerning his blind friend's experience of being dropped off at the wrong stop. After that, John said we needed to eat. I had no real meals ready to go in the apartment, accept for some beer. John had spotted a donut shop when he was driving to my apartment, so we picked up a dozen donuts, washing them down with beer.

There were many evenings when I would sit with Hoyt in my living room, and the television set from the unit above me could easily be heard in my apartment. There, Hoyt and I would be sitting in the dark. Why should I pay for cable when I have access to the neighbors' TV for free? I could tune into the program with my ears. There were certainly evenings when I did not agree with the program choice that I was listening to. I wanted to call upstairs and request the station be changed to something more of my liking.

CHAPTER 40:

A TANDEM BICYCLE, SEPARATED FROM MY BROTHER DURING AN ORGANIZED RUN

& ANNUAL FISHING TRIPS

Around this same time, my former optometrist, Dr. Giannotti, who was an active member of the Scotts Valley Lion's Club, knew that I was no longer riding mopeds and that my vision was gone. He worked with the local club and arranged for me to have a tandem bicycle purchased for me. This was not some low-end bike; it was a high-end mountain bike tandem made by Gary Fisher, which I still have to this day. There are many stories of various adventures and rides, which almost always involved me as the blind dude sitting in the backseat. The term *pilot* is for the person who rides in the front seat and is responsible for steering, breaking, and shifting of gears. The term *stoker* is for the person who sits in the backseat, and as I always say, gives the pedal power to the bike. Although various pilots have accused me of putting my feet up and not pedaling at various times, but to be successful riding a tandem, both the pilot and stoker need to be in synch. I have offered on many occasions to perform the pilot role, but none of my sighted or blind friends have ever taken me up on that.

Early on, Amy was a willing pilot, and we went on many fun rides around the neighborhood and would regularly participate in the annual Bike for Sight event that was held every year in Napa in the 1990s. It was for a worthy cause, supporting the Light House for the Blind and the Enchanted Hills Camp. The event in the 1990s was smaller and organized locally. In the mid- to late-1990s, the local ride was cancelled for approximately 10 years and then it was reintroduced as a much-larger event with third-party organizers in 2007.

Riding on a tandem takes a lot of communication between the pilot and stoker. It can both make and break a relationship. Amy was a great pilot, and I was able to pick up on her nonverbal cues, like when she would reduce the pedaling rate or I would sense her leaning one way or another in order to execute a turn, which was more complicated on the longer tandem. These types of bikes also take longer to stop, and to get going again requires that both riders push off and pedal at the same time. Later we had some memorable family rides, which included our infant daughter Megan. We had purchased a special side-cart that attached to the back of the tandem. Megan loved to take rides with us on the bicycle. She would be placed in the cart with her helmet on, her stuffed animal Ted and a bag of snacks. I am sure we were quite a sight as we peddled down the road on this already longer bike with a side-cart and a baby on board.

My brother went through a period of time when he was a very competitive cyclist, where he competed in races and various events, including triathlons. In his quest to bring me into this competitive world of his, we began signing up for various riding events. Early on, we participated in rides that supported the Multiple Sclerosis Society. These rides would usually be one- or two-day events, consisting of a Metric Century, which is 100 kilometers, or about 62 miles, pedaled each day.

Somehow my brother talked me into signing up for Cycle Oregon IV; this was a weeklong bike ride that covered around 500 miles. That year's ride started in Beaverton, where we pedaled west to the coast, to Nehalem, then south to Tillamook, and then headed back to the east, toward Hood River. Cycle Oregon is a supported ride; participants are provided with meals, camping facilities, shower and restroom facilities, and sag wagon support. My brother definitely took on the caregiver role for me on this trip.

I guess much like our guide dog partner, folks with vision loss appreciate consistency and routine. Having a location for storing special things, such as the cane or harness, but also everyday items need a place as well, i.e., one's toothbrush, keys, wallet, box of cornflakes, etc. For someone with sight loss, a consistent environment equals independence.

I used to tell people, jokingly, the way Amy got my attention was by moving the furniture around. Since I was not able to see facial expressions, which can be a big part of communication, one way to get my attention would be to move the furniture. I always knew if I came home and the couch had been moved, that was a clear sign I was in trouble.

I also liked to tease my mom because she would get bored with consistency. She needed to rearrange her rooms every so often because she liked a new look. Of course, I got to experience the rearrangement in a whole different way. My shin might find the coffee table's new location or my drink might end up on the floor where an end table used to be. Cupboard doors were another hazard; if left open, painful consequences would be the result.

For me, having a familiar and consistent environment, knowing where my bed was, the bathroom, the dog's food, etc., meant I could move around independently.

During Cycle Oregon IV, every day meant a new home. We were in a different campground every night, surrounded by different tent neighbors. For me, the evening sounds would change from night to night. Based on what activity they might be engaged in or how much beer they had consumed, the sound volume would also fluctuate. It was impossible for me to move through the camp independently because it was never the same. To find the bathroom, showers, or meals, I needed my brother to guide me. It is fair to say that in this type of environment, I was pretty much dependent on my brother to lead me from location to location. I very much appreciated the assistance, but I also very much missed my independence and freedom of movement.

For this particular road bike tour, we removed the mountain bike tires and replaced them with slick tires. The first two or three days of the trip for me were fond memories of riding out to and along the Oregon coast, but things began to change for the worst. First, we started to have mechanical issues with the tandem, with the front wheel spokes breaking as we were riding. One spoke would break, then another and another. I was concerned that the wheel would become unstable and then unsafe. This is not a repair that could easily be made while you were riding, and my brother would always be the reassuring voice, saying we needed to keep pedaling and get to camp, where the rim could be repaired. Once we made it to camp for the night, the rim was taken to the mobile repair shop, where the broken spokes were replaced.

We started out on day 4 of the tour and the spokes once again began breaking early on our ride. My brother did not believe in using the sag wagon, which was a truck-like vehicle used to pick up riders who had mechanical or physical issues preventing them from continuing with the tour. Instead, he pushed us to continue pedaling to camp, where we could once again get necessary repairs. We were not talking much at this point, and not working together. We reached camp, broken spokes and all. The rim was brought to the same mobile repair guy, and he recommended an entire replacement of all spokes on the rim, but he also went on to say that he did not have the resources to complete this full repair now, as he had responsibilities to all the riders on the tour. The two or three broken spokes were replaced again, but it was our understanding that every spoke on the rim was weak and subject to breaking.

This was probably day 5, and truth be told, I was hurting from the multiple days of riding. I was not having fun anymore, and was ready to quit the ride. My brother did not want to hear this from me. He was ready to ride the tandem by himself in order to finish the tour. This would mean taking the sag wagon for the final day of the tour. Many angry words passed between us. My brother agreed to abandon the tour. That was day 6 of our tour. I remember needing to leave a note in our tent as to why it was still standing when all the other tents had been broken down and loaded into the trucks for transport to the final destination.

My brother and I still needed to return to our departure point of Beaverton, where our truck was. We had made previous arrangements with our parents to pick us up in Hood River, where the tour was going to end. We needed to get back to the truck before my parents would pick it up and drive it to the end point in Hood River. This actually involved my brother piloting the tandem on very busy roads as we pedaled back to our departure point.

Perhaps a year prior to the Cycle Oregon Ride, my brother had convinced me to run a 10 K with him through the redwoods at Henry Cowell Park in the Santa Cruz Mountains. It was called the Redwood Run and it started in the small town of Felton. This was pretty close to the end of me having any useful vision. Shortly after the run began on surface streets, it turned onto a country trail, which consisted of an uphill climb with a sandy surface. Shortly after turning onto the sandy trail, my brother and I lost each other. So, I was on my own to complete this run. This was a new unfamiliar environment that I could not really see to navigate. This was another one of those "eye opening" experiences for me. I was running on a trail that I had no knowledge of. It was an eventful 10 K. I missed a turn or two, ending up running straight off the trail into the brush, not seeing the curve in the trail, ending up falling on my stomach. Roots and uneven surfaces proved to be another tripping hazard that

I could not see to avoid. My shirt was soaked with sweat and was covered in dirt, but I am proud to say I did cross the finish line upright. There was a gentleman who wanted to challenge me at the end of the run when there was like 100 yards to go. After all I had been through on the run, there was no way this guy was going to beat me to the finish line. I sprinted to the end, and since it was a straight shot from where I started running full out to the end, I made it before my challenger did.

The other full memory I have from the tandem times with my brother involved the "Death Ride." It was properly named because riders who signed up for this event actually paid for the opportunity to challenge themselves in a one- day marathon to pedal over up to five mountain peaks. Let me set the stage. My brother lived in Santa Cruz, and once or twice a week, he would drive to my apartment in Santa Clara for what we called training rides up Mt. Hamilton, which was the closest and highest peak to my apartment. The elevation of this peak at the highest point was 4,200 feet, but the road we were pedaling on was actually lower than that. We might have trained like this for perhaps three months, but the peaks of the Death Ride started at 6,000 feet and climb to above 8,000 feet.

The highest point of the training rides that we did were a good 2,000 feet lower than the starting point of the Death Ride. In addition, we traveled from sea level, where we lived, to 6,000 feet in one day. There was no acclimation to the elevation change, so we were used to breathing air at sea level, and now we had suddenly jumped to 6,000 feet.

We began the Death Ride, pedaling up Monitor Pass, immediately becoming deprived of oxygen, gasping for air. Our legs were carrying a 50-pound tandem along, with two men, to the top of Monitor Pass. Breathe, pedal, was the pattern, as we crawled our way to the top. It was such a relief when we made it to the top. After a short break for some snacks, we got back in the saddle and coasted our way down the other side of the pass. The descent happened so quickly and we were at the bottom in no time. The reprieve of being able to coast with the wind hitting us in the face gave us renewed energy.

We needed to turn around and pedal back up the same mountain highway we had just come down. Probably not necessary to say, but going up sure took a lot more time and energy than coming down. Our legs were on fire and our chests were aching from all our labored breathing, but we did manage to pedal our way to the top of the peak once again. During what was our final descent of the day, my brother informed me that the odometer mounted on the tandem's handlebars displayed our coasting speed of 50-plus miles per hour. Fortunately, the highway had been closed to traffic, so my brother had lots of maneuvering room. Because of our increased weight, we were passing all the other riders, as we descended the mountain. I just held on for dear life, because I could tell that we were moving faster than I had ever gone on a bike, for sure.

A benefit of being categorized legally blind means the annual fishing license is free. I am not what you would consider a sophisticated fisherman, but I was so fortunate to have a life-long friend (the late great John Lusk) who was an incredible fisherman. From the time we first met in the fourth grade, until his tragic death from cancer at age 46, John lived and breathed fish. He could have easily been a professional fishing guide, but his passion was to be on the water himself, reeling in fish. He had a beautiful boat with all the high-end equipment one would need for any kind of fishing or crabbing as well as for tubing and water skiing. I remember a funny story when John and I were at the store picking up supplies before we headed out to the coast. We always had a variety of stuff in the cart, from nets, to poles, to bait, hooks, line etc. As the clerk was ringing up our purchases, I began feeling someone tugging on my white cane. I naturally held my ground and pulled back against this resistance. I started to think my friend John was messing with me, but that did not make sense since John was in front of me and the pull was coming from the side. I learned the store employee had been trying to get her hands on my white cane to ring it up as part of our purchases. Since I was not giving up this item and not responding to visual cues, John, realized what was happening, and gave the clerk a back and forth head gesture to indicate "no" to taking my cane. I think the message got through and the tug of war ended with me still in possession of my cane.

Those annual trips to Oregon for salmon fishing and crabbing bring back such amazing memories. Prior to my October visits, John would always research what section of the river we were going to fish, and we would be sure to schedule around slack tide, as to not miss the best crabbing opportunities as well.

John was familiar with the hatchery on one of the rivers that we regularly fished. What he discovered adjacent to the hatchery was an accessible platform area for disabled anglers. This immediately became our favorite shore fishing spot. The platform area was so nice with paved access from the parking lot right up to the edge of the river. From the platform, you could literally cast your line to the point where the hatchery's fish ladder met the river, and that was the ideal spot to be. To have the opportunity to be so close to these fish was an unbelievable experience.

Additionally, John took me on fishing trips to Alaska and Queen Charlotte Island, Canada. He would set the table, so to speak, when it came to fishing, finding the location, preparing the gear, baiting the line, casting out or telling me where to cast my line. John did all the hard work, and my job was the fun part, reeling up the fish. Even if I cast the line astray or tangled it in the bushes or snagged it on the bottom of the river, John would patiently fix the mess.

When we would meet our daily limit of salmon and crab, John would drive to a secluded beach on the Oregon coast. Then it would be my opportunity to get behind the wheel and take a turn driving the truck on the beach. Those trips provided so many memories that will live on forever.

CHAPTER 41:
DEGREE, CERTIFICATION
& SEARCHING FOR A JOB

I had successfully completed my internships and had earned my BS degree in Occupational Therapy. Amy had passed the OT National Board Certification and had accepted her first OT position, in Concord, California, at a facility designed to assist injured workers, called Comprehensive Health and Active Rehabilitation Training (CHART). I needed to prepare for my OT National Boards Test and find a job as well.

My certification exam would need to be proctored, meaning the questions would be read out loud to me and my answers would be transcribed. I needed to request accommodations from the testing board. I would have preferred a proctor in the OT field, only because they would have familiarity with the terminology and proper pronunciation of the vocabulary. As it turned out, the testing board appointed a neutral third-party person who did not seem to have a medical background. The test went okay for me, and since I passed, I really did not have anything to complain about. There were a couple of times, though, during the test, questions were read to me incorrectly. I recalled the word *hypertension* being spoken by mistake, and when I asked for clarification, because the question did not make sense, the question was reread with the correct word, which was actually *hyperextension*. Of course, when you hear something like that during a test, you start wondering and worrying how many other words might have been misread that could have affected your answer. With tests like this, the results take weeks to be sent to you. The time between taking the test and receiving the results was an unsettling waiting period.

Now the real hard work would begin. I had always heard that looking for work is a full-time job. Being a new blind therapist certainly complicates getting that first professional job that will launch your career. The big question for me was when to disclose my blindness to a prospective employer. I sent out many resumes during my initial job search disclosing in the cover letter that I was blind.

I always felt that my blindness made me better prepared to assist people, as I was a walking example of adapting to my disability. I was a problem-solver and trouble-shooter. My journey to become an occupational therapist had required me to compensate for my progressive sight loss, both on an academic and practical level. I had developed non-visual methods for learning the required subject matter. During treatment sessions, I utilized my patient's vision to compensate for my lack of vision. I might have them read the goniometer when measuring their range of motion or the recipe when they are combining ingredients when preparing a dish. When patients are involved in their own therapy, in this case, providing visual assistance, patients become more engaged and empowered in their recovery. Now to convince a sighted colleague to hire me and give me the opportunity to work with clients was another matter.

I found that being honest and up front about my blindness did not equate with being contacted for follow-up interviews. If I did not disclose my blindness with my initial inquiry into a position that was of interest, then I would often be asked to come for a face-to-face interview. This approach would get me in the door, so to speak, but the interview could often be characterized as uncomfortable once they discovered that I was blind. In my mind, the interviewer would immediately jump to the conclusion that there is no way that a blind therapist could perform this job. The interviewer's mind would already be made up, so I would not have a chance to be considered. This type of rejection would not be direct, but the message was clear. First of all, there would not be any follow-up interest after this initial meeting, and when I would follow up, my phone calls were rarely returned. And you knew when the face-to-face interview focus would suddenly change to a discussion of practice areas that I should be pursuing. This was a clear message that I was no longer being considered for the actual position that I had come here to apply for.

I did actually make a positive impact on one human resource representative because she ended up offering me a position that she stated would be without benefits. She indicated that they did not want to worry about my eyes and blindness. The position that I had applied for and that was advertized stated full- or part time positions with immediate benefits upon hire. This sure felt like discrimination based on my blindness. I was being offered something different from what was advertised. It seemed so blatant. This company's hiring tactics did not sit well with me, the position was not ideal for what I wanted or needed, so I did not accept. It definitely felt like discrimination to me, but my priority was getting a job, so challenging the company was not where my energy needed to go. And bringing attention to the issue could have a negative impact on me regarding future employment opportunities.

Amy's brother Jeff was kind enough to drive me to another interview. I remember that I had disclosed my blindness in the cover letter, and surprisingly, to me, I was contacted. The prospective employer treated Jeff and me to lunch while the position was discussed. An employee informed me that a customer had complained about my guide dog. The message was clear to me that the complaining party expected Hoyt and me to leave the restaurant. I did not want to make a scene, particularly with a potential employer. In my mind, if the customer had allergy issues, then it was up to them to leave. Fortunately, I did not hear anything further about the issue, but it made the interview more stressful.

My buddy, John, had married his college sweetheart, Gwen, and they had moved to the Pacific Northwest where he eventually worked for the Intel Corporation. He would regularly call me, reading off job prospects from the local *Oregonian* newspaper. He was in favor of me moving to Oregon, saying I could get out of the expensive Bay Area. This motivated me to regularly look in the *Oregonian* newspaper for OT job listings. After a few weeks of looking, I found a listing that interested me. It was in Eugene, Oregon, at the Center for Neuro Educational Therapies (CNET). I did some further research concerning the facility and discovered their focus was neurological disorders. The majority of the clientele had experienced some type of traumatic head injury, which can express itself very differently, depending on what part of the brain was affected. Clients with encephalitis and epilepsy were other conditions commonly treated in the program.

There was a center where the clients would come during the day for therapy. CNET had three levels of care that clients could be placed in with the goal of progressing to the most independent level. The program offered two board-and-care group homes, where different levels of assistance were available to the clients. At the highest level of assistance, the board-and-care provided for 24-hour supervision, shopping/cooking support, and overseeing of one's finances. The second-level board-and-care home's working goals were for cooperative living, independent shopping, independent meal preparation/cooking, and independent financial management. The final level of support involves clients living in their own studio apartment without any formal support.

With this particular application, I had disclosed my blindness as part of the cover letter. Surprising to me, I received a call from Jan at CNET. She proceeded to conduct an interview with me over the phone. I was able to articulate my qualifications using my voice without the physical face-to-face meeting. Jan knew of my blindness from my initial contact with CNET, but I was able to speak with her without blindness being in the forefront. My words made up my first impression. Hopefully, I would be considered first as an occupational therapist rather than a blind guy who needed occupational therapy.

I was offered a position and accepted it. This meant a move to Eugene, Oregon, for Hoyt and me. My buddy, John, seemed thrilled with my new job, but Amy not so much. We would have the classic long-distance relationship. I needed to prove to myself that I could get a job and support myself in spite of blindness. The thought that CNET was willing to hire me, looking at the qualifications that I had to offer, and not focusing on the fact that I was blind felt really good.

CHAPTER 42:
MOVING OUT OF STATE FOR MY FIRST OT JOB

Once again my parents were right there giving me the support with the big move to Eugene. My mom and I made a trip to the area to scout out my new workplace and potential rental apartments and discover shopping opportunities nearby. We were very productive with the initial two day/night trip to Eugene. I managed to meet my coworkers and tour the CNET facility and found and rented an apartment that was a half mile from my workplace. I visited the Eugene Commission for the Blind and was referred to an Orientation and Mobility instructor who could help me learn about this new city.

This was a big move for anyone starting out on their own. It was exciting but at the same time very scary. My apartment this time was not just a short drive and city away from family. I was moving out of state, starting a new job, and coming to a city that I knew nothing about. My support system would be a phone call away, but my closest face-to-face assistance was a good two-hour drive away from John and Gwen, who lived in the Portland area. I did have my canine companion, Hoyt, so at least I would not be alone during this relocation.

I knew from experience that employers' bottom line was billable time. This meant that I needed to have a system in place where I could complete the necessary paperwork independently using my computer. I had requested that CNET provide me with any and all forms that their therapists were required to complete when services were provided to the clients. This substantial stack of forms was sent to me. Now I needed to figure out how to make all these materials accessible to me, so I could complete them independently.

Len Burns to the rescue: I had been introduced to Len, a blind gentleman, who also lived in Santa Cruz. Len was a practicing psychologist who was also a computer whiz. My family and I hired Len to assist me with the task of converting these forms into an accessible format. Word Perfect was the mainstream word-processing application at the time for those who were using computers. Personal computer usage in the early 1990s was the exception rather than the rule. Most small businesses like CNET were still completing all of their paperwork manually, meaning all of the forms were handwritten, copied, and mailed out.

I became very acquainted with Word Perfect and learned about the power of macros. Macros were a series of command line instructions that could be typed into Word Perfect and a desired form would be created real-time right on the computer screen in front of you. The different macros that were created represented the various forms that I would be responsible for completing on my job. The macros were triggered by pressing the Enter key. It was amazing to see how the form would just start appearing on the screen when the specific macro was opened. The text of the form would auto-fill on the screen and the cursor would be placed in the field ready for the answer to question #1. Once I typed in the answer and pressed the Enter key again, more of the form would auto-fill and the cursor would be placed in the field where the answer to the next question could be typed in. If you press the Enter key enough, the entire form will eventually be created on the screen. It can be saved, edited, and printed out as a hard copy for the client's file. It took many hours of macro programming to get the forms to visually look like the originals, but my having access to these documents provided me with additional confidence as I prepared to kick off my career.

Moving time came in November of 1991. My parents' mid-size truck was filled with any hand-me-down furniture and accessories that would help to fill a bachelor pad with anything free or donated.

There was an old bright-orange-colored vinyl couch from the 1970s that I remember growing up with. It would fill space and be functional in my new apartment's living room. Cosmetically, it was most likely an eyesore, but I was not worried about the visuals. I applied for my own Sears charge card and proceeded to purchase a new bed, as well as a washer and dryer. It was nice to discover that Oregon had no sales tax.

We ended up placing bump dots on these new appliances, so I would be able to operate them independently through touch. My clothes were organized and matched up, so they would be ready for work. Most of my pants and shirts were interchangeable, so whatever combination I picked would look okay together. I learned the way to the office of the apartment complex so I could drop off my rent check each month. There was a grocery store near my work that I had learned the route to, but shortly after starting my job, I discovered that the store was going out of business.

My new job would officially start the Monday after Thanksgiving. We made the all-day eight-plus hour trip to Eugene from the Bay Area, arriving on Wednesday evening. Amy and I had driven up separately as she was planning to stay a couple of extra days to help me get settled in. We had a simple Thanksgiving meal with my parents and Amy on Thursday, as everyone helped me move in to my apartment. I needed to learn the route through the complex, to the main road. Interesting how most sidewalks meander as they wind their way past each of the complex's buildings. While the actual road has a pretty straight route out to the main road, walking the road would have been the most direct route, but definitely the most dangerous, particularly for a blind guy. My parents and Amy were very patient and worked with Hoyt and me to learn the route. There was a bus stop right outside the apartment complex, where I could catch a ride, being dropped off right in front of my workplace. I also learned the route from my apartment all the way to my workplace, as I preferred to walk rather than waiting for the bus.

For the first couple of weeks, when I traveled to my job, I took the bus, along with several children, who were taking the same bus to school. I got to know the kids at the stop a little bit, as we all waited for the bus. Of course, Hoyt, being the dog in the group, was the most popular one. The kids understood that I was blind and that Hoyt was trained to guide me safely to wherever I was going.

After the first couple of weeks, I was feeling more confident and really did not like waiting for the bus when I could just walk the half mile to work. On the first day that Hoyt and I kept going beyond the bus stop, I remember a young boy running to catch up to us, saying, "Mister Jeff, you have passed the bus stop."

I was touched that this boy had run down the street chasing Hoyt and me, thinking we had accidentally passed the bus stop. I let him know that we were going to walk to my job and thanked him for looking out for us.

Saying goodbye to Amy on Sunday after Thanksgiving was very hard. She had made some of my favorite meals, placing them in my freezer, so I would have things to eat during the next month before I was planning to travel home for Christmas. Amy had a long drive ahead of her on Sunday returning to the Bay Area and her job on Monday. She stayed as long as she could, but by early afternoon, she needed to get on her way.

There we were, Hoyt and me, living in an apartment in Eugene, Oregon, 400 miles away from home. I was starting a new job in my chosen field as an occupational therapist. Those first several days were particularly quiet, lonely, and scary, as I was truly on my own, but, of course, I did have my 4-wheel drive dog by my side that was willing and anxious to guide me wherever I needed to go.

I also got to experience the Oregon winter weather, and two words come to my mind: *rain* and *wet*. Getting to and from work was an ordeal trying to keep myself and Hoyt as dry as possible. There was nothing worse than getting to work and being soaked from the walking commute, knowing we still had eight hours of work ahead of us. Of course, Hoyt was the one that everyone fussed over, worrying about the poor wet dog. I quickly transitioned from a California fair-weather guy to a seasoned Oregonian. I immediately obtained foul-weather gear and kept a supply of dry towels at work for Hoyt and me.

I remember one morning after arriving at work through a steady rainstorm, one of my coworkers said that we were lucky this season because Oregon was experiencing a drought. I remember thinking I do not feel too lucky right now, as water was dripping off Hoyt and me. If this is a drought year, then I would hate to experience a "normal" rainfall year, as dealing with rain every other day like I had since relocating to Eugene was more than enough for me.

The time between Thanksgiving when I began my new job and Christmas when I went home for the holidays went by quickly, as I was focused on learning the new job and navigating the city of Eugene.

CNET has one main office where clients come during the day to receive speech and occupational therapy to assist them in building the skills needed for independence. In addition, the OTs, who were John, whom I had met on my initial visit, and me, were tasked with providing assistance to the clients in the home(s) where they were living while at CNET. John and I would assist with budgeting, shopping, meal prep/clean up, laundry, and general home management.

Before I could support the clients with their activities of daily living, I needed to learn the routes to these homes where the clients lived. During the day, I was involved in my OT work at CNET, facilitating group and one-on-one classes to develop skills necessary for independence. After work and sometimes weekends, I would work with an Orientation and Mobility Specialist to learn the local transit system in order to travel to my desired destinations.

During much of my travels, I had the opportunity to interact with clients more on a peer level, rather than the formal therapist-to-patient level. We were on the bus together, and the clients were empowered to assist me. They were not focused on themselves, but rather my sight loss and the needs around that. Having this kind of relationship with the clients provided for opportunities where higher-level skills could be practiced. For example, I could have the clients identify where we were or describe various businesses we were passing, notifying me when traffic lights change color or the sidewalk ended. This allowed them to focus their attention and be more aware of their surroundings. I could relate to their frustrations as we waited for a bus and envied the freedom of others who could jump into a car whenever the need arose.

The standard route of the Lane County Transit Bus that clients would take to CNET each weekday had a stop across Centennial Boulevard from CNET. At that particular bus stop location, there was a very complicated intersection, where Centennial Boulevard. merges with another major road right where the bus stop was. The pedestrian crossing required activating two separately controlled signal lights. The crossing also involved navigating across several lanes of traffic. Many of the clients had perceptual deficits, visual field limitations, and impaired judgment, so making this crossing was unsafe.

I remember that my Mobility instructor felt the intersection was unsafe for a blind pedestrian to cross, as well. The next sentence out of his mouth really bothered me, though. Why did he feel the need to state that he was confident with his cane skills as an instructor, but questioned my abilities? He has not walked in my shoes, and did not need to suggest that his mobility skills are better than those who actually have vision loss. I was so ready to hand him my cane, put him under a blindfold, and let him attempt the crossing.

CNET and Lane County Transit agreed for the bus to deviate from its usual route once in the morning and once in the afternoon. This would avoid the intersection during times that clients would likely be traveling to and from CNET. I was well aware of the alternate schedule, so I planned accordingly. I taught a class each week in downtown Eugene at an apartment complex for transitioning head-injured tenants. I would travel by bus to and from there.

On one of my return trips to CNET, I confirmed with the driver concerning the deviation of the route, and he was adamant that the modified route was only scheduled once each weekday morning. Panic immediately took over. I explained to the driver that there was also a scheduled alternate route, one in the afternoon, as well. I let him know the crossing at the drop-off location was unsafe, particularly for me and for the clients we serve.

Out of desperation, I also played the blindness card (which I do not like to do), telling the driver it was outright dangerous for someone who does not see to attempt to cross at that intersection. "If you were blind like me, would you attempt to cross the street at the designated bus stop?" I said to the driver.

The driver began showing compassion with my situation, as I was pleading with him to please deviate from the usual route and drop me off at the alternate safe location. He agreed to call the transit office to obtain special permission to go off-route. The distance from the downtown transit center where I picked up the bus to my drop-off stop was only a few minutes, so all of this negotiation would need to be settled quickly.

Visions of my experience in Santa Clara, where I was dropped off at an unfamiliar location, flashed into my mind. I am like my guide dogs, I thrive on routine and consistency, and if that is disrupted, it is a very unsettling feeling.

Fortunately for me, the dispatcher gave the driver special permission to go off-route. I never heard that I had been correct about the afternoon deviation, but when I contacted the Lane County Transit Office it was confirmed.

CHAPTER 43:
ENGAGEMENT & RETURNING TO CALIFORNIA

The Christmas holiday was approaching and many of CNET's clients would be returning to their homes to be with family. I also was making reservations to be with my family and Amy.

It was reassuring to have landed my first OT job, and the position seemed to be a really good fit for me. Now I was going home for the holidays to see my family and long-time girlfriend, Amy. Amy was still working and living in Concord. Questions had been coming up, even prior to my move to Oregon, about our relationship long-term and what our plans were.

Upon returning home for the Christmas holiday, I took Amy on a date back to Carl's Jr., where we had gone on our first date. I had a dozen red roses delivered to the table where we were sitting together and that is where I proposed to her. She said yes, and the rest is history, as they say.

During the remainder of the holidays while we still were together visiting at home, we had many discussions about organizing the wedding and where we wanted to live. Planning the wedding seemed to fall into place easily. Our long- term plans, though, were a bit more complicated. Amy was not excited about moving away from family, out of state to Eugene where I was. I was not too interested in living in Concord, where Amy was currently.

We had had the opportunity to visit my sister in Santa Rosa, where she had moved to follow her boyfriend Paul, who later became her husband. We really liked the Santa Rosa area, as it reminded us of where we had grown up. It was close to the ocean and a short ride to the countryside, both places where we enjoyed spending time. Our plan would be to settle in Santa Rosa to begin our life together.

PRESSURE

We were targeting summertime of 1992 to relocate to Santa Rosa. This meant we would have to give notice to our current employers and find a new place to live. I so appreciated the opportunity that CNET had given to a blind therapist. Let's face it, hiring a blind OT felt like a risk, I am sure. They did not know me nor did they know if I could actually do the job. Approaching my employer and letting them know that I would be leaving was not an easy thing to do. I had landed a job where all things were falling into place in terms of my blindness and ability to work as a therapist. I really had mixed emotions about leaving a place where I felt I had proven that my blindness did not interfere with my ability to provide OT services to the clients.

I had returned to Oregon for a few more months of work, and Amy had gone into wedding-planning mode. She had found and reserved the place where we would have our ceremony and reception. It was a beautiful location at Silver Mountain Vineyards, which was a winery in the Santa Cruz Mountains close to where I grew up.

On September 19, 1992, Amy and I were married, surrounded by our wedding party of my brother, Michael, and Belinda, John, and Jenny, Dave and Leisbeth, my sister Cheri, and my brother-in-law, Paul. There were approximately 120 of our family and friends, including both of our maternal grandmas. Hoyt was the best dog, and he performed his duty, leading this groom down the aisle to the gazebo, where Amy and I exchanged our vows.

We had both done the apartment-rental thing and knew that a rental home would be more to our liking. We found a three-bedroom two-bath home on the west side of Santa Rosa in a quiet neighborhood that became our residence for a year plus.

Amy applied for and was hired as an OT for North Coast Rehabilitation Center. One of her roles was to evaluate people who had been injured on the job, i.e., Workers' Compensation cases. Having to participate in depositions and a trial concerning patient/

employee's functional capacities was not part of the job she enjoyed. After a year or so, Amy was able to transition to a more specific traditional role.

Finding employment for me was not as easy. My job-hunting experience as a blind applicant had taught me, finding practical opportunities worth pursuing took considerable time.

After submitting multiple resumes and participating in several interviews, I remember being offered a position at Friends House, which was a retirement community in Santa Rosa. The position was designated as contract work part time. This meant I would be working independently, providing therapy services to patients in the assistive-living unit. As a new graduate without having a more-experienced therapist to mentor me, I did not feel this position was the best fit or environment for me.

Let's just say I was pretty much striking out as I hunted for a job on my own. After a couple of months with no real prospects, I reached out again to the State Department of Rehabilitation. This was the agency that had supported me during my college years.

I was introduced to Geoff Perel who was the Rehab Counselor in the Northern California area assigned to work with the visually impaired caseload. Geoff was a true advocate for making sure his clients had all the resources and tools to be successful pursuing their vocational goals. He made sure that I obtained all necessary equipment that would assist me to perform my job duties.

I remember receiving a computer system, including a monitor, mouse, keyboard, speakers, printer, and scanner. Along with all of this hardware, software was also purchased for me, including: upgrades to Word Perfect and Vocal-Eyes, which was assistive-technology software designed for people with sight loss, providing access to the DOS platform. Flipper, the software that I had been using during my internships and position in Oregon, was good software, but the company was very small with limited hours of operation. Being given the opportunity to obtain this better-supported Vocal-Eyes software was the right move for me at the time. This kept me current with available mainstream and assistive software.

One of the issues that I discovered with all this amazing assistive software at the time, though, was the lack of training resources. You can have the greatest hardware and software available, but if you do not know how to use it, it is pretty much worthless as a tool to assist you.

Geoff had referred me to a private contractor in the area, who claimed to be a trainer. It was very evident to me during my initial appointment with this guy that he did not know what he was doing in regard to providing training services. It was clear to me that I knew a lot more about the assistive technology then he did. This first appointment with the so-called trainer was spent listening to his monologue about the poor quality of synthetic speech in these computer systems.

I remember asking Geoff if there were other trainers available for me to work with, but at the time, this technology was pretty new and DOR did not have other options to offer to me. This lack of training resources was something I kept in the back of my mind, and would become a real idea later in my career. I let Geoff know that I would train myself with the technology that had been given to me and there would be no need for DOR to pay for these services in my behalf.

Geoff had referred me to job-readiness workshops, where resume writing and interviewing strategies were discussed and practiced. The million-dollar question of when to disclose your disability to a prospective employer was constantly under debate with no definitive answer.

I remember scheduling informational interviews with people in the community who I felt could be a resource for me in assisting with finding work. I had always known about the hidden job market and unadvertised positions. Often it was who you that who would let you know about an opening or get you in the door for that initial interview.

A wonderful lady who I connected with was Lois who was working for the Community Resources for Independence (CRI); later, their name was changed to Disability Services and Legal Center (DSLC). Lois was a very kind person, a good listener, and well-connected in the community. She had relocated from New York and was friends with and had gone to school with Dr. George Flores, who was the Public Health Officer for Sonoma County at the time.

Lois had provided me with the names of several Sonoma County programs where OTs were utilized to provide therapies for disabled children. This gave me an opportunity to meet professionals working in the therapy field.

During the time that I was participating in this job readiness workshop, I discovered an opening for an OT through the Pacific Career Center, which was part of Goodwill Industries of the Redwood Empire. Upon further investigation, I learned that they had been looking to fill this position for over a year. When the OT position had been vacated during the early part of the previous year, it had not yet been filled.

Goodwill Industries is known for assisting people with disabilities by raising money through donations and providing employment opportunities. The Pacific Career Center's purpose was to provide vocational services to employees who had been injured on the job and for people with disabilities looking for employment. Standardized testing was used to determine an individual's strengths and weaknesses, as well as their aptitude for various types of employment. The OT position was primarily responsible for evaluating a person's functional capacities when considering the physical demands of a position. Additionally, the Pacific Career Center had offered services to Workers' Comp. cases, where most commonly, a muscular, skeletal, or neurological work-related injury/accident would be evaluated.

My resume and cover letter did get me an interview. I remember in this case I thought it would be best to disclose my blindness in the cover letter, thinking this is an organization that works with disability. My strategy must have worked, as I did land an interview.

For me, just the act of traveling to the unfamiliar interview site would increase my stress level. I knew I was being watched, being the blind applicant entering the office, finding the reception desk, and locating a seat, while I waited to be called in for the interview.

Most of the time, I would arrange a ride with a family member when it came to interviews. In this case, though, my interview was in the middle of the day and Amy was at work. For whatever reason, I never considered taking a taxi, probably because of the cost. The weekend before my interview at the Pacific Career Center, Amy played the role once again of an Orientation and Mobility instructor, familiarizing me with the route from where the bus would drop me off to the Goodwill Office where my interview would be. To complicate things even more, the location was in an industrial part of Santa Rosa with limited sidewalks and right next to the railroad tracks.

Walking from the bus stop to the office required that I cross the railroad tracks. The train had to come down the tracks right when Hoyt and I were crossing, and it was terrifying! Hoyt did fine when the bells sounded around us, and I am assuming the lights were flashing and the bars were coming down. I, on the other hand, panicked, and instinctively grabbed the leash, tightly dragging Hoyt and me away from the tracks as quickly as possible.

With my body full of adrenaline, hyperventilating and heart pounding, we did make it to the office for the interview. Since Hoyt and I had just avoided being run over by a train, the actual interview itself did not seem so bad.

My interview must have gone well, and I was offered and accepted the position.

I was able to let my prospective employer know that I had the backing of the State Department of Rehabilitation, and they were willing to assist with any accommodation needs that I might have.

Unfortunately, from the first day I started this position, referrals to the Pacific Career Center for OT services were very limited, and in the six-plus months that I worked there, the referrals never picked up. I might have had a referral or two each week from the Department of Rehabilitation, but none of the third-party private pay insurance carriers were making referrals like they had historically done. I suppose the lack of referrals could have been attributed to being uncertain about a blind OT performing Functional Capacity Evaluations, but I really felt like these referral agencies had needed to find other resources for their injured workers when Pacific Career Center stopped offering this service during the previous year. They were most likely happy with the services they were now getting and had no reason to switch back to Pacific Career Center.

Goodwill Industries had encouraged me to research and find a training opportunity that would help me grow professionally in this new practice area.

When I contacted the first professional seminar company, I requested that I be able to send out an announcement to other attendees in order to find someone who might be willing to assist with note-taking for a fellow attendee with sight loss. That request was not well-received by the seminar organizers. The message that came back to me was pretty clear and direct. They did not want someone with sight loss to attend their training session. Furthermore, they did not think that a blind person could perform Functional Capacity Evaluations. They did not even acknowledge the fact that I was a Registered Occupational Therapist and simply dismissed my abilities because I was blind. With that type of attitude and response, I was not about to pay for their course. I remember that several messages went back and forth between my supervisor and the seminar organizers, and the bottom line was they did not want me in their class and I did not want to be in their class. Fortunately, I did find another training-course opportunity through a competing organization that was more than willing to work with me.

The course itself was being held out of state, and it was three days and two nights in duration. This was a big deal for me, as I would be traveling alone to Dallas, Texas. I would be riding on buses, planes, and taxis. Although it would have been nice to have Hoyt on the trip, it meant more responsibility, for me, meeting his needs.

CHAPTER 44:
A CAREER CHANGE FOR MY GUIDE,
A LAY-OFF & OUR FIRST HOME

Shortly after returning from the training seminar in Texas, an instructor from Guide Dogs was scheduled to perform a follow-up visit with Hoyt and me. Guide Dogs likes to check in annually with working teams to make sure everything is going well. Usually, newly graduated teams will have a face-to-face visit from Guide Dogs particularly in the first year or two. These follow-up visits typically involve a brief discussion of how things are going and then we actually work a route while the instructor watches.

It turned out that Amy had visited her brother in San Francisco, and her car had been vandalized with one of her windows being smashed out. The window repair was going to take place at the same time as the follow-up visit from GDB. While we were away working the route with the instructor, the window repairman arrived with his pet dog. When Hoyt guided me back home, he spotted the other dog and growled. Of course, Hoyt's behavior was observed by the instructor. It took a bit of time for me to fully get Hoyt's attention back. The instructor asked me to keep the school informed about Hoyt's behavior with dog distractions while working. Unfortunately, Hoyt had a couple more experiences where he exhibited aggressive behavior around other dogs that were nearby.

It was decided that Hoyt would be returned to the school for re-evaluation. When I was without my guide dog, it meant that the cane would be my only mobility tool for the time being. I always tell people that not having your 4-wheel drive dog available for mobility assistance is like not having a car available to drive you places. By now, my preferred mobility choice was definitely a dog, particularly when it came to traveling any distances, like going to work, the store, or just a walk.

The school worked with Hoyt for a week or two, but at the end, it was decided that Hoyt should be retired as a guide dog. It was also recommended that I not keep Hoyt if my plan was to get another guide dog. The school felt that bringing a new guide dog into my home with Hoyt, who had exhibited aggressive behavior toward other dogs, would not be a good fit.

Hoyt and Amy were particularly close, so the idea of not keeping him as a pet was difficult to accept. I had always felt I would keep any of my guide dogs as pets if they were no longer working. Guide dogs that retire or are career-changed have several options. In some cases, the dog stays with the handler, or goes back to their puppy raiser, or is adopted by a person who has been pre-screened and is on a waiting list for one of these dogs. My sister was like eight months pregnant with her first son. She and her husband agreed to take Hoyt into their imminent growing family. So not only were they going to have a newborn baby, they were also willing to take on a dog. It's a good thing that guide dogs are so well trained, but having a new baby and a dog had to be so overwhelming for them. I was grateful, and it was very reassuring to know that Hoyt would be living with family, and the bonus was that we were practically neighbors, just a couple of miles apart. That meant visiting Hoyt would be so convenient for us.

I applied for a new guide dog, and was accepted, but was told it would be many months before there was a class opening. Santa Rosa, where I was living now, was only 45 minutes from the Guide Dog campus, and because of a last-minute student cancellation, I was asked if I wanted to attend class the following week. So instead of having to wait months, I could be in class training with a new guide dog by next week.

My work situation was slow, and my new baby nephew Paulie was now home, with his mom, dad, and new dog, Hoyt. So I decided to accept the offer to attend class.

At the time, the "retrains" as they are called, who come to class for a successor dog, could take a two-week class instead of the full four-week class. I was paired with a coated German shepherd named Hale. He had been raised in Ogden, Utah, by Kristen Emmert. The name "Hale" certainly represented the environment during our first two weeks of bonding and training together.

During that February, 1993, class, it must have rained 12 of the 14 days that we were in training together. It really made for a miserable experience in terms of the weather. Hale and I both survived what I will refer to as the "Hale Storm." This accelerated two-week class (#CA519R), along with the stormy weather, secured our partnership immediately. Hale had the reputation of being a big bad German shepherd, but in reality he was a furry teddy bear afraid of his own tail.

Coming home with Hale, returning to work, I was met with the news that I would be laid off. Amy and I had just put down an offer on our first home. So despite my current unemployment status, we became homeowners.

CHAPTER 45:

NEW JOBS: BENEFITS COUSELING & HOUSING ACCESS MODIFICATION COORDINATOR

Following my position at Pacific Career Center, I ended up learning about a position at CRI/DSLC, where I had met Lois previously. Unfortunately, Lois had moved on from her position at CRI/DSLC, so I would not have the privilege of working with her, but I had my introduction because of her.

The position that I had accepted would not require my OT degree. I would be a "Benefits Counselor," assisting people with disabilities when applying for or maintaining government benefits. This often involved the Social Security Disability Insurance (SSDI) or the Supplemental Security Income (SSI) programs, as well as In-Home Support Services (IHSS), and MediCal and Medicare. At the time I began this position, I was filling in for a lady (Cheryl) who was out on maternity leave.

This is where I learned about government programs available to assist people with disabilities. I also learned that individuals with sight loss (legal blindness) sometimes had different benefits from other disabling conditions. This could be positive when it came to work history/eligibility, payment amounts, and work incentives. The necessary devices to assist a person with sight loss, though, such as magnifiers, glare shields, long canes, along with training, etc., were not covered by medical insurance, while other disability groups requiring devices such as walkers, wheelchairs, shower benches, and commodes are typically covered items.

As Cheryl's maternity leave was coming to an end and she would be returning to CRI, I began working with the Executive Director at the time (Mike). We had been in contact with another Independent Living Center in California, which had recently developed a Housing Access Modification (HAM) Program. This is where income-eligible homeowners and renters with a variety of disabling conditions could receive grants to make their apartment or home more accessible. We took this idea and applied for Community Block Grant (CDBG) funds from Sonoma County and other larger municipalities in the county.

My OT background did come into play with this newly-developed position. CRI was successful in repeatedly being awarded these CDBG funds. For the four years that I coordinated the HAM Program, each year the available funds to assist residents would increase.

My job was to perform on-site assessments at disabled residences. I would consider their physical and/or sensory limitations and make recommendations to improve access. I would write up project descriptions and put them out to bid. Typical installations that were completed through this project involved placing grab bars in the bathroom, widening doorways, building ramps, adding visual alerting systems for those with hearing loss, and placing color contrasting and tactile warning strips on steps, etc., for those with sight loss.

While working at CRI, my eye that still had a Molteno Valve implant began causing me a lot of discomfort. Since my active treatment at Stanford was now many years in the past, I did not have a current ophthalmologist. My medical insurance was now Kaiser, so returning to see Dr. Egbert was not really an option. When I contacted Kaiser Eye Clinic for an appointment, as a new patient I was given an appointment for about a month later. Even though I explained that I was a glaucoma patient with eye pain, I was told I needed to see an optometrist first. My eye was becoming more and more painful. It did not seem fair to be dealing with eye issues once again. After all, I had already battled this disease for 10-plus years, it had taken my sight, and now one of my eyes was acting up. This time, though, I was not trying to save my vision. That was already gone. I needed to figure out why my eye was hurting and what could be done about it.

The discomfort was intensifying, and waiting for my appointment with an optometrist did not seem like the best approach. I made a trip to the Kaiser Emergency Room and saw an ER doctor, who took one look at my eyes and got me fast-tracked into seeing an ophthalmologist. I saw Dr. Hake, and after she took a quick look at my painful eye, she said the Molteno Valve implant was failing. She was obviously familiar with this procedure. I remember back in the early 1980s when I had my first Molteno Valve implant, the doctors at Stanford were lining up to examine my eye, as it was something they had never seen before.

Dr. Hake said the Kaiser Eye Clinic here in Santa Rosa did not handle glaucoma patients with valve implants. I was referred to the Oakland Kaiser facility. Unfortunately, the referral process was going to mean yet another appointment in Oakland before a final resolution would be decided. As it turned out, the doctor who examined me at Kaiser Oakland remembered seeing me as a patient at Stanford when he was completing his residency.

It was reassuring to know that this ophthalmologist was familiar with my case and history of treatment. I was scheduled later that week for yet another surgery to remove the valve. After surgery, I was given the Molteno Valve that had been removed from my eye, I guess as a souvenir, which I still have today. It was an interesting piece of silicon hardware that had been in my eye for around 10 years. It was experimental plumbing that had acted as a drain for my eye, and had helped to prolong my eyesight during the end stage of my battle with glaucoma.

I was ready for a career change and was looking for more advancement opportunities, along with working more directly with people. I had felt good about being involved with developing the HAM Program and knowing many people had benefitted. Every project that was completed under this program had a requirement that any improvements be permanently affixed, so it would remain for the benefit of others. And as far as I know, the program is still available to assist people.

CHAPTER 46:
THE EARLE BAUM CENTER OF THE BLIND

Around this same time of job transition, I was hearing about a center for people with sight loss that had recently been opened on the west side of Santa Rosa. Upon further investigation into this organization, I learned that it was called the Earle Baum Center of the Blind. It was named after Earle Baum, who was a blind farmer, who was born and raised on his family's farm and later ran the farm on the piece of property where the center is now. When Earle died in 1986 at the age of 90, he donated his land, so a place for blind people to gather and learn could be established. Thirteen-plus years after Earle's death, the Earle Baum Center of the Blind opened its doors to the community in October of 1999.

I remember scheduling an informational meeting with the director early in 2000. I was given a tour of the property. There was Earle's original two-bedroom house, which was serving as the office. There was the original garage, which was used for storage, and later had exercise equipment brought in, as well. In addition, there were three portable classroom buildings, a mobile home, and a couple of sheds on the center's grounds.

It was explained that there was a small staff of three: Marlene who provided office/clerical support, Denise who worked part-time as a Vision Rehabilitation Therapist to provide direct services and the director. At the time, Orientation and Mobility services were being offered by contract employees. Susan was a contract employee at the time, and she provided life coaching to those adjusting to sight loss.

I was encouraged to enroll in braille classes with Denise. My Department of Rehabilitation case that had been opened with Geoff

Perel had been successfully closed several years prior when I had been working at CRI/DSLC in the HAM Program. My case was reopened by Ilene, a counselor who worked with non-vocational cases. I qualified for services under the "Home Maker" catagory. This meant I would be supported once again by the Department of Rehabilitation in learning braille. The Department of Rehabilitation had also provided me with a Perkins Brail Typewriter, along with a large supply of paper, allowing me to produce braille.

During the time that I was enrolled in braille classes, I also attended a weekly support group called the "Thursday Thinkers." This is where I had met Larry (one of the original founders of the EBC), Beryl (a volunteer/advocate), and my future coworker Patricia (who was bringing her mother with sight loss to the meetings).

In my mind, there was a huge service missing from the Center's offerings. There was no technology program, and that was a critical resource for those people experiencing sight loss. I had a discussion with the director about the need for the establishment of technology services. I think he understood the importance of technology for those with sight loss. In order for the center to be reimbursed for assistive technology services, EBC's current vendorization would need to be upgraded for technology services. This would mean that the Department of Rehabilitation would pay the EBC to provide assistive technology assessment and training services. Dealing with the State is a bureaucratic process that takes time.

In the interim, as the technology program was being formalized, I regularly volunteered my time developing and facilitating a weekly discussion group called Tech Club. The purpose of the group was to demonstrate computer technologies designed to assist people with sight loss. I also worked on getting computer systems donated, along with the specialized required assistive software, so visually impaired people could have firsthand experience with this solution that could provide access to this new world of computers.

My knowledge of software at the time was pretty good, but I had limited experience with hardware. Sometimes the used computer systems that were given to the EBC needed updating or repair to make them compatible with the assistive technology software that we were going to install. My dad and father-in-law were always willing to assist, and having them as a resource while I was trying to prove my value to EBC in the early days was so helpful. Many hard drives and video and sound cards required upgrading on the donated systems before they would be compatible with assistive technology applications.

I remember that computer systems were moving away from the Disk Operating System (DOS) into Windows with its Graphical User Interface (GUI) and the challenge of developing access for magnification and screen-reader users. There were many people with varying degrees of sight loss. Some did well with magnification, while others needed a full screen reader.

The transition from DOS to the Windows Operating System was initially a technological challenge for screen-reader manufacturers. The DOS Operating System was text-based, so the screen-reading software could pretty easily be developed to speak the information that appeared on the screen. A text letter is represented by a specific ASCII value, so communicating to screen-reading software was pretty easy.

Windows, however, was a Graphical Operating System, meaning, that what was presented on the screen was actually pictures that represented specific applications. Once a program is opened, additional graphic pictures were presented showing various tasks that could be performed.

I have been told that a picture on a computer screen is actually a combination of various pixels that represent various colors, shades, and shapes. Every picture is represented by a different combination of pixels. Even if two pictures are similar visually, the combination of pixels representing each could be quite different.

Screen-reading software developers needed a method for understanding what a specific combination of pixels was meant to represent. This meant developers of the actual mainstream software needed to include code that the screen-reading software could communicate with, under the hood, so to speak, letting the screen reader know what this specific combination of pixels is representing. This required cooperation from the mainstream software developers to include coding language in their applications.

In the early days of Windows, educating the mainstream programmers as to the need for this underlying code that could communicate to the assistive technology software, and getting it actually implemented was an uphill battle, and without this cooperation, those with sight loss were being left behind. Early on, updates to mainstream software could often make the screen-reading software stop working. If you were using assistive technology software, it was not advisable to update to the newest version of the operating system or application. This definitely put the visually impaired computer user at a further disadvantage because they could not benefit from the newest mainstream features.

Because there were people with varying degrees of vision loss, I wanted to be able to show both magnification and screen-reader solutions. Configuring a single computer to work with both of these access features was challenging because the applications did not play well together. The magnification software was developed by one company, while the screen-reading software was created by a different company. There were device drivers and configuration settings that needed to be installed in a specific order in order to have both access solutions available on the same system. And if there was an issue with one of the assistive technologies, then you needed to uninstall the applications in a specific sequence in order to troubleshoot whatever the issue was.

Earle Baum was born in 1896 on his family's farm just west of Santa Rosa. This homesteaded property had been in the Baum family since 1856. By age 17, Baum had lost substantial sight, most likely from retinitis pigmentosa, the number-one cause of congenital blindness. A star pupil at Santa Rosa High, Earle had dreamed of a writing career.

With his sight loss, pursuing a career in journalism did not seem practical at the time. Earle Baum spent his lifetime working the farm, tending the animals and planting, cultivating, pruning, and harvesting the farm's seasonal bounty. He used baling wire as a guide to assist with navigating the property. The wires were located outside the back door of the farmhouse. One of the wires might lead to the barn, while a different wire would lead him to the orchard of fruit trees, and another wire would take him out to the farm's well. Earle had a bathtub placed in the barn, not for bathing purposes, but to assist him with measuring the amount of hay he would feed the animals.

He remained on the farm until his death in 1986 at age 90.

CHAPTER 47:
THE POWER OF BRAILLE

Denise was successful in teaching me grade-1 braille. I remember after learning grade-1, card games became accessible to me once again. I purchased a couple of decks of braille cards and was able to play with my sighted family members and friends. I preferred the games that had fewer cards to handle, but I was willing to try any game, as it was so empowering to be able to play without sight. The more cards that the game required, the slower I was at playing because it took time for me to feel/read each card. It did make me a bit self-conscious thinking I was slowing down the game for the other players, but there seemed to always be a willing competitor.

I remember how I created and placed braille labels on my CD collections, and how cool it was to be able to independently find the music that I wanted to play.

I had always been able to write braille faster than reading it. Braille consists of a six-dot configuration called the braille cell, three vertical dots next to three more parallel vertical dots. The letters of the alphabet were made up by different combinations of these six dots. The top left dot was considered Dot 1. The dot below Dot 1 was Dot 2, and below that was Dot 3. Dot 4 was in the second column on the top right, Dot 5 below that, and Dot 6 was the bottom right.

So, for example, if only the top left dot was present, that represented "a." If Dots 1 and 2 were present, then that represented the letter "b." The letter "c" was represented with Dots 1 and 4. To be efficient with braille, an individual needed not only to develop tactile awareness, but in addition, you needed to memorize what letter the specific pattern referred to. You would need to spell out the words letter-by-letter.

PRESSURE

Denise went on to teach me grade-2 braille. This was yet another level of that touch language, but now I was beginning to understand how sophisticated this language can become. Grade 2, or what is called contracted braille, required even more memorization. It uses the same letters, punctuation, and numbers as grade-1 braille, but adds a series of special signs to represent common words or groups of letters, a bit like a kind of shorthand. For example, there are braille contractions for words such as *the, for,* and *will* and braille contractions to represent common letter combinations such as *ing, er,* and *sh.* This means it's quicker to read and write than grade-1 braille, and also takes up less space. In grade-2 braille, one needed to not only distinguish what dot pattern was presented, but also where the dot pattern appeared in the word. You needed to understand the rules of contracted braille, and the dot patterns had different meanings based on where they were placed in the word or sentence.

I never became very proficient with grade-2 braille, but I have a lot of respect for those who did, like Denise. Grade-1 braille has served me well with my needs, and just the continued advancement of technology has allowed me a variety of methods for labeling and identifying items. I think braille literacy is a necessity for children with significant sight loss. For those learning the English language, sentence structure, subjects, predicates, nouns, verbs, and punctuation are concepts that need to be visualized, so to speak. And for someone with sight loss, feeling the letters, words, punctuation, and how they relate to one another in a sentence is really the only way to understand the language non-visually.

CHAPTER 48:

A VOLUNTEER, A CLIENT & AN EMPLOYEE

My Department of Rehabilitation case had been transferred back to Geoff, as he was the counselor who worked with vocational clients. I was going to be hired as the first Assistive Technology Specialist for the Earle Baum Center of the Blind. Because I was unemployed when I started volunteering at Earle Baum, I was receiving Social Security Disability Insurance (SSDI). Geoff wanted me to obtain whatever technology could assist me in this new developing position. Geoff understood that any and all equipment purchases needed to be made while I was receiving Disability benefits; otherwise, I or EBC would be responsible for any needed equipment.

California State University Northridge (CSUN) had been hosting an annual conference in Southern California for the past several years. The conference had been growing each year and it was considered "the conference" for people with sight loss. I had mentioned this conference to the director , thinking it would be a great opportunity for EBC to learn about and meet the manufacturers who were developing technologies to assist people with sight loss.

The director thought it would be a good idea for him and me to attend the CSUN conference together; further, I learned that we would be sharing a hotel room for a couple of nights at the Embassy Suites. Being the new guy on the block, I went along with the plan, but I must say it was a little weird sharing a room with your boss. I remember the couch bed was where I slept, and I wasn't about to complain. After all, I wasn't the one financing the trip.

The director had brought his guide dog with him for the trip. I had chosen to leave Hale at home because traveling for me was already stressful enough, and having the added responsibility of traveling with a dog was not what I wanted to take on. The director's vision loss was from retinitis pigmentosa, which meant his visual field was limited; but there was what I understood were sweet spots, where his tunnel vision had pretty good acuity. Remember, I am a blind guy telling you this, so in my mind, having any amount of vision is better than none. This available vision allowed for successful navigation of the unfamiliar hotel environment, identifying such things as elevators, conference rooms, relieving areas for his guide dog, etc. Following the director and his guide dog around the Exhibit Hall proved to be successful, as we visited many vendor tables and learned about a variety of technologies and services available to assist people with sight loss.

Upon returning from the CSUN conference, things at EBC were starting to move rather quickly. I remember my first actual EBC student was Larry. As I had said previously, Larry was instrumental in transitioning Earle Baum's farm into his dream of being the Earle Baum Center of the Blind. Larry's background was law, and he had been a practicing attorney. It was very important to Earle, Larry, and other founders that the Center be "of the Blind" as opposed to "for the blind." The idea was that people who have lived with sight loss are in a unique position and can assist people dealing with sight loss.

The original EBC bylaws mandated that 51 percent of the Board should be visually impaired. Larry was one of these on the original Board of Directors who happened to be blind. One of his responsibilities on the EBC Board was to review the EBC Financial Report. This was provided to Larry as an electronic spreadsheet file. My teaching skills would be tested right away because this was like learning how to swim by jumping into the deep end of the pool. What I learned early on as an Assistive Technology Specialist was not only do you need to know how to use the screen-reader and magnification software, you also need to know the mainstream application. Students who you are training are interested in knowing how to complete a task on the computer, and the assistive software is actually secondary. For example, let's say the student wants to create a financial spreadsheet to track spending. The student's goal in this case is really to be taught how to use Excel for developing column and row headings, formatting cells, as well as creating formulas. The student appreciates that the AT software will speak or make the information easier to read, but the end goal is the actual spreadsheet.

Larry had been provided with an electronic document that had been exported from Quick Books into an Excel spreadsheet. It was a summary of what the EBC received in terms of donations/payments and what was paid out in terms of salary/bills. The first problem that I saw with this file was that the data did not export cleanly from Quick Books. The column headings with the category names were on different rows. This meant that the data would not read well as you moved through the spreadsheet. Jaws has the ability to be set to automatically read column headings as you move from column to column. However, in order for this automatic feature to be configured, all the column headings need to be on the same row. This meant before Larry could read through the expense report, he would need to be shown how to edit the spreadsheet's data.

I began the training with Larry by introducing the keyboard commands for navigating and editing content from within a spreadsheet. Mouse access for screen-reader users like Larry is not useful because the mouse is a visual tool requiring positioning of the pointer on the portion of the screen you want to work on. Fortunately, there are keyboard commands available for almost all of the things that can be performed by mouse point and click.

Larry was shown how to select data from one cell and paste it into a different cell. With cuing, Larry was able to get all the column-heading data into the same row. Once the column headings were in the same row, I was able to show him how to set Jaws to automatically read the column and row headings as he navigated the spreadsheet. This instruction took several sessions before Larry was comfortable with the entire process. The ongoing issue, though, was each time he was given an exported spreadsheet file, this process would need to be repeated to make it readable.

Larry was frustrated with the amount of work required to make these monthly spreadsheets accessible. He felt it was EBC's responsibility to provide the financial information in an accessible format. He claimed he discussed these concerns with the director, but it seemed to fall on deaf ears in terms of any supportive action being provided.

Larry requested that I explain the issue to the director. It put me in the middle and in an uncomfortable position. I was a new hire and did not want to rock the boat with the director, but Larry did not feel he was being understood. The exported files that were provided to Larry for his review as a Board member took significant effort for the data to be formatted so that it would read well with Jaws.

The director seemed to be of the opinion that Larry's computer skills were lacking and that was the main reason he had difficulty reading the financial data. I do not think the director was really interested in Larry having access to this detailed financial information.

He was the type of CEO who liked to make all of the decisions himself. It seemed like the fewer people who knew about donations or expenditures the better. I knew he did not encourage staff members to contact Board members directly, and any communication of this type needed to go through him.

It was awkward for me because I provided training services for several of the EBC Board members. In addition to Larry, there were Erik, Beryl, Barbara, and probably others. When we would meet, I tried to keep the conversation focused on the training at hand, rather than talking about any EBC business.

Early on with my employment at EBC, the Board of Directors had mandated that the director assign a staff person to provide technology services at a Board member's home because they were having computer issues. I, being the new and only technology guy on staff, was the chosen one for this job. I could tell that he was uncomfortable asking me to perform this task, but I was not really given a choice. I knew EBC was not formally being paid for my services, and it felt more like an EBC entitlement, since it was for a Board member.

A different Board member's husband would be assisting with this computer repair and driving me to the Board member's home with the computer issue. This assistant worked during the day, so it was expected that I would make myself available in the evening to help. It was a long evening at the Board member's home, as his computer required reformatting of the operating system and reinstallation of Jaws and other applications. Having sighted assistance with this project was invaluable because there was no assistive technology software available during the reformatting process. As it was, I did not get home until after midnight.

The majority of my training services were conducted on-site at the EBC, but there were various times when I would travel to a consumer's home or workplace in order to provide instruction. This meant I would be working in an unfamiliar environment, which was uneventful most of the time. There were a couple of situations, though, that I recall that were very frightening. One of the leading causes of sight loss is diabetic retinopathy, so those who are dealing with this disease need to regularly measure their blood-sugar levels. The level needs to stay within a range that is neither too high nor too low. When levels drift outside of the normal range, medication and/or dietary intervention is immediately needed. If the imbalance is severe, it can quickly become a life-threatening situation.

During one of these off-site training sessions, Hale and I had arrived at my consumer's (Mickie's) mobile home. Mickie was not only a client, but also a long-time volunteer at EBC. She had been volunteering at EBC since the Center opened, and I considered her my friend, as well as a student.

Hale and I followed Mickie to the room where the computer was located. It was just the three of us (Mickie, Hale, and I). I had no concept as to the home's layout. I had an understanding of where the front door was, as I could mentally retrace my steps from where I had entered, but that was the extent of the awareness that I had about this place that I was in.

My consumer and I had been working together for about an hour, when I noticed she had become very quiet and was no longer focused on the lesson. When I attempted to engage her in simple conversation, all I heard in response was unintelligible mumbling. I knew she was in trouble and assumed this sudden crisis was related to her blood-sugar level.

I reached out and grabbed her arm, looked her directly in the face, and with a distressed voice I asked her what I could do to help. At this point, she was no longer responding in any way, as far as I could tell.

My heart was racing and I was in full-on panic mode. There I was in a house that was completely unfamiliar to me, with a client who was in medical distress. In 2002 when this happened, cell phones were still pretty new, and not very accessible to people with sight loss, and I did not have one with me. I did not know where the landline phone was located in the house nor did I know where the kitchen was, where perhaps I could find juice or something else that could help.

I was not sure what I could do, but I knew I needed to do something, fast. I could retrace my steps back to the door, where I had entered, but then I would have to find a neighbor to help. It was a mobile home park with no sidewalks, and once I got outside, I would not know what direction to turn to find the closest neighbor. I began by looking around the room that I was in for the phone. Oh how I wished someone would have called my consumer's number right at that time, as the ring sound would have been my audible beacon, allowing me to find the phone and get help.

As I began exploring various surfaces around the room, looking for the phone, what I can only describe as divine intervention occurred.

My consumer's daughter-in-law happened to come over for an unplanned visit as this calamity was taking place. Her arrival on the scene probably saved my consumer's life. The daughter-in-law raced to the kitchen, found some juice, and gave it to my consumer, which slowly brought her back to consciousness.

This was a huge learning experience for me. From that point on, I made a point to always carry a cell phone with me when I was teaching, and to identify where the landline phone was located when I was at an unfamiliar place. Carrying a long white cane as a back-up, using my guide dog, and also asking about important medical conditions that could require assistance, is valuable information for me to have.

These preventive measures that I continued to follow from that point forward paid off several years later, when I was working with another consumer at her workplace.

This lady also had diabetes, and her workplace was in an industrial warehouse setting where several businesses had manufacturing space. There were the three of us, my consumer, my guide dog, Lucas, and me. During the training session, my consumer was becoming less and less responsive, and once again, I was seeing the signs of dangerous blood-sugar levels. This time, I had my iPhone with me and I let my consumer know I was calling 911. She was still communicating with me and could articulate words and said, "No," to my idea for getting help. This stopped me for a minute and I pleaded with her about what action she wanted done to help her.

When she was unable to articulate a complete sentence and the only word I continued to hear was "No," I knew it was time to make that 911 call. I grabbed my long cane and cell phone from my bag and stepped outside to summon assistance. I also used my cane to locate the doorway to the business next door and was able to get additional assistance while we waited for emergency services.

The paramedics arrived and were able to stabilize my consumer. They recommended that my consumer be transported to the Emergency Room (ER) for further evaluation, but my consumer refused to comply with this recommendation. She needed to sign a form declaring that she was refusing to be transported to the ER.

She requested that she and I continue with training together, acting like this entire emergency event was no big deal. I was in no condition to even consider continuing with our lesson. I wish I could have been transported out of the situation by the emergency services, but I was able to contact someone for a ride and eventually got out of there.

CHAPTER 49:
BLIND PARENTING

Amy and I had been trying to start a family for several years. We were working with specialists at this point. The dream of becoming parents was not coming true for us. The lack of success and cost of each procedure was becoming a concern and added much stress to our lives. Amy never gave up on her quest to become a mom. After about six years of pursuing almost every test and procedure available, we were elated when we found out that Amy was pregnant.

Megan Marie Harrington entered the world on August 15, 2003. Megan was one week past the due date, so it was decided that Amy's labor would be induced. Megan was 25 inches long and weighed in at nine pounds, nine ounces.

Amy was on maternity leave for the first three months, but after that, I would be fully in charge of child care on Fridays when Amy was scheduled to go back to work. I was excited and worried at the same time. It was going to be my responsibility to make sure all of Megan's needs were met. There was no manual for Parenting 101 and being a blind dad, as well, made it even more interesting.

Megan and I fell into a routine together. Knowing if and how to change diapers was pretty easy. Using your sense of smell and feeling how full the diaper was worked well. I remember the onesies that I typically dressed her in were simple and easy to work with.

Megan was really good about verbalizing when she was hungry. Feeding her was easier than I thought it might be. Initially, bottle feeding was no problem, and moving her to a solids diet required a little more consideration, but it was not a big deal. Not being able to see exactly where her mouth was in order to place the spoonful of food pretty much solved itself. I just needed to get the spoonful of food close to her mouth, and Megan would do the rest, placing her mouth and lips around the spoon. The biggest issue as far as Megan was concerned involved the speed that each spoonful of food appeared in front of her mouth. I could rarely keep up with her demand. Hale loved Megan's feeding time, as well, because he was really good about positioning himself right under the highchair in order to catch whatever might fall from Megan's tray. Having the dog there helped a lot with cleanup, as well.

Walks were daily occurrences and an activity that the three of us (Megan, Hale, and I) looked forward to each day. Megan was strapped into a baby backpack, and I found the best method for getting her in and out of it was to place the empty backpack on the counter, lift and strap Megan into it, and then I could place the backpack straps over my arms and fasten the waist belt. I always made sure to have Hale harnessed up, ready to go, prior to getting Megan in the backpack.

Ted, as I called him, was Megan's stuffed animal from early on in her life, and he, without fail, was part of any walk that we took. Megan was on my back, and there were a few occasions when Ted or the hat I had placed on her head were not present when we returned from our walk. I am guessing Megan had decided it would be a good idea to toss these objects at some point during the walk. It seemed like when this would happen, Amy would get home from work, and even though our walk had been several hours previously, we would drive the route that we had walked, and I do not remember a time when we did not find Ted or the strayed hat during this rescue mission.

My guide dog, Hale, had turned 12 years old a couple of months before Megan was born. He was such a loyal dedicated dog who continued to guide me and now Megan on walks around the neighborhood. Even though his hearing and hips were starting to fail him, he always led us safely on our walks; it was really difficult, but I knew the time had come for Hale to retire, as one of his back hips was starting to drag during our walks. If any dog had earned his retirement, it was Hale. It was time for him to relax and not have to worry about leading Megan and me around anymore.

Because of having a newborn baby at home, I qualified for home training with my next guide dog. This is a customized opportunity reserved for students with special circumstances.

The week of Thanksgiving 2003 I was introduced to Charlie, my third guide dog. I remember we celebrated that holiday at Grandma's cabin, which was in the Sierra Nevada Mountains just outside of the town of Arnold. I have fond memories of being there with our new baby daughter, Megan, my retired guide dog, Hale, and in training with my new guide dog, Charlie. When you are in training with a guide dog, you are usually not allowed to take your dog away from the campus without the supervision of an instructor. I had been given permission to take Charlie out of town to the mountains, but I was asked not to work him during that time, as we had not trained together for very long at that point.

I graduated with Charlie in November of 2003, and even though I had not participated in traditional campus-based training with the other students, I was asked to attend the graduation ceremony with class CA640D. This was always a great opportunity to thank everyone who made it possible for people with sight loss to obtain a guide dog. There were the generous donors, the instructors, the support staff, including Charlie's puppy-raiser, Jessica Knox, who was from Scottsdale, Arizona.

Early on before Megan was walking, our routes involved either a short loop, medium loop, or long loop. The loops were one mile up to perhaps two-and-a-half miles in distance. I did not always know what she was doing in the backpack. Sometimes she would fall asleep; other times I would hear her giggling or making different noises, and when we would encounter other barking dogs, as we passed their yards, I remember chuckling, as I heard Megan bark back at the barking dogs.

I remember one time when we were leaving the garage for one of our walking adventures. I regularly used a remote control to open/close the garage door. When returning home, simply pressing the button on the remote provided me with a reassuring audio cue as the garage door opened. On this particular occasion, unknown to me, the garage door had stopped after only opening three-fourths of the way. As Charlie led me out of the garage with Megan on my back, my forehead smashed into the partially open garage door, forcing me to fall backwards on my back, which is where Megan was. I was a little bit stunned from the whiplash, but even more concerned about Megan's well-being. I was a bit traumatized from the experience, but Megan was fine. She did not even cry. I think she thought this falling-over-backwards thing was really fun.

When Megan was a bit older and had begun walking, the neighborhood park became a favorite destination. When we would arrive, she would help me find a bench, so we could attach Charlie to it. She would play on the equipment, and when it was time to go, she was so helpful in cuing me about where we had left Charlie.

Another favorite destination was Mom's workplace. For a couple of years, when Megan was a toddler, Amy was fortunate to work at a facility that was only a half mile from our home. The route to get there did involve Charlie, Megan, and I crossing two major intersections. Fortunately, these intersections did have audible signals, meaning after the pedestrian button was pressed, you would get a *tweet tweet* (for an east/west crossing) or a *cuckoo cuckoo* noise (for a north/south crossing), cuing me that the pedestrian light was green. I still needed to rely on my Orientation and Mobility training to identify when my parallel traffic surge had started, but having the audible signals helped to reinforce that the pedestrian crossing was green.

Amy often would be able to come home during her lunch break, but Megan, Charlie, and I would occasionally walk to her workplace for a visit. Megan would get so excited when her mom would greet us in the waiting room of the rehabilitation unit. Mom and daughter would often go together for a quick visit with coworkers and patients. Charlie and I would wait for Megan to complete her tour of Mom's work.

I am sure we were quite a sight - - harness in my hand, a guide dog leading the way, and a baby on my back. Anytime you travel in public with a guide dog, it makes you the center of attention, whether you want to be or not. Statistically, approximately only around 5 percent of people with sight loss will use a guide dog as a mobility aid, so to actually see a working team in public is not very common.

It would always make me smile when we were leaving a restaurant, and hear the surprised comments from other diners when my guide dog would appear from under the table. They were unaware of the dog's presence until then, which is a testament to the dog's temperament and training. I remember dining in a café, with Hale under the table, when I accidentally dropped my napkin and it ended up falling on him. Now most dogs would be interested in sniffing and possibly eating this food-scented object that landed on them, but not big bad Hale. He was startled by the unexpected object and let out what I can only describe as a high-pitched scream. Let's just say that everyone now knew that there was a dog under the table.

CHAPTER 50:
GUIDE DOG ACCESS ISSUES & TEAM BUNGEE

Over time, I have had a few experiences where the business that I entered was not welcoming to my guide dog. Sometimes this "discrimination" is very passive, and other times it was more blatant. The passive experiences were more difficult to call people out on and might involve being led to a table in the back of the restaurant or being led to a table in a different room from other diners. Other times, it was very direct, and I was told that no dogs are allowed. It was surprising to me that some of the establishments were refusing me access with my dog.

I remember stopping at a McDonald's in the Central Valley of California on our way up to Grandma's cabin. I was standing in line waiting to order, when someone from behind the counter said, "No dogs allowed."

I answered back, letting whoever had made the statement know that this was a guide dog. I do not think the term *guide dog* meant anything to the employee, and the next thing I knew, he was standing in front of me pointing his finger into my chest, telling me to get my dog out of the restaurant. I repeated the fact that this is a guide dog and we have the right to be here. At this point, the other customers in line began speaking up to support us, and I appreciated the backing. Our initial plan was to get to-go food, and eat as we continued our drive. However, when they assumed it would be a "to-go order," I let them know that we would be eating here at the restaurant with my dog.

I did follow up with a letter to the McDonald's corporate office and received a very apologetic response regarding the treatment that I had received with my guide dog. In these situations, I try and take the diplomatic approach. I want to educate the public about the access laws concerning guide dogs. Yelling and making a scene, in my mind, does not send a positive message about guide dogs or blindness. Now if they had insisted that I leave the restaurant because of my dog, I would not have left and would have insisted that they call the police.

I remember another time when camping with our friends, Larry and Chris, at a state park. When checking into our campsite, the ranger insisted that I pay a fee for my dog. I tried explaining the law concerning guide dogs, but she was adamant that I was to pay. For me, it was not about the $1 or $2 dollar fee, but rather the principle. I did not want to make a scene in front of my friends and simply asked the ranger to check with her supervisor. I was pleased when around an hour later the ranger had come to our campsite, giving us a refund of the fee that I had paid for my guide dog.

And then there was the time I was working Hale on the beach at another state park, walking with my brother-in-law Paul, when a ranger drove up in her truck to intercept us. This ranger had been told that there was a dog on the beach. Apparently, this state park did not allow dogs on the beach. I let the ranger know that this was my guide dog. I think the ranger understood what that meant, but the next statement out of her mouth was "The people up there"—I think probably gesturing toward the parking lot—"do not know that." So it seems to me then that the issue is actually with those people "up there," as I gestured toward what I thought was the parking lot, and not with me and my guide dog walking along the beach.

When I began losing my vision and competitive team sports were no longer an option for me to participate in, I began running with my dad, neighbors, and other family members on the country roads around our home in the Santa Cruz Mountains. Throughout high school and during my college years, I was able to see well enough to jog, particularly on those roads that I was familiar with and had grown up traveling on throughout my childhood. My dad and I even signed up for several organized 10k run events.

Probably one of my family's favorite events was the annual Wharf to Wharf run that was held in July each year. The run started at the Santa Cruz Wharf and followed the coast line, ending at the Capitola Wharf. All along the route, there were people cheering you on, there were bands playing at different locations along the route, and the overall party atmosphere made you forget that you were even running. Following the run each year, my parents would have a big barbecue at their home.

When I graduated from San Jose State, I figured my running days were over because I could no longer see. The annual Wharf to Wharf run was coming up again and several of my family members were once again signing up to participate.

My brother-in-law, Paul, came up with the concept of Team Bungee. Paul attached one end of a bungee cord to a belt loop on the back of his shorts, and I held onto the other end of the bungee cord. I do not remember practicing too much with this setup, but on the day of the Wharf to Wharf, we put this idea into practice. It worked really well. The bungee cord kept us far enough apart so our feet did not ever get tangled, and there was just enough tension in the cord so that I could feel when Paul changed direction or speed. Fellow runners did not always know that I was blind, and many thought that Paul had lost some type of bet with me, and his payment meant that he would have to pull me all the way to the finish line.

CHAPTER 51:

MY YOUNG DAUGHTER'S UNEXPECTED FALL INTO THE SWIMMING POOL

Our house had an in-ground swimming pool in the backyard. For safety reasons, my dad had assisted us in installing a fencing system around the pool prior to Megan's birth. We had made it clear to Megan that she was not to go into the fencing area without permission. We also did not ever let Megan go out back unsupervised at her young age.

I remember an incident when I was working inside the fenced area, performing some type of maintenance with the pool. Megan, who was probably around two years old, asked if she could come into the fenced area just like she was supposed to. I was already inside the pool area, close to the gate where you enter/exit, so I had given her permission to enter the area where I was. I remember hearing the pool gate swing open, and a couple of seconds later, I heard the gate latch click shut. At that same time, I heard the alarming sound of a splash noise. I immediately knew Megan had fallen into the swimming pool just a few feet off to my left. In just a matter of a second, I was transformed into full panic mode, and knew I needed to act fast. Megan was in the swimming pool without a life jacket and not knowing how to swim. During the time of hearing the pool gate close, immediately followed by the sound of a splash, created an adrenaline rush throughout my body like I had never experienced before. I immediately jumped into the pool, trying to land right next to where I had heard the splash noise. Fortunately, my jump aim into the pool had been a good one.

I was completely freaked out, but so relieved when my extended flailing arms and hands made contact with Megan's body as soon as I hit the water. Megan once again did not seem to be fazed by her unexpected fall into the swimming pool, and just like the whiplash-backpack incident, when I ran into the half-opened garage door, she was fine. Dad, on the other hand, needed significant time to calm down.

I granted extra TV time that particular afternoon following the swimming pool experience. Amy and I tried to limit the amount of time each day spent watching TV.

Megan loved her TV time, and when she was older, claimed that she figured out how to turn down the volume and turn on the captioning feature. There could be some truth to this confession of Megan's because I know her grandpa, Del, would turn on this feature when he was visiting us, as Grandpa had trouble hearing the TV. I suppose she could have learned the procedure from watching her grandpa. So I guess there were times when I thought TV watching time was over, but Megan was apparently taking advantage of her dad's blindness. Megan said she could turn on the TV without me knowing and be able to watch/read the screen. I told myself that at least the reading part made the extra sneaky TV watching time an educational experience.

CHAPTER 52:
THE MT. WHITNEY CLIMB

My uncle John, my cousin Mike, my brother Mike, and several friends of my cousin, including the late Mark Davis, planned a back-packing trip to Mt. Whitney, which has an elevation of 14,505 feet. I was encouraged to be part of this quest to the highest point on the continental United States. My uncle John, in an attempt to build my confidence, said he would be the best human guide that I had ever had. Now my uncle John is a stand-up comedian who would say anything for a laugh. He had limited training with human guide technique. If you have heard the expression, "the blind leading the blind", that was my Uncle John and I on Mt. Whitney. But for some reason I was intrigued by the idea and agreed to go on this adventure.

Each person was expected to train on their own since none of us lived near each other. To train for this mountain climb, I used Megan's weight as my simulated backpack. I used Charlie as my canine leader, as we hiked various trails in the Santa Rosa area, attempting to prepare my body for this trek up Mt Whitney. Santa Rosa has primarily flat terrain, so finding hilly trails to hike meant you needed to travel outside of town for more challenging training opportunities.

Initially, as I began my workout regimen for this climb up Mt. Whitney, my plan was to have Charlie be my primary leader to follow during the trek. When I had shared this thought with my cousin and brother, they did not think that was the best plan of action. They did not think using Charlie as a guide on the type of terrain that we would be required to cover would be safe for either of us.

I knew nothing about this Mt. Whitney trail, and both my brother and cousin had previous experience, so I was easily persuaded to follow their better judgment. That was the first indication that this hike was going to be way more challenging than I had expected. I continued to use Megan and Charlie as my training partners up until we actually left for the climb.

Just getting to base camp where the trek would begin was a 500-mile drive from Santa Rosa. The route took us across California, through the high Sierra Mountains via Yosemite National Park, to the eastern side of the mountain range, near the town of Lone Pine, locating Whitney Portal, where we literally reached the end of the road at the campground.

It is an 11-mile walk to the very top, along what is considered a trail. The starting elevation is 8,375 feet. Our group plan was to make our way to High Camp that first day, where we would spend the night. High Camp was a six-mile trek from the Whitney Portal, at 12,000 feet, so that would be a significant elevation gain in one day.

Initially, the standard human guide technique worked well, as I walked next to my brother, grasping his left arm just above the elbow. The first couple of miles were pretty easy to negotiate on what I considered to be a real path that we were able to follow. Then things began to change. The trail had narrowed to single track, the ground under our feet became uneven, and walking next to my brother was no longer possible. Now I was walking directly behind him, touching the middle of his backpack, which kept me pretty much lined-up on the single track trail.

Walking that close to someone for many miles becomes very tiring. Your feet can easily get tangled up, creating opportunities for tripping and loosing your line of travel.

Then we encountered the first of many stream crossings. Sometimes I would need to follow my brother, using a fallen tree to get across the rushing water; whereas, other times I would need to follow my brother's footsteps, as he moved from rock to rock across the stream.

My cousin, acting like Superman, would stand in the middle of the freezing water providing assistance as I searched for stable footing. The footholds that I would find were not consistent in size or shape, so each step was somewhat of a surprise. There was no time to relax during these maneuvers, as you were always on the defensive, trying to prevent yourself from falling.

There was definitely a time or two when my feet did get soaked, but for the number of stream crossings that we did, our success rate was pretty darn good, thanks to the team.

As we continued to climb this mountain, the conditions became more challenging for me. In my mind, there was no longer a trail to follow. We were in what I would describe as a continuous boulder field that needed to be negotiated. Initially, the rocks that we passed over were ankle-high tripping hazards, but now there were boulders as high as your waist and shoulders that we needed to crawl over and slip around, while we continued to move upward with backpacks on our back. This was the highest I had ever been above sea level, and I was depleted of oxygen, as well, due to the elevation.

As we were nearing high camp, I had reached the exhaustion point. There was a fellow hiker resting on one of these boulders that we were approaching. The hiker realized I was blind and he began clapping for me, and when I reached the boulder that he was sitting on, the hiker stood up and gave me a standing ovation. That outward expression of congratulations by a stranger while I was climbing Mt. Whitney gave me the inspiration to push the final distance to High Camp.

When arriving at High Camp, I was completely spent of energy, and I was not real useful when it came to setting up camp. Fortunately, my brother and cousin were efficient with establishing our camp and getting the tents set up. Honestly, not a minute after the tents went up, an afternoon hail storm pounded the camp, but we were all protected as we lay in our tents.

Someone in our group actually packed in a case of beer to share. Drinking that beer, along with munching on a burrito, food and drink had never tasted so good.

That night in the tent at High Camp trying to sleep was difficult. My exhausted physical state, adjusting to the thin air, and lying on the ground did not equal a restful night for me. As I pondered the idea of moving onto the summit, doubt had entered my mind. I knew the very top was still five miles further up. I also knew that getting to the top would only be halfway, and there would still be 11 miles of hiking down to complete this journey.

I knew how much it had taken out of me to get this far, and to press my luck any further did not feel right to me. My brother and cousin were very supportive of my decision and we hiked down the mountain together.

Congratulations to my uncle John and everyone else in our group for making it to the summit of Mt. Whitney on this trip. I certainly have regrets about not reaching the summit, but I am proud of how far I did get with my team of support.

Now that I have had that experience with hiking Mt. Whitney to High Camp and back, I would consider making a second attempt, knowing firsthand how challenging it really is.

CHAPTER 53:

BALANCING THE NEEDS OF AN EXPANDING STAFF WITH THE CONSUMER'S NEEDS FOR SPACE

Throughout my 20-plus years working at EBC, there always seemed to be a level of tension between the clients and the CEO; there were 3 different people that held that position during my employment.

The clients, who were people with sight loss, either had previously or were currently receiving services to assist them with adjusting to their sight loss. Some of these clients had an entitlement mentality, and in their mind, services at the EBC should be free to them, because of their sight loss—that is, up until the passing of the Workforce Innovation and Opportunity Act in 2014, which changed the federal government's vocational rehabilitation funding priorities for every state and was no longer funding the goal of the Home Maker.

The term *Home Maker* refers to an individual who has experienced sight loss, and their goal is to learn the skills necessary to maintain their independence. Often Home Makers are people in their seventies, eighties, or nineties, and they are not interested in competitive employment at this stage of their life. Instead, they want to learn how to manage all of their activities of daily living, as their vision is diminishing.

The majority of clients receiving services from EBC were pursuing a Home Maker goal. The average age of a client at EBC was around 78 years of age. I often tell people if you live long enough there is a high probability of developing Age-Related Macular Degeneration (AMD) or some other eye condition. These individuals were not looking for a job, but rather wanting to learn skills and obtain the technology that was going to allow them to maintain their independence. The goal for these people experiencing sight loss in their retirement years was to continue living in their homes, rather than being placed in some sort of an assistive-living situation simply based on diminishing visual acuity.

The legislation in the Workforce Innovation and Opportunity Act meant the majority of EBC clients would no longer qualify for Department of Rehabilitation services under the Home Maker designation. This meant a significant funding loss to EBC since this target population would no longer be able to receive financial assistance for the services that they needed to maintain their independence.

EBC is always on the search for grant dollars to offset the existing budget deficit in terms of revenue versus expenses. Now without the Home Maker revenue, the deficit would only increase.

EBC introduced a more formal Private Pay process, where clients requesting services would be asked to pay out of pocket. This was not received favorably by many of the existing or previous clients, as they were being asked to pay for services that had previously been covered by a government agency.

Educating the EBC clients and family members about the new focus on Private Pay reimbursement was and continues to be an ongoing effort. Trying to calculate a fair rate for EBC services was also a challenge. EBC receives different reimbursement rates depending on the funding source.

EBC's second CEO came up with a figure of $150 per hour for EBC services, which is a more realistic dollar amount that reflects what it actually costs EBC to provide an hour of service. The $150 hourly rate was initially used as the Private Pay rate, but this high rate scared off many of the Private Pay clients. Many of the clients EBC serves are on fixed low incomes, and the $150 hourly rate was overwhelming for them to comprehend.

In all the years that I worked at EBC, no one was turned away from receiving services based on ability to pay. A person's training needs could be prioritized, as well as utilizing group classes when possible and placing them on a waiting or on-call list.

Eventually, the Private Pay hourly rate was modified to $50. It was also emphasized that clients did not need to pay their bill in full each month, but rather pay what they can and spread it out over as many months as necessary. This more manageable hourly rate did prove to be more successful in terms of getting the majority of clients to pay something toward the services they were receiving. It was true that the $50 rate did not come close to covering the actual EBC costs, but that is the reality for many nonprofit agencies.

For the first seven years or so, the EBC Administration offices were located in Earle Baum's original farmhouse, with its two bedrooms, a bathroom, living room, kitchen, and sun porch. The directors office was in the back bedroom and the Office Manager's office was in the front bedroom. I remember Orientation and Mobility (O&M) instructors, along with other Vision Rehabilitation staff members, utilized the living-room space for their workstations.

I was fortunate and had a semi-private office located in Classroom 2, which was the Tech Center and where my training sessions occurred. Denise also had a private office space in the Rehab House, where she did the majority of her teaching.

From day one, the demand for technology services was immediate and ongoing. I soon had a day of students scheduled, then two days, and within the first year or two, my entire week was scheduled with technology clients. Typically, a client learning technology would be scheduled for a two-hour session during the week. My calendar was running out of open time to schedule clients, so it was time to recruit additional tech staff.

In 2003, Jennifer joined EBC's Technology Department, and as a result, I became a manager. She was also a client of Geoff's through the Department of Rehabilitation and came to EBC highly recommended. Jennifer had sight loss like me and was a user of assistive technology, including braille. I was excited and relieved to have Jennifer as another instructor. Not only did she immediately help with the backlog of clients needing training, she also was another colleague from whom I could seek advice from, as the EBC Tech Department continued its development and growth.

Later in 2003, Barb joined the Tech staff as a contract employee, as well. I had been working with Barb since 2002, when she was referred to EBC as a Department of Rehabilitation client also through Geoff. Barb's vocational goal was to be an Assistive Technology Specialist. Barb was another person who was blind and a user of the technology that she would be teaching. Geoff supported Barb by providing training hours to learn the technology, but also developing her teaching skills in order to become an instructor for EBC. This was a win win for everyone involved. Barb received on-the-job training, and EBC received reimbursement for assisting her to achieve her vocational goal.

The majority of clients who received technology services at EBC actually had some degree of functional vision. This meant that these clients could most likely benefit from visual enhancement strategies, i.e., magnification, color and contrast changes, and font style and size. Currently, EBC had three blind instructors who could not experience the benefit from these types of accommodations. EBC was also experiencing more of a demand to provide training off-campus at a client's home or workplace. And simply having someone in the department with vision to help troubleshoot issues and provide more visual-based instruction became another priority.

Jacques joined the EBC Technology Department in 2005 and gave EBC the opportunity to offer even more technology services, including a focus on low-vision options.

The number of EBC staff was steadily increasing. But EBC had run out of office space in Earle's original farmhouse.

In 2006, a brand-new office building was constructed, which included a small reception area, eight separate offices, and a staff kitchen. The additional office space was divided up into specific departments. There was originally an Administration Department for the Office Manager and Office Assistant, a Conference Room, a Technology Department, an Orientation and Mobility Department, a CEO Office, a Development/Public Relations Office, a Technology Management Office, and a Copy/Fax Room.

This created much more needed building space on the EBC campus. Now each staff member had an actual office space to work from, and Earle's farmhouse was transformed into the EBC Visitor Center. This gave clients waiting for class, family members, and other visitors a place to hang out.

Some of the actions taken when Earle's farmhouse was converted from Administrative Office space to the EBC Visitor Center did not sit well with those clients/visitors/volunteers who were now occupying this new space. The gas supply to the oven and stove, as a rule, was turned off in the Visitor Center. A locked cover was placed over the thermostat. I do not recall being told the reason for these modifications, and I would regularly hear displeasure expressed regarding these types of decisions. These adult clients felt like they were being babysat, and they felt as if they could not be trusted to operate the stove or thermostat.

There always seemed to be a power struggle concerning the use of Visitor Center space. The clients/volunteers who regularly occupied the Visitor Center seemed to want control over the entire house space. The management staff, on the other hand, had their own priorities regarding the space, which often created a conflict.

From my observations, the majority of those who occupied the Visitor Center were there to socialize before or after a scheduled class that they had. I could always count on a hot cup of coffee being available no matter when I would show up at the Visitor Center. Most of the people who hung out at the Visitor Center identified themselves as EBC Volunteers. I did not always know what task was being performed in behalf of EBC, but with the title of "EBC Volunteer," certain entitlements seemed to be expected.

The volunteers seemed to want a say in EBC personnel and hiring decisions. They felt left out when employees' hours were reduced or a new hire was made without their knowledge. The volunteers felt like the communication from EBC management was lacking when it came to Center happenings. They would suggest activities or classes and get upset if their ideas were not implemented. The volunteers would come up with ideas, and it seemed like the expectation was that EBC staff was to develop a program around the idea that was suggested. Volunteers would also get frustrated saying there were not enough volunteer tasks for them and that they expected EBC staff to come up with tasks for them to complete.

Part of the responsibility of offering to be a volunteer is to share with the organization what your strengths and interests are, letting the organization know what you can do to help. Some volunteers would request complementary training in order to complete the task that they agreed to perform. Some volunteers felt this type of training support should apply to their home equipment, as well, since they were emailing and calling people on behalf of EBC sometimes outside of normal business hours.

Being that the EBC was located in a rural setting more than a mile away from any commercial businesses, meant there was no easy way, for people who did not drive, to travel to a store/restaurant.

Even if someone wanted to walk from EBC, it was an unsafe activity with no sidewalks or shoulder of the road to follow. I have jokingly called the Earle Baum Center, the EBC Island. It is beautiful, but quite remote if you are on foot.

Client's and staff who are unable to drive were encouraged to bring their own snacks/lunch and use the Center's refrigerator and/or microwave. The idea of having a vending machine was brought up many times, but the director never fully embraced this idea. He felt like there was not enough foot traffic to support a vending machine.

I took it upon myself to research and schedule a visit from a vending machine supplier. The supplier came out to meet with me at the EBC. He asked questions about the number of clients that we served and felt like the location could work for the installation of a vending machine. The vendor would be completely responsible for the machine and stocking it. EBC's commitment would be to provide a location along with electrical power. I connected the vendor company with the EBC Director, but no formal agreement was ever made.

I took it upon myself to search for and find a vending machine that could work at EBC. I eventually found a used old-fashion style vending machine for sale in Santa Rosa. It was the kind of machine that you place the coins in the slot of the item that you wanted and you would spin the knob to get the item to drop out. Amy and I borrowed a truck, went to see the machine and ended up personally purchasing it. We delivered it to EBC. In order to get the machine into the EBC Visitor Center, the exterior door needed to be removed.

Amy provided all of the initial set-up along with the ongoing support, clearing the machine of coin jams, purchasing product and stocking the snacks/drinks. Braille labels were created to assist with identifying each item. A digital recorder was magnetically attached to the machine with an audible message that could be activated to list the items available.

The machine was managed by Amy and me for approximately 10 years. The second CEO had legal concerns about the income generated from the products sold. The vending machine at best was a break even proposition, and if you factored in our time for shopping, stocking and repairing, it cost more to operate then it actually made. My goal in obtaining this machine was never to make money, but rather provide clients, staff, family and friends the option to have a snack or drink.

I officially donated the vending machine to EBC in 2016. The dollar change maker, which was a separate piece that attached to the vending machine giving you 4 quarters for a dollar began to malfunction. Finding replacement parts for this older technology was unsuccessful. EBC ended up removing the machine and giving it away.

CHAPTER 54:

THE EBC CAMPUS RESPONSIBILITIES INVOLVE MORE THAN SERVING PEOPLE WITH SIGHT LOSS

The Earle Baum Center was located outside of Santa Rosa on the western border of town approximately a mile west of the city limits. The campus was situated on 17 acres in a beautiful setting. Ray, who was an acquaintance of the original director when they were both part of a kayaking group, became a friend of the EBC early on. Ray heard the plea for help and volunteered to donate his time to assisting EBC with managing the property.

Besides the Center buildings and courtyard, the expansive property consists of walking pathways, vernal pools, orchards, gardens, a picnic area, and a completely fenced-in play yard for the working dogs.

Officially, Earle Baum had left his farm to The Redwood Lions Memorial Foundation; the Foundation rented out the farm to the Earle Baum Center, which was a 501c nonprofit organization. The $1 annual lease was truly a bargain.

Developing the EBC and providing the training and social opportunities for people with sight loss to get the necessary assistance is an invaluable community resource. Having the additional responsibility of managing the 17-acre property where the center resides requires significant resources of money and time that is not directly related to the mission.

This is where Ray's willingness to volunteer for EBC is one of those donations that is so valuable to an organization. Ray actually became an employee for EBC after several years of volunteering, and he is still working for the organization as far as I know.

I know that initially two large dumpsters were used simply to collect debris that had been abandoned all over the property. I know that Ray recruited friends of his (who were also volunteers) to assist with the installation of an irrigation system to help with watering the property.

Just keeping up with the mowing needs on the property was a full-time job. Ray created and maintained a trail system at EBC, which encouraged clients and family members to walk along the property. It was a safe way for people experiencing sight loss to get out and use the cane skills that they were learning or get their guide dog out on a walk. There was a shorter accessible guide rope trail and a much longer trail that covered the entire perimeter of the property.

Groups of clients would have regularly scheduled walk times, and I was a consistent daily walker of the long trail, with my guide dog leading the way. Hale, Charlie, and Lucas were my canine guides who became very familiar with these trails.

EBC has partnered with the Laguna Foundation, which is a nonprofit organization working to preserve, protect, and restore the wetlands of Santa Rosa. The two organizations have secured cooperative grant funding that has been mutually beneficial. EBC received financial assistance to help with managing the property, and the Laguna Foundation has access to Earl's farm land to preserve and rehabilitate the property back to its original natural state, which is right in line with their mission.

Another amazing and special use of the EBC property was the installation of a labyrinth. My coworker, Patricia, who had started at EBC around the same time as I, had worked as a Vision Rehabilitation educator. Like many EBC staff, Patricia wore multiple hats in terms of job duties. Her primary role was to lead classes in the community focused on available resources to assist people with sight loss. The classes that Patricia facilitated were provided in four different counties. In addition, Patricia developed and offered art/craft activities, as well as occasional field trips to museums, state/county parks, the beach, etc.

Because of Patricia's efforts reaching out to people with sight loss, she would regularly receive financial donations in behalf of the Earle Baum Center.

One of these anonymous donors had left Patricia a significant amount of money. This donation inspired and gave Patricia the opportunity to have a labyrinth constructed.

EBC, with its available land, provided the location for the labyrinth. Patricia would not only be responsible for directing the funding for the project, she was also the lead in the labyrinth's design. Traditionally, labyrinths are visual in nature, and those with sight loss cannot fully appreciate their beauty or navigate them independently. Patricia wanted the labyrinth at EBC to be accessible, which meant having a 39-inch-wide smooth concrete surface with a brick curb on each side of the path, suitable for cane users, guide dogs, two people walking as human guides, and most walkers and wheelchairs. Details concerning the EBC Labyrinth can be found on the World-Wide Labyrinth Locator website (https://labyrinthlocator.com).

Kati joined the EBC staff in 2014. Her extensive employment experience with startup companies, as well as large corporations, and her work ethic and compassion were immediately apparent. Kati was originally hired to replace the retiring EBC Office Manager, but her role became much bigger. Her current title is Director of Operations for EBC, where she oversees the core services, which include Assistive Technology, Orientation and Mobility, Independent Living Skills, and many recreational programs. In addition to her formal title, Kati has fostered a beneficial relationship with the Boy Scouts of America, and has overseen the completion of many Eagle Scout projects at the Center. This has resulted in major improvements, including a standalone staircase for teaching safe travel, removing dangerous tree roots, construction of a garden shed and several new outdoor tables.

CHAPTER 55: WHO IS THIS GUIDE DOG?

A true and funny story did occur between me, my guide dog, Charlie, my coworker, Jennifer, and her guide dog, Jam. We would regularly plan playtime for our working dogs, and EBC had dedicated a large area of land for a dog play yard. The play yard was enclosed with fencing, so the dogs could run around off-leash in a safe controlled environment. Half of the yard had a dirt surface and the other half of the yard had a grass surface. There was fencing down the middle of the two yards with a gate that could be opened or closed, allowing the dogs to have full access to both yards, or it could be closed off, to separate the yards from one another.

On this particular day, both Jennifer and I were guided up to the play yard by our guide dogs. We removed their harnesses and leashes, which let the dogs know that formal work time was over for now, and it was time to play. The dogs always enjoyed this opportunity to be free and run around independently.

After around 15 or 20 minutes, Jennifer needed to leave for an upcoming appointment that she had. She located her dog's harness and leash, reattaching the equipment to the dog. Jennifer was then guided back to her office.

I left the play yard a minute or so later, gathering up my harness and leash, and placing it on the remaining dog. I was guided back to my office at EBC. A paratransit bus that I had scheduled previously came to pick me up and take me home. Occasionally, I would have paratransit drop me off at the grocery store on my way home, which was only a couple of blocks from my house. This gave me an opportunity to pick up anything that might be needed.

The dog and I were dropped off in front of Raley's, and after shopping, we walked home. I try to be consistent when it comes to verbal commands and hand gestures for my guide dog. Even though we had walked this particular route many times together, on this occasion, it felt like the dog was a bit uncertain. It really got weird for me once we had made the crossing from the shopping center into my neighborhood. For whatever reason, the dog would not turn into my driveway when we were walking down the street. That was really strange because normally the dog gets very motivated when he sees home, knowing this is the place where dinner will be served shortly.

After a bit of a struggle to get the dog to turn right into my driveway, I entered my home through the garage entrance.

Amy was in the kitchen, which was right across from the garage door that I had just come through. There was a moment of silence when we entered, which I realized later was due to the unfamiliar four-legged canine partner that was with me. Amy let me know that the dog I had with me was not Charlie.

I had no idea that Jennifer's dog, Jam, and my guide dog had been switched when we left the play yard, but now all the indecisiveness we were experiencing together on the walk home made sense.

When I called my coworker, Jennifer, and asked her how Charlie was doing, she had no idea what I was talking about. I laughingly said that her dog, supposedly lying on the floor under her desk, was here. When I told her how our dogs had been accidentally switched when we left the play yard, Jennifer could not believe that had actually happened. This would have been a perfect story for some TV show, but it was not rehearsed or planned; it just happened. I told Jennifer that I was the last one in the play yard and there was only one dog left, so that is the one I used.

CHAPTER 56:
MY CANINE ALUMNI

I graduated with my current guide dog, Lucas, in December of 2011, with class # CA732. Lucas was raised by the Wing Family in Rocklin, California. This was the final class of visually impaired students that occupied the original San Rafael Campus dormitory before it was completely demolished, relocated, and reconstructed.

The original dormitory housed two students per room with a total of 12 rooms. Between the California and Oregon campuses an average of 350 students graduate each year. The new rebuilt dormitory has 20 single-occupancy rooms (plus two instructor rooms) to better accommodate future students, whose average age is 50.

Lucas, in true yellow Labrador Retriever style, is completely motivated by food. He never forgets to remind me when it is feeding time, and to my knowledge, has never missed a meal, unless there was a planned medical procedure that prevented him from eating.

For the first week of class #732, I had been partnered with a different guide dog. This dog's name was Vegas, and when it came to walking routes together, we did not always agree on pace. I wanted to move a little bit faster, and Vegas was happiest working at his current moderate pace. My instructor and I decided that changing to a different guide dog would be a better fit.

Lucas entered my life at the beginning of my second and final week of training in class #732. We literally and figuratively hit the ground running. Lucas had one speed, "fast." There were no more concerns about pace. Never again would I be complaining about guiding speed. Our accelerated formal training together was limited to a week in duration before graduating, but we traveled a lot of routes, and bonded quickly.

PRESSURE

My third guide dog, Charlie, was also a yellow Labrador Retriever, that also had a good appetite and had no trouble cleaning his bowl at meal time. Charlie's claim to fame was a sock fetish. In his mind, the dirtier they were, the better they were. Charlie was not too picky, though, and freshly laundered socks seem to go down just as easy as dirty ones. If the socks were not on your feet, then they were fair game for consumption, as far as Charlie was concerned.

One of the more memorable Charlie sock stories occurred when my mother-in-law, Molly had agreed to dog-sit for Charlie, when we took a vacation to Maui. Molly had put out a pair of socks she was planning to wear. She could not find her socks after we had left for the airport, but knowing Charlie's reputation for devouring socks, Molly had a pretty good idea where the socks had gone. Obviously, Charlie thought this was a special snack left just for him. Molly contacted Charlie's veterinarian for help, not wanting to alarm us about the socks. The doctor's office advised her to give Charlie a dose of hydrogen peroxide. That remedy did the trick and the socks came right back up.

Charlie was also known as the cuddler in the family. You would find him curled up with anyone or anything that was at ground level, whether it was his bed, the cat bed, a loose pillow, or just a conveniently placed human companion lying on the floor, Charlie would roll up in a ball, making himself right at home.

My second guide dog, Hale, was a coated (long-haired) German shepherd. Loyalty was his middle name. Hale was always at my side, following me from room to room. If we were stationary for a prolonged period, Hale would strategically place himself, lying against a wall, which would give him a full 360- degree view of anything that might be approaching us.

Hale was not a big-time eater when it came to his meals, and often when his routine was changed, he would not eat at all. Getting Hale to eat when we traveled was an ongoing issue. He had a very sensitive stomach, and if his diet was ever altered, i.e., providing him a bone or some other treat, then things could get really messy out the other end.

Because of his German shepherd breed and police dog image, people in the public were less likely to interact with him when we were out working together. Truth be told, though, Hale was a big, fluffy teddy bear that was afraid of his own shadow.

Hoyt, my first dog, was a Golden Retriever. He will always hold a special place in my heart, as he was the canine leader that showed me independent travel was possible again. Most of my guide dogs had a working life of 10+ years, but unfortunately, Hoyt's career as a guide dog was ended early. He had no trouble transitioning into his role of being a regular dog in my sister's family. He was a tennis-ball-chasing fanatic. My nephew's arms would tire out from throwing the ball before Hoyt was ready to stop retrieving it. Hoyt's life was cut short by illness, but he made up for it with the excessive fun that he always had with his family.

CHAPTER 57:
IN CLOSING

It has been 43 years since I first noticed my failing vision and the diagnosis of glaucoma. Then there was the 10-year medical battle to control the pressure and attempt to save my eyesight, and my journey into and living with blindness.

Writing this story has allowed me to look back and realize how fortunate I have been. I am not promoting blindness for anyone and would have definitely preferred to have been able to see during my entire lifetime. I consider myself lucky that I had pretty much normal vision for the first 13 years of my life, and my perception of the world is going to be based on my limited snapshot of seeing. I have had the opportunity to work with people who have varying degrees of visual acuity, from those who are still driving and reading, to those who need magnification or color enhancements, to those who cannot see at all. Then there are those who have been blind since birth and those who lost their sight later in life.

I have experienced vision and know what it means to see. People who have been blind from birth do not have a frame of reference to draw upon, so I would think they would have trouble fully understanding what it means to see. For me, losing my eyesight created a great deal of sadness in my life; perhaps if you never had vision to lose, because you were born blind, your emotional experience would be different from mine.

I have visual memories that I can recall that help me when relating to the visual society that we all live in. If someone references a color or a scene, I have a visual reference to draw upon.

Describing color to someone who has been blind from birth feels indescribable to me since I am drawing upon my visual memory. I cannot think of descriptive words that could fully describe color if you have no frame of reference to draw upon.

One question that I regularly am asked is about my dreams. How are my dreams presented to me? Are they visual in nature or do they present through other non-visual types of sensory input?

From those dreams that I do recall, I am aware that I am blind, but it is as though I am observing the dream through a camera or a third person. So I am watching myself act out the dream as a blind person. I can see the scene that I have been placed in, but the actual person in the dream is blind. So I might know, for example, from the camera or third person that someone with a knife is chasing me, but at the same time, I am aware that I am struggling to get away because I cannot see where I am going.

I think my dream experience is unique to me based on the fact that I could see throughout my childhood and that my brain has visual memories. I remember reading the book, *Crashing Through*, about Mike May who was blinded at age three from a chemical accident. In his forties, he underwent an experimental stem-cell surgery to restore his eyesight. The surgery corrected his eyes' ability to see, but his brain could not interpret the new visual information that it was receiving. There was no visual memory for his brain to reference to let him know what a particular image represented.

I hope this story has been interesting, entertaining and informative. My wish is that people with sight loss are given the same opportunities to succeed or fail as anyone else and that preexisting assumptions do not prevent someone from being given an opportunity.

Here are some photos I have added...

The first is a photo of me playing Little League Baseball.
And a picture of me recovering from one of many surgeries.

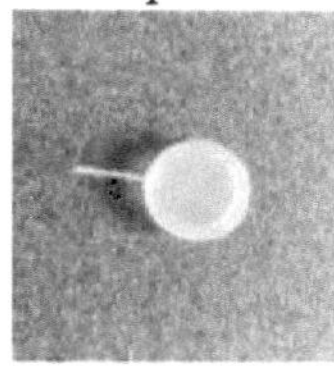

Above, the experimental Molteno Valve implanted in my eye to relieve pressure.

This is one of me graduating from San Jose State University. My sister Cheri

and brother Michael are standing with me.

Here are Amy and I with Guide Dog Hoyt at our wedding.
And another with Hoyt and I.

This is graduation day with Guide Dog #2 Hale.

Hiking Pikes Peak with my dad and Hale.

Daughter Megan is born.

Here I am graduating with 3rd Guide Dog Charlie.

Charlie guiding me with Megan in the backpack.

PRESSURE

I enjoy my family time and here are some pictures of special memories. Skiing, tandem bike riding, parasailing, Disneyland.

JEFF HARRINGTON

From fishing to marathons and skydiving, life is an adventure and my lack of sight has not stopped me from living it.

EPILOG

It was May, 2021, and it was clear to me that it was time to move on from the Earle Baum Center of the Blind, where I had worked for more than 20 years.

The pandemic, which officially started in March of 2020, is still prevalent, with infection rates continuing to rise, as schools and restaurants are reopening to in-person business. Statistics clearly show that those who have been vaccinated are avoiding serious illness, while those who are not are taxing the medical delivery system. The virus variants are changing from the original COVID 19 to Delta and now Omicron. Fortunately, the recent variant does not seem to be more severe in terms of critical symptoms, but it is much more contagious.

The basic tasks of existing in society during the ongoing COVID pandemic, i.e., walking down the sidewalk, entering a business, riding a bus, are all activities that people take for granted. But if you cannot see, these simple tasks continue to take on a different level of concern. Restaurants have expanded their outdoor serving capacity, which means sidewalks that were designated for pedestrian travel are now being occupied by tables and chairs for dining customers. In some cases, visually impaired walkers have been forced to travel in the unfamiliar and unsafe street in order to reach their destination.

You cannot see that an individual might be approaching you with or without a mask, you cannot see the signage or visual markings on the floor indicating where you should line up or sit to maintain a socially safe distance from those around you, and when someone actually approaches you, should you greet them with a hug,, handshake, or fist bump? What is politically correct for the situation that you find yourself in? And not being able to see any of the visual cues around you gives you little insight as to how to best respond. The answer can vary based on the city/state that you are in, the event that you are attending, and whether you are inside or outside.

Developing the Technology Program at EBC back in 2001 was a busy and exciting time. Being the lead person for putting together a new service offering to benefit those with sight loss was very rewarding. As I have often told people, "There is never a good time to lose your vision, but if it happens, now is a good time." What I am referring to is the speed at which technology is changing. Many of the devices and services that are being brought to the market are hands-free and in some cases without a screen. These types of advancements are designed to be used without the need for seeing, so this type of interface is ideal for someone with sight loss.

I must say, though, that working during this time of COVID has been definitely the most demanding of my career. The entire EBC service delivery system needed to be changed to accommodate the pandemic. Clients were no longer permitted to come on campus to receive either group or one-on-one instruction. EBC services would need to be transformed into a remote delivery system. Further, the remote system needed to be accessible to people with sight loss and it needed to be a simple solution.

Researching and finding the conferencing solutions that are currently being utilized at EBC involved a great deal of testing and trial-and-error. It was one thing to find the solution that would allow EBC to continue delivering services, but getting staff and clients comfortable with this new system was probably the biggest and most time-consuming part of the transition.

Detailed documentation concerning conferencing procedures were created and distributed in various formats, including large print, braille, audio, and electronic, to assist people with learning this new platform.

The second EBC CEO, had gone on medical leave in mid 2018, and I took over the position of interim CEO, and with the other managers support, kept the EBC moving forward.

Back in 2003, when Megan was born, I had reduced my workweek from 40 hours down to 35. When I was interim CEO in 2018, the EBC Board had approved increasing my hours to a 40-hour workweek.

The second CEO's employment with EBC was ended in late 2018. I let the Board know that I was not interested in taking on the CEO position permanently, as my true passion was working with the clients, but I would stay on until the CEO position was filled.

During an executive meeting in early 2019, I was informed by a fellow manager that he was now the CEO. I received no formal communication from anyone on the Board regarding this decision. I did send an email to the Board President, at the time, expressing my disappointment with not being provided the courtesy of being told about this change. Even after my email message, there was no response from the Board.

This manager had aspirations to be CEO, so behind the scenes, he had made his desires known, and he was now the interim CEO, and later that year, was appointed permanent CEO.

Around that same time, I let the management team know I did not want the expectation to be that I would physically be present all day on Fridays. I agreed to be present during the Low-Vision Clinic Fridays and work remotely during other Fridays.

I remember preparing to leave on a Friday in 2019 around noon, and I popped my head into the directors office, where he was meeting with Kati, letting them know I was leaving and would see them at the next day's Bike for Sight fundraiser event that my family and I would be participating in.

The directors response to my announcement of leaving was what I would describe as pure anger. I was yelled at as I stood in the office hallway right outside of his office. I was confronted with a barrage of questions, "Don't you have training scheduled? There is work that needs to be done. Why didn't you tell me you were leaving?!"

I was shocked by this uncontrolled outburst. No one should be talked to in this manner, and doing it publicly was even worse. I felt completely disrespected and was furious.

I no longer wanted to participate in the Bike for Sight event, since I knew the director would also be present. My sister and I had trained for this upcoming event, along with my brother-in-law. Amy, my mom, and mother-in-law had also purchased tickets to attend the event. We had already paid for the tickets, so not wanting to let down my family, I attended the event.

I never heard from the director during the event or at any other time during the weekend. I thought he might acknowledge his inappropriate outburst, but there was no communication or apology from him.

On Monday following the weekend, I was still very angry about how I was treated. I actually sent an email to the executive team as well as the Board President, resigning from EBC. That did get Kati's, and the directors attention. Interestingly enough, I never heard from the Board President concerning my email resignation.

The director denied yelling at me, but he seemed to be genuinely apologetic for the unfortunate interaction that we had had. I agreed to withdraw my email resignation.

The director reduced my working hours and compensation from 40 hours back to 35 hours a week, saying it did not set a good example to the rest of the staff if I was not physically present all day in the office on Fridays. I let the director know that I was no longer interested in managing the Tech Department primarily because I did not want to work that closely with him anymore.

When the worldwide shut-down began in March of 2020, due to COVID, employees were transitioned into working remotely. EBC was no different from other companies. I was working as much as other full-time EBC employees. I asked the director to reconsider my weekly hours, as no EBC employees were physically working from the office anymore, and that was the reason given for my hours being reduced.

The director scheduled a meeting with me and truly acted like he wanted to resolve the 40-hour workweek question that I was asking about. The director said he wanted me to work 40 hours per week, but he was unwilling to pay me for the increased hours. Instead, he tried to entice me into agreeing to work 40 hours per week, saying I would accrue more PTO time if I did so. That statement about accruing more PTO time was true, but what he did not say was that I would be required to take more PTO time if I wanted a day off (eight hours instead of seven) or an entire week off (40 hours instead of 35). What the director had attempted to con me into was to increase my working hours to 40 per week without any additional compensation. Well obviously, I did not agree to these terms and was insulted that the director would even offer such an unfair proposal.

After this conversation with the director , I really felt like a devalued employee and made a conscious effort to avoid interacting with him as much as possible. I reminded myself that what I valued was helping people with sight loss, so that is what I chose to focus on, moving forward.

The final insult came in December of 2020, when raises were given out to EBC staff. Let me preface these circumstances by providing some historical reference. Over the years while employed at EBC, my job performance has been reviewed by three CEOs and one Director of Programs. I have always received the highest of ratings (Exceeding Expectations) in the various categories, i.e., Job Knowledge, Communication, Team Work, etc. With the exception of 2019, when I was reviewed by the new director for the first and only time, I received the lowest ratings ever (Meeting Expectations) from an EBC supervisor. When this fact was pointed out, some of the ratings were changed to be higher.

In November of 2020, I had my employee review with Kati, and all of my ratings were Exceeding All Expectations.

However, when EBC raises were given out at the end of the year, for the first time ever as an employee at EBC, I was not given one. I would have fully understood if no raises were given that year due to the ongoing economic hardship experienced by businesses as a result of the global pandemic. But instead, for whatever reason, I appeared to be singled out to not receive a raise.

I could not rationalize this decision in my mind. I had never worked harder for the EBC organization, and I'm not sure what more I could have done. Due to the COVID crisis, it had been an overwhelming year of change for EBC.

When the director heard about my resignation, he contacted me to thank me for my service and wish me well. He did not seem to have a clue about why I was leaving. I did remind him about how I had been treated and disrespected.

The EBC Board of Directors did host a very nice catered lunch in April of 2021, honoring my 20-plus years of service to the organization. The new Board President provided the audience, which included Amy, my mom, sister, coworkers, and Board members, with a very entertaining summary of my life, career, and arrival at EBC in 2000. Another Board member (Hoby) provided a very touching tribute to me, describing how he came to EBC during his senior year of high school, receiving technology instruction from me. Hoby was gracious with crediting me with helping him acquire the skills, as he prepared to move on to college. Hoby went on to earn his PhD from the University of California Davis (UCD) in Organic Chemistry. Hoby is involved with several business ventures, and I know, without a doubt, he will be successful.

PRESSURE

The EBC Board of Directors honored me by naming a campus trail after me (The Jeff Harrington Trail).

EBC had the Michelle Trail, which was named to honor one of EBC's original Orientation and Mobility instructors. This was an Eagle Scout project, where a specially designed trail for the visually impaired was constructed on the property that included a guide rope that could be touched and followed.

The mile-long trail that was named after me follows the perimeter of the property, through the orchard, winding around the vernal pools, and passing the accessible labyrinth, garden, and dog play yard. I cannot tell you how many times I have walked this trail. Every lunch hour, while working at EBC, I could be found on it, being led by one of my 4-wheel drive guide dogs, Hale, Charlie, or Lucas. There is a new beautiful sign mounted next to the dirt pathway that I now pass by each time as I continue to walk the trail, on a regular basis, usually on the weekends. The words printed on the sign are both in braille and raised lettering. The words are so kind and meaningful, and I am truly honored.

> *"The Jeff Harrington Trail*
> *in recognition of Jeff's 20*
> *year service to Earle Baum*
> *Center is an inspiration*
> *to all, a generous friend,*
> *his optimistic attitude,*
> *perseverance, and*
> *humble spirit shines*
> *through, he is a true*
> *trail blazer".*

About the Author

Jeffrey Harrington is a first-time author who shares, in this book, his personal story, transitioning from being sighted to becoming blind. He grew up in the Santa Cruz Mountains, attended Soquel High School class of 1984 and graduated from San Jose State University with a degree in Occupational Therapy. He has been living in the Santa Rosa area for the past 30 years with his wife Amy, daughter Megan, guide dog Lucas, pet dog Quincy, and cat Harley, surrounded by close family, including his mom (Carolyn Harrington), sister (Cheri Sharp), brother-in-law (Paul Sharp), nephews (Paulie and Devon Sharp), and mother-in-law (Molly Stanton).

Mr. Harrington can be contacted at: pressure.story@gmail.com